Breaking Through to the Other Side

Breaking Through to the Other Side:
*Essays On Realization
in Modern Literature*

by
Donald Gutierrez

The Whitston Publishing Company
Troy, New York
1994

Copyright 1994
Donald Gutierrez

Library of Congress Catalog Card Number 93-60176

ISBN 0-87875-435-0

Published in the United States of America

To

Father "Ted" Hesburgh, C. S. C.
President Emeritus
University of Notre Dame

—for being there for us

Acknowledgments

I wish to thank the following book publishers and literary executors for granting me permission to quote from the books listed below:

Laurence Pollinger Ltd. and the **Estate of Frieda Lawrence Ravagli**, for permission to quote from D. H. Lawrence *Selected Poems*, NY: New Directions (1947).

Bradford Morrow, Literary Executor, the Kenneth Rexroth Estate, for permission to quote from *The Collected Shorter Poems of Kenneth Rexroth* (1966) and Kenneth Rexroth's *Flower Wreath Hill: Later Poems*, (1991).

New Directions Publishing Corporation, for permission to quote from *The Collected Shorter Poems of Kenneth Rexroth*, Kenneth Rexroth's *Flower Wreath Hill: Later Poems* and Robert Duncan's *The Opening of the Field*.

Penguin USA, for permission to quote from *The Complete Poems of D. H. Lawrence* (1971).

The following essays first appeared in the publications listed below:

"Bringing to Light the Labyrinthine Mind: The Maxims of La Rochefoucauld," in *The Liberal & Fine Arts Review*, v. 5, no. 1, 1985.

"D. H. Lawrence's 'Spirit of Place' as Eco-Monism," in *D. H. Lawrence: The Journal of the D. H. Lawrence Society* (Nottingham, England), Fall, 1991. The piece appeared in *Santa Fe Poetry* (1981) in shorter form.

"Breaking Through to the Other Side: D. H. Lawrence's 'New Heaven and Earth' as Apocalyptic," in *Paunch*, no. 62-63, 1990.

"Sex in D. H. Lawrence's Fiction," in *The Liberal & Fine Arts Review*, v. 3, nos. 1-2, 1983.

"The Champ of the World and the Champ of the Word: Norman Mailer's *The Fight*," in *Arete: The Journal of Sports Literature*, v. 5, no. 1, Fall 1987.

Acknowledgments

"The Discrimination of Elegance: Anthony Powell's *A Dance to the Music of Time*," no. 34, 1975. This essay has been enlarged for the book.

"'The Holiness of the Real': The Short Poems of Kenneth Rexroth," in *Re Arts & Letters (REAL)*, v. 17, no. 2, Fall 1991.

"The Beautiful Place in the Mind: Robert Duncan's 'Often I Am Permitted to Return to a Meadow,'" in *American Poetry*, v. 6, no. 1, Fall 1988.

"The Mass-Media Celebrity: Big Star, Little Fan," in *Common Sense* (University of Notre Dame), v. 5, no. 2, 1990, and *The Wilderness Outlook*, no. 53, 1990 (Silver City, NM). This essay has been enlarged for the book.

"Wanted: A Unified American Intelligentsia," in *Common Sense*, v. 3, no. 4, 1989 and *The Wilderness Outlook*, 1989. This essay has been substantially enlarged for the book.

Other Books by
Donald Gutierrez

*Lapsing Out: Embodiments of Death and Rebirth in the Last Writings of
    D. H. Lawrence* (1980)
The Maze in the Mind and the World: Labyrinths in Modern Literature,
    The Whitston Publishing Company (1985)
Subject-Object Relations in Wordsworth and Lawrence (1986)
The Dark and Light Gods: Essays on the Self in Modern Literature, The
    Whitston Publishing Company (1987)

Contents

Acknowledgments vi
Preface 1

I. A 20th Century 17th-Century Frenchman
Bringing to Light the Labyrinthine Mind: *The Maxims*
   of La Rochefoucauld 8

II. Three on Lorenzo
D. H. Lawrence's "Spirit of Place" as Eco-Monism 24
"Break On Through to the Other Side!": D. H. Lawrence's
   "New Heaven and Earth" as Apocalyptic 36
Sex in Lawrence's Fiction 53

III. American Pugilism, British Elegance
The Champ of the World and the Champ of the Word:
   Norman Mailer's *The Fight* 72
The Discrimination of Elegance: Anthony Powell's
   A Dance to the Music of Time 99

IV. Two San Francisco Poets
"The Holiness of the Real": The Short Poems
   of Kenneth Rexroth 116
The Beautiful Place in the Mind: Robert Duncan's
   "Often I Am Permitted to Return to a Meadow" 144

V. Culture Criticism
The Mass-Media Celebrity: Big Star, Little Fan 152
Wanted: An American Intelligentsia 161

Index 183

"And so I cross into another world
shyly and in homage linger for an invitation
from this unknown that I would trespass on."
                D. H. Lawrence "New Heaven and Earth"
                from *Look! We Have Come Through!*

"Break on Through to the Other Side!"
        Jim Morrison

Preface

This book is a collection of mainly literary essays centered on a D. H. Lawrence (and Jim Morrison) metaphor of breaking through to a new world of sensibility. That Lawrence describes this intensely private, even hermetic experience in public ("world") as well as private terms conveniently broadens its applicability, for, with Lawrence, the revelation, the breakthrough, the "New Heaven and Earth" is at best a private *and* public experience. If, in his long mid-period poem of that title, he has primarily a symbolic marital event in mind, it is a microcosmic transcendence meant to point the way—society should follow, imitate the tiny exemplar. Another term for this metaphor of breaking through is realization, which not only signifies understanding or perception but making more real, achieving, if one can so put it, reality. Kenneth Rexroth endows the idea with a kind of sacramental character in his memorable words the "holiness of the real" from his outstanding poem "Time Is the Mercy of Eternity." As subjective and elusive (or illusory) as reality may be, human beings nevertheless seem to know when they have so engaged reality as to rise, in Northrop Frye's superb phrase, from reality to realization.

The ten essays in this book exhibit a variety of breakthroughs and/or realizations. They may be only potential breakthroughs, possible transcendences, as intimated in the two final essays of culture criticism, in which the transcendence depends on realizing the dangerous falsity of the mass-media celebrity or the different danger of a non-existent or inadequate intelligentsia in American society. Realization can take the form of apprehending the new Golden Ages suggested by the creative imaginations of poets like Lawrence, Rexroth and Robert Duncan. Or, more prosaically and soberly, realization occurs in an acute 17th century mind like La Rouchefoucauld's, that can jar us with the sense of our own moral and psychic frailties like alcohol on a cut. In Norman Mailer's densely figured world of professional boxing and his subtle rivalry with Muhammad Ali, we observe a breakthrough in the "paradrama" of the hero as prizefighter, race champion, iconoclastic wit and comeback artist. On another plane is Anthony Powell, the British novelist who stands today as the greatest rival in 20th century English prose style to Mailer's formidable American prose baroque. The title of Powell's twelve-volume novel, *A Dance to the Music of Time*, suggests realization through recognizing and assimilating the ironic discrepancy between art and reality. Powell's aristocratic elegance and austerity align him with the physical and symbolic integrity implied by Mailer's Ali and the athletically ascetic wit of La Rochefoucauld. On the other hand, the love-and-nature cosmos of Rexroth and the dream landscapes of Duncan appear relatable to the romantic apocalyptic of Lawrence. The essays, then, suggest different and even antithetical orders of breakthrough, realization, transcendence.

The 17th century aristocrat and philosopher Duc de La Rouchefoucauld is modern in the almost Freudian acuity of his sagacious *Maxims*. In his *mot* "Self-love is subtler than the subtlest man in the world," La Rochefoucauld provides the humbling realization from which moral and psychological understanding could more soberly begin.

The essay on D. H. Lawrence's famous phrase "spirit of place" involves the monistic idea underlying not a little of Lawrence's significant work that humanity and nature are enclosed in each other. Lawrence is one of the early 20th century "modern masters" whose work suggests, among other things, that our primary breakthrough, upon which all the smaller ones crucially depend, is the realization of the utter primacy of the earth itself. Further, he combines his subject-object, subject-subject awareness with a powerful metaphysical sense of the human place (a combination I term "eco-monism"). If Lawrence is thus a kind of proto-ecologist, it is a status enriched by both a philosophical dimension and dramatization in literary art.

The second essay on Lawrence in this collection (from which it takes its title) offers a lengthy scrutiny of his key middle-period poem "New Heaven and Earth" from his book of verse *Look! We Have Come Through!* This long poem, embarrassing at first in its ostensible exhibitionism, embodies a profound vision of a symbolic love relationship, and, obliquely, of the disintegrating universe of World War One. "New Heaven and Earth" assumes this deeper significance if regarded as apocalyptic, that is, as an artistic use of a crisis theology of beginnings and ends. Lawrence, who was highly conversant with this whole tradition of eschatology, implemented its mode in some of his major works. Thus it is not surprising to see him resort to this sensational medium of religious crisis for an event which, issuing from a complex and tumultuous marriage, culminates in an aftermath of mutual realization. Rather than being a poem of inexcusable emotional dishevelment, "New Heaven and Earth" is both a work of art of considerable sophistication and overwhelming emotional force. The "other side" reached in this long (and long underrated) poem is a New Jerusalem with a population of two, like that of the little world of Birkin and Ursula in Lawrence's profoundly apocalyptical *Women in Love*.

The third Lawrence essay deals with sex in four fictions: *Sons and Lovers*, *Women in Love*, *The Virgin and the Gypsy*, and *Lady Chatterley's Lover*. Lawrence's treatment of sex in his work is, at its best, ontological: we see through, as it were, the medium of sexuality into the roots and depths of human being. Thus Lawrence avoids superficial or "sexy" renditions of sexuality by integrating it with emotions, instincts, subtle reverberations of mind and body which vividly exhibit symbolically weighted dark and light areas of character. This complex integration locates, to my mind, the source of deepest force and originality in Lawrence's fiction, a body of work dramatizing both realization and non-realization.

A vastly different breakthrough from any in this collection occurs in the essay on Norman Mailer's book *The Fight*, which deals with the 1974 Muhammad Ali-George Foreman prizefight in Zaire. The transcendence occurs (unsurprizingly for Ali) in a boxing ring, but at a very special moment as Ali the Challenger awaits the very formidable champion, but awaits him with controlled exultation. The great boxer, wit and Black activist had been barred from the ring for three years for refusing induction during the Viet Nam War, stripped of his world-championship belt by the prize fight authorities, and after a long break was now confronting a fighter that many thought could possibly maim or even kill Ali during the bout. Yet Mailer's account is as much about the primitivist or vitalist modes of thinking and its (close) relation to Mailer's own sense of the prime energies comprising reality and a potential for realization as it is about one of the most dramatic boxing matches and prizefight buildups in ring history.

Anthony Powell's prose style (especially his tone) is one big reason why people read him, going like devotees of some fanatical cult through volume after volume of the twelve novels comprising *A Dance to the Music of Time*, depression if not thoughts of suicide looming for them at the prospect of the series ending. Indeed, some place Powell's series novel among the significant fiction of the century. The power, the impact of *Dance* is, to be sure, keyed through the style (and complex point of view), and integrally effected in the tone, which is urbane, composed, "classical":

> The image of time [in Poussin's painting "A Dance to the Music of Time"] brought thoughts of mortality: of human beings, facing outward like the Seasons, moving hand in hand in intricate measure; stepping slowly, methodically, sometimes a trifle awkwardly in evolutions that take recognizable shape; or breaking into seemingly meaningless gyrations while partners disappear only to re-appear again, once more giving pattern to the spectacle: unable to control the melody, unable, perhaps, to control the steps of the dance.
> *A Question of Upbringing*, v. 1 in *Dance*

The realization here and throughout the series resides in the esthetic experience a reader can have of the tension between Powell's sense of the order and perfection of art and the disorder of and imperfection of life. Often the tension breaks and comedy or satire results. If esthetic tension can be beautiful or pleasurable to experience, it can also test the limits of the satire itself when dealing with character types that might be impervious in art and certainly in life to satiric resolution.

It is tempting to suggest nature itself as the locus of realization in Kenneth Rexroth's exquisite love and nature verse. Certainly some of this West-Coast poet's best verse occurs amid such concentrations of nature as the Sierra Nevadas and the Coast Range mountains. But realization in Rexroth's work (prose as well as verse) has more to do with the intense communalism of love in which the "naturalness" of the wilds is reflected and climaxed in the potential naturalness and insuperable mystery of sexual love. As Rexroth puts it in his four-part poem "Inversely, As the Square of Their Distances Apart," "Invisible, solemn, and fragrant, / Your flesh opens up to me in secret, / We shall know no further enigma." Rexroth's breakthrough manifests itself in the golden awareness that "the holy *is* the pile of dust," that is, that the sacred resides in the common, everyday, even lowest phenomena of life, and to perceive this is to intensify and enrich and thus to realize life through immanence.

The title of the 20th century American poet Robert Duncan's famous poem "Often I Am Permitted to Return to a Meadow," manifests the basic idea for this collection in metaphorical and philosophical terms. Duncan implies a monistic idea of breaking through as intensified and mythicized human experience of a place and thus of humanity itself. Arising from this "magical" association is the sense of its apotheosis of human life and creativity and their interdependence with place. It is a vision, a realization of a revered place or state of mind one can return to, as one must, for the refreshening of body, mind, and soul.

The final two essays in this collection, culture criticism meant to be readable, point towards the need for individuals in mass societies to take over their societies, either through deposing false deities or by learning to respect or achieve intellection and to harness it to social ends or values. The first concerns a world phenomenon—the mass-media celebrity—that represents a psycho-social malaise in modern mass societies. Making super-stars of entertainers glorifies, even deifies, such persons at the expense of the rest of a mass population, especially those people with at best limited opportunities for achievement. Such celebrities virtually thwart the breakthrough that would be possible for larger numbers of people did they not have such sham gods and goddesses dazzling them as pernicious substitutes and thus blinding them from their own self-realization.

The second essay, supplementary to the celebrity piece, presents a plea for a community of intellectuals (both academic and non-academic) to occupy a larger role in American society. I suggest that intellectuals can become the moral, imaginative and intellectual conscience of our far-flung, heterogeneous, morally disoriented nation, and indicate what some of the barriers to this goal are and one general way of creating and enlarging such a class or community. Were this enhancement of role to occur, perhaps realization could be made a little more accessible and enduring even in the everyday life, or even especially in the everyday life.

I

A 20th CENTURY 17th CENTURY FRENCHMAN

Bringing to Light the Labyrinthine Mind:
The Maxims of La Rochefoucauld

> "Vanity of vanities, saith the Preacher; all is vanity." Ecclesiastes 1:2

> "We have as much right to complain about those who teach us to know ourselves as that Athenian madman who complained about the doctor for having cured him of thinking he was rich." La Rochefoucauld, *The Maxims*

During the last few decades the United States has been overwhelmed by fads, doctrines, and business enterprises designed to persuade people to become more content with themselves. One shortcoming in this recent commercialization of self-affirmation is that it usually does not penetrate human nature very deeply. Viewing ourselves superficially, we try to be convinced that we like, or should like, what we see. Pleased that self-acceptance or self-development is not really hard at all, we remain half blind and half conscious, ignoring the mazes of our inner darkness and outer confusions.

We know that Freud at the beginning of this century probed these darknesses and confusions and posited the existence of an inner realm of psychic checks and balances, of thrusts and extremities. What is not so well known, however, is the fact that the seventeenth-century maxim writer and aristocrat Francois, Duc de La Rochefoucauld, had explored similar terrain in broad, trenchant generalizations that illuminated deep illusions and delusions in a most disconcerting way:

> Self-interest speaks all manner of tongues and plays all manner of parts, even that of disinterestedness.
> (maxim 39, p. 40)

Though we may be struck by La Rochefoucauld's psychological modernity here and elsewhere, a more important characteristic of *The Maxims* is the universality and timelessness of his provocative insights. According to Henri Chamard, " . . . La Rochefoucauld's outlook is one-sided," though, adds Chamard, "he [La Rochefoucauld] nevertheless gives us from time to time precise, profound, penetrating views of human life" (p. 12). The qualification appears to outweigh the stricture. Not all of us may fit into the iron maiden of one of La Rochefoucauld's sayings. However, he is not making personal analyses. His concern, as that of any traditional moral philosopher, is to achieve as much scope as possible: the "human condition" is bound to be a center or norm of behavior and being. Yet, "extreme boredom provides its own antidote" (maxim 532, p. 103) applies both broadly and with formidable accuracy. Our "shock of recognition" and not always amused chagrin at one maxim after another confirm this accuracy.

La Rochefoucauld has often been accused of cynicism, and even some of his friends in the famous salon of Mme. de Sablon, a center of maxim-making, were quite shocked when *The Maxims* was published. His close friend, Mme. de La Fayette, accused La Rochefoucauld of projecting his own morbidities on humanity (p. 12). Chamard himself defines a conventional position on La Rochefoucauld's alleged cynicism: his morbid maxims were the result of his embittering experiences. La Rochefoucauld's world, states Chamard, was full of "a never-ending series of plots, deeds of violence, greed, and duplicity" (p. 11).

Yet, even in La Rochefoucauld's time some people felt that his *Maxims* were not cynical or morbid. Since the work had appeared in five editions during his lifetime, clearly it must have had readers and, quite possibly, admirers. Chamard states that " . . . in the seventeenth century no one believed . . . in the goodness of human nature" (p. 11). Thus Odette de Mourgues's assertion becomes highly relevant: "There is no simple approach to *The Maxims*. Everyone studying the work is tempted to suspect previous criticism of having chosen the wrong angle" (p. 3). The diversity of interpretations of *The Maxims*, therefore, suggests their depth and complexity.

According to W. G. Moore, La Rochefoucauld had ample grounds in experience for being embittered: " . . . [A] study of La Rochefoucauld does not enforce the notion of the cynic; it increases our respect for the writer" (p. 7). Moore further elaborates a significant point about *The Maxims*:

> It is a mistake to judge *The Maxims* by their truth. Whoever said that the Maxim should express a statement with which we must all agree? This if logically applied would turn [*The*] *Maxims* into truisms . . . What else the seventeenth-century reader could see or expect to see in the Maxims . . . is . . . something directly opposed to a truism. "Revelation" would be a better word, . . . truths that are unwelcome, unpalatable . . . (p. 84-85).

My thesis in this essay is that *The Maxims*, far from being cynical, are acutely revealing about the real, involuted nature of the psyche. They antedate Freud in their perceptiveness about the darker regions of human motive and behavior; this is a fertile parallel which, however, I do not intend to develop. A corollary point, seldom mentioned in La Rochefoucauld studies, that I will develop is that, despite a pessimistic cast to *The Maxims*, some of the maxims also contain an affirmative character in implying space for change or growth. I will first focus on some of the maxims dealing with the "passions," because they by their protean character lead quite naturally to La Rochefoucauld's major theme of vanity, an area with which much of this essay will be concerned.

Often enough, we assume La Rochefoucauld to be a "classical" author, one full of well-turned, even pleasing numbers such as "Hypocrisy is a tribute vice pays to virtue" (maxim 218, p. 62). The fine balance and antithesis of moral components held together by the golden middle term "hypocrisy" as well as the maxim's urbanity and conciseness so charm us as to soften the pungency of the thought; the glittering syntactic and semantic ingenuity partly blinds us to its sharp edges. Thus it can be a shock to confront the saturnine La Rochefoucauld of maxim 527:

> The human condition is so wretched that while bending his every action to pander to his passions man never ceases groaning against their tyranny. He can neither accept their violence nor the violence he must do himself in order to shake their yoke. Not only the passions

but also their antidotes fill him with disgust, and he
cannot be reconciled either to the discomfort of his disease or the trouble of a cure (p. 102).

This is a state of conflict indeed. In fact, it is an oxy-
moronic condition of vital paralysis, of desire warring endlessly
with conscience, cravings with self-improvement. Written in
the age of the Sun King, a period extolled for suave rationality
and decorum, this maxim (longer than most of La Rochefoucauld's) depicts the "human condition" as an abysmal torment
of dividedness; it would even serve as an appropriate motto for
Dostoyevsky's Underground Man. Any creature so conflicted
would scarcely seem capable of performing the various basic activities of life, and perhaps it is testimony to noble effort that
humanity can even function while riven by such brutal opposi-
tions of energy.

What should mitigate the charge of cynicism against La
Rochefoucauld—though it often adds to it—is that, like all superior moralists, he exhibited acute insight rather than a heavy
hand to assert his authority. He knew that beneath the skin of
rationality, grace, and etiquette marking any civilized era or culture or class, human beings could be seething cauldrons of
chaotic feelings and bedeviled impulse. It is thus no surprise
that some of his more memorable aphorisms concern feelings
or, as he called them, the "passions," a subject upon which he is
both eloquent and concise:

> The passions are the only orators who always
> convince... (maxim 8, p. 36)

> The passions set aside justice and work for their own
> ends, and it is therefore dangerous to follow them and
> necessary to treat them with caution even when they
> seem most reasonable. (maxim 9, p. 36)

> In the human heart new passions are for ever being born;
> the overthrow of one almost always means the rise of
> another. (maxim 10, p. 36)

> Passions often engender their opposite. Avarice some-
> times begets prodigality and prodigality avarice; a
> man is often resolute through weakness and bold
> through timidity. (maxim 11, p. 36)

> Whatever care a man takes to veil his passions with appearances of piety and honour, they always show through. (maxim 12, p. 61)

The figure in maxim 8 of the emotions as powerful persuaders suggests both their force and a certain artful dexterity: feelings have eloquence and can even scheme. In maxim 9 the emotions can displace or overrule the conscience or superego ("justice") and have their own way. Thus, one must guard against them, even and perhaps especially when they, in all their Mephistophelian cunning, infiltrate reason and try to resemble it. Emotions, like any form of rudimentary life extending its being, continually regenerate themselves; the repression of or victory over one, like some law of energy, engenders another. By indicating in maxim 11 how opposite qualities can be linked or can even induce each other through the magical shortcuts of the emotions, La Rochefoucauld offers a generalization worthy of the future psychological novel.

If the five proverbs above suggest a classical rationalist's antipathy to the emotions, maxim 404 suggests a positive role for the "passions":

> Nature, it seems, has buried deep in our minds skill and talents of which we are unaware; the passions alone have the function of bringing them to light and thereby sometimes giving us a clearer and more comprehensive vision than ingenuity could ever do (p. 84).

"Ingenuity" here means ratiocination, excessive reasoning. The passions (surely a more attractive word than "affects") serve as middlemen or midwives for bringing to birth capacities or functions like intuition, memory, even impulse that would aid cerebration in sharpening and completing our vision of reality. This is a large role for the emotions; the Romantics would later applaud it. If La Rochefoucauld's earlier maxims on the feelings warn us that "it is necessary to treat the passions with caution," maxim 404 warns us that if we are too cautious with them our spontaneity and perceptiveness, as well as any dedication to intellectual discovery, may diminish, even cease. Emotions, for all their dangers, regenerate and inspire.

La Rochefoucauld regards the emotions as disguised aspects of a central element of human nature: "The passions are merely the various whims of self-love" (maxim 531, p. 102).

Self-love, or vanity: this is a prime subject in *The Maxims*, one that he treats with irresistible penetration and wit, and to which we now address ourselves.

Vanity is a profound, relentless, seemingly invincible force. Its power, its depth, its virtually biological thrust is memorably registered throughout *The Maxims*:

> The virtues lose themselves in self-interest like rivers in the sea. (maxim 171, p. 56)

> Vanity may not quite overthrow the virtues, but it shakes them all to their foundations.
> (maxim 338, p. 77)

> The most violent passions sometimes let us relax, but vanity keeps us perpetually on the go.
> (maxim 443, p. 89)

Time after time La Rochefoucauld's insights into vanity are so sure, so "right," that they make us wince. His concise exposures of the insidiousness, vice, and folly of excessive self-esteem are like sharp dabs of alcohol on an unsuspected wound. Of all human tendencies, vanity is the most centrifugal. It is the human trait most rooted in the inner physical life because it is so intricately interlinked with our basic biological being and survival.

If vanity, then, is linked with survival and our physical existence, why should we castigate it? Like neurosis, one could argue, it keeps us going, just as whiskey did Ulysses S. Grant (during the American Civil War). But like neurosis, it keeps us going at half speed; it bars us from more ambitious growth and achievement. We allow ourselves to be controlled by it: "Man often thinks he is in control when he is being controlled . . . " (maxim 43, p. 40). As we glance at a number of La Rochefoucauld's aphorisms on vanity, we are struck by the endless subtlety of this mysterious life-clinging yet soul-warping force. Noteworthy first is the invincible deftness and bottomlessness of narcissism:

> Self-love is the greatest flatterer of all.
> (maxim 2, p. 35)

> Whatever discoveries have been made in the land of self-love, many regions still remain unexplored.
> (maxim 2, p. 35)

> Self-love is subtler than the subtlest man in the world.
> (maxim 4, p. 35)

In confronting self-love in *The Maxims*, then, we encounter what is most intimate, most deceptive, and, to complicate matters, most "human" in ourselves. No one loves us as much or as intimately as we do, no other person turns our head with such resourceful cleverness. Our self-love is amazing in the involutedness of its self-deceiving vanity, our arms wrapped so fondly and frequently around our own backs that we do not even notice the pressure.

La Rochefoucauld, who was a generous and chivalric man, despised this self-infatuation. He was himself willing to confront the charge of vanity in a passage of candor and typically deft insight from his "Self Portrait":

> I am intelligent, and I make no bones about saying so, for what is the good of being coy about it? So much beating about the bush and toning down when it is a question of stating the advantages we possess looks to me like concealing a bit of vanity behind externals of modesty, and resorting to artful wiles to make others think much better of us than we actually claim (p. 24).

And in characteristic Rochefouldian irony of behavior-reversal, he confesses in "Self Portrait" that: " . . . I stand up so passionately for the cause of reason that I become unreasonable myself" (p. 25). The nobleman who knew something of the world and its ways in the highest reaches of seventeenth century European court life, the battlefield, and the salons had come to know something about himself as well. Whether or not "It is more important to study men than books" (maxim 550, p. 104), La Rochefoucauld undoubtedly studied many men, and himself foremost. Perhaps, as he suggests in "Self Portrait," he was not always pleased at what he saw: "My expression has something melancholy and aloof about it which makes most people think I am supercilious, although I am nothing of the kind" (p. 23). Is the end of that sentence prompted by justifiable self-defense, or by vanity?

La Rochefoucauld's moral austerity is tempered sometimes by a rich sense of comic irony. He might have had trouble surviving in the salons and company of such grand ladies as Mme. de Sablón, Mme. de La Fayette, and Mme. de Sévigné without the wit underlying the famous maxim 19—"We all have strength to endure the troubles of others" (p. 37)—or the deep if quiet sympathy of "For a woman hell is old age" (maxim 562, p. 106). The point of the irony, of course, is that we do not suffer enough; this is not out of noble strength but because of a lack of empathy or humanity. Though partly humorous, this little saying cuts deeply into the thick flesh of our self-interest.

A less acerbic humor suffuses "We would rather run ourselves down than not talk about ourselves at all" (maxim 138, p. 52). An offspring of "Self-love is subtler than the subtlest man in the world" (maxim 4, p. 35), this "sentence" also suggests that we would rather run ourselves down than have someone else do it for us. We know how subtly pleasurable self-criticism often can be, in vivid contrast to receiving open criticism from a friend or enemy.

Another form of this vanity suggests either a "friendly" conscience or just the sort of ignorance or slothful self-content these maxims are designed to prick:

> We cannot get over being deceived by our enemies and betrayed by our friends, yet we are often content to be so treated by ourselves. (maxim 114, p. 49)

One encounters some of the dark complexity of human nature in people who are consciously aware of deceiving or betraying themselves. When we encounter this involuted dishonesty in ourselves, self-esteem makes it less outrageous, and not necessarily because our various selves are on good terms. Our "selves," still being part of our "Self," generally makes self-deception easier to take, whereas deception by another person, no matter how close, is basically part of the "Other," and thus it is unavoidably distanced from us. Another maxim about vanity and self-deception re-evokes Georg Groddeck's "It" in the form of vices: "When the vices give us up we flatter ourselves that we are giving up them" (maxim 192, p. 58). All this should give us pause. If La Rochefoucauld's sense of an inner world suggests vast murky spaces of illusion, delusion, ignorance, and egotism, it also suggests that forces beyond our control might prevent us from being self-destructive. The "decision" to abstain issues from esoteric energies a long remove from willfulness or moral promptings.

Related to the humbling if humorous maxim 192 but more harrowing is a maxim that confronts our individual misery and demands that we expunge from it any craven self-pity and delusive self-enoblement:

> Often we believe ourselves long-suffering in adversity when in fact we are merely prostrated, and we undergo such adversity without daring to face it, like cowards who let themselves be killed for fear of defending themselves. (maxim 420, p. 86)

This aphorism withdraws any anodyne from the pain. It is easy when free of adversity to say that we should face our troubles rather than making those troubles seem worse because we have narcissistically submitted to them. Yet this is certainly not one of La Rochefoucauld's darker sayings, harboring as it does the possibility of heroic resistance to misfortune. We fully apprehend it, though only in adversity; that is the crucial moment in which our own vulnerability is tested by the vanity of self-debasement from which La Rochefoucauld would shame us.

Let us consider briefly the other end of the gamut (assuming one exists): can a human being be disinterestedly generous? Is altruism possible? La Rochefoucauld more than once suggests that we should closely examine the motives beneath our generous gestures: "We would rather see those we do good to than those who do good to us" (maxim 558, p. 105). Though few enjoy remaining grateful, more than a few of us can readily tolerate having the "object" of our kindness visible. Gratitude is not easily borne with dignity or grace. Being grateful for too long (but how long is "too long"?) can diminish a person; his gratitude pleasantly reminds us (at his expense) of our generosity, thus feeding our vanity. But we are, most of us, not perfect—are we not allowed a little pleasure from our magnanimity? Emerson's "The only reward of virtue is virtue" (Cohen p. 54) is a hard saying because a person has to be careful about the quality of the experience of his own virtue.

Vanity, as suggested earlier, does help us to survive, to maintain some kind of stabilizing self-identity. But we can make too much of that, in view of our relative ignorance of what life, society, and the world could be like if we learned to master our vanity. Vanity in *The Maxims* appears to be so close to our basic existence that to deny, express, condemn, and cut it away seems like opening our veins. The only suitable answer to this in La Rochefoucauld is to quote parts of the great maxim 563 at length, perhaps one of the most devastating definitions of vanity or self-love ever conceived:

> Self-love is love of oneself and of all things in terms of oneself; it makes men worshippers of themselves and would make them tyrants over others if fortune gave them the means. It never pauses for rest outside the self and . . . only settles on outside matters in order to draw from them what suits its own requirements. Nothing is so vehement as its desires, nothing so concealed as its aims, nothing so devious as its methods; its sinuosities beggar the imagination, its transformations surpass metamorphoses, its complications go beyond those of chemistry. No man can plumb the depths or pierce the darkness of its chasms in which, hidden from the sharpest eyes, it performs a thousand perceptible twists and turns, and where it is often invisible even to itself and unknowingly conceives, nourishes, and brings up a vast brood of affections and hatreds. Some of these are such monstrosities that on giving them birth it either repudiates them outright or hesitates to own them (p. 107).
> . . . .
> [Self-love] can keep its pride intact while doing the most despicable things . . . (p. 109).

One does not need a Freudian schema, which violently compartmentalizes the fluid universality of a La Rochefoucauld maxim, to see that this maxim describes an elemental area of human nature. In this area we associate our survival with self-love. In some respects this is an undesirable association for personal development at certain stages and for society itself; yet, as I shall soon try to show, it bears an affirmative aspect. It is also natural, but natural in a way that a number of philosophies, whether rightly or not, warn us to guard against and transcend.

In any case, what forcefully comes across in this maxim is a survival drive, a ruthless selfishness, and a power of mind for satisfying these urges and goals so pervasive as to occupy the entirety of human nature. A vanity so integral to our deepest being makes the consolidation of the virtues seem very difficult. La Rochefoucauld's concept of vanity suggests how alarmingly formidable the transformation of basic human energies into constructive values might really be.

Maxim 563 was among seventy-eight withdrawn by the author, possibly, according to La Rochefoucauld's editor L. W. Tancock, because they were similar to La Rochefoucauld's earlier maxims (p. 18). One can indeed detect some motifs in the quoted fragments, and, as these aphorisms go, maxim 563 tends to be too long. Yet it is a magnificent set piece, for it virtually presents the human psyche as a labyrinth in which the minotaur and the propitiatory victim are one, combined in the self but also divided in conflict. Is there any solution to this condition? Can minotaur-victim recognize a potential oneness or unified identity which could discover the exit from the labyrinth and gain entry to the open light, the free and responsible place?

A pessimist usually sees the worst side of something, and a cynic usually suspects its good side. The crucial word in the two definitions is "usually." Certainly there is something warped about a person who *always* distrusts the motives of others. On the other hand, we brand as fool or Pollyanna anyone who accepts everything at face value or sees good everywhere. La Rochefoucauld clearly belongs within the darker shades of this spectrum. Yet the color metaphor is misleading, for it discounts the brightness of the wit and clarity irradiating these maxims. Further, considering the destructiveness and genocide perpetuated by human societies over the centuries, and especially in the twentieth century, La Rochefoucauld hardly seems accurately described, and thus dismissed, as a cynic or pessimist. Indeed, one of the underlying tenets of modernist art is, to utilize Thomas Hardy's lines from "In Tenebris II": "Who holds that if way to the Better there be, it exacts a full look at the Worst" (Williams p. 22). Like the great modernist artists, La Rochefoucauld exacts a full look at the Worst.

Yet this look is not nihilistic. There is scarcely a maxim of La Rochefoucauld that says or implies that the human condition is rigidly limited or that self-development is useless or devoid of value. A number of aphorisms overtly indicate, even encourage room for growth, improvement, or fulfillment:

> Perfect valour consists in doing without witnesses what one would be capable of doing before the world at large.
> (maxim 216, p. 62)

> If we never flattered ourselves the flattery of others could do us no harm. (maxim 152, p. 54)

This does not say that we all largely flatter ourselves. If never flattering ourselves is an impossible ideal, there are significant gradations between the two extremes. But not being overly attached to ourselves is a constructive character trait and superior, through the striving its achievement demands, to the wishful-thinking willful egotism of modern fads like Positive Thinking.

Even an aphorism as hard to swallow as maxim 458, "Our enemies are nearer the truth in their opinion of us than we are ourselves" (p. 90), is more acceptable and even affirmative in its suggestion that we at least are willing to consider what our enemies charge us with. The inability to see our own faces without a mirror has its analogous facets in our character and conduct.

Though La Rochefoucauld compares the emotions and self-love to a sea, he still recognizes a kind of moral logic in human experience and behavior: "It is to the credit of virtue, we must admit, that men's greatest troubles are those they fall into through their misdeeds" (maxim 183, p. 57). That sentiment might give only cold comfort, especially to a miscreant, but it does offset the observation that "Chance and caprice rule the world" (maxim 435, p. 88). Rather than contradicting each other, these two maxims indicate a sense of a life and world in which virtue and evil count.

Even vanity is not seen exclusively from a dark perspective. In one of his greatest perceptions, one also counterbalancing a host of severe maxims about vanity, La Rochefoucauld declares:

> Self-interest, blamed for all our misdeeds, deserves credit for our good actions. (maxim 305, p. 73)

That sentiment makes La Rochefoucauld's architecture of vanity complete. Is one *not* going to donate money to a worthy cause if he realizes that it inflates his self-esteem? Whatever vanity there may be in such behavior, some objective good is accomplished, and the realization of the motive of vanity could lessen the vanity. A writer may become conceited for writing an important novel, yet the accomplished literary work transcends the conceit (and mortality) of its author. In showing concern for someone else's poor health, we may be "feeling our own sufferings in those of others . . . " (maxim 264, p. 68), yet, again, effective virtue is rendered. If *The Maxims* emphasizes that many of our kindly gestures are not necessarily or entirely disinterested, in maxim 305 selfishness harbors altruism. Still, is La Rochefoucauld harsh towards our vanities?

Like some of the great satirists, La Rochefoucauld felt that getting to know ourselves better should be beneficially humbling. Still, recalling his formidable elaboration of vanity in the disquisitional maxim 563 and vanity's endless powers of self-transformation, how can one be sure that any humility experienced is the real thing rather than vanity playing Tartuffe in order to control, dominate, and finally enslave others? The link in maxim 563 between self-love and the desire for power over others embodies a key insight into political motivation and the lust to acquire leadership.

If vanity can lurk within our humility, perhaps this linkage is an inescapable tendency of human biology. Though saints may transcend this subtle weakness, most people are not saints. Yet, lacking the gifts to be a saint would not, by La Rochefoucauld's lights, excuse us from being responsible for what we are and do. Self-expression can often be meaningless if we have nothing worth expressing or do not understand (or try to understand) ourselves or others. The crucial consideration, however, is that if anyone were to scrutinize himself as carefully as the great satirists and psychologists imply he should, he would seriously hesitate to strive for any position of great power. The ironic tragedy and possible catastrophe of our time may well reside in the fact that the people who should not control modern power, in view of its perilous political and military dimensions, are the ones most "full of passionate conviction" about their ability to wield it, and least concerned about their own motives.

It has often been said that an open society has continually to be fought for to be preserved, that its vulnerability to greed, apathy, and power monopolies also constitutes a strength in the form of freedom. This is likewise true of the Good Life residing within the negative exterior of *The Maxims*. Genuine virtue and full consciousness are qualities to be striven for, like an athlete's regimen for breaking a record. If we have the misfortune to live in a society in which the dominant values frequently resemble the Seven Deadly Sins, another apothegm by the French maxim master might partly suggest why: "Little is needed to make a wise man happy, but nothing can content a fool. That is why nearly all men are miserable" (maxim 538, p. 103). This sentiment is put more winningly in maxim 439: "There are few things we should keenly desire if we really understood what we wanted" (p. 88). As we lurch towards the end of the most genocidal, massively destructive century in the history of mankind, La Rochefoucauld's sentiments might finally distress us not because they are severe but because they are too mild.

Works Cited

Chamard, Henri. "La Rochefoucauld." Rice Institute Pamphlets, 18, 1 (January 1931).

de Mourgues, Odette. *Two French Moralists: La Rochefoucauld and La Bruyére.* London: Cambridge University Press, c1978.

Emerson, Ralph Waldo. "Circles," *Essays,* cited in *The Penguin Dictionary of Quotations.* Ed. J. M. and M. J. Cohen. New York: Penguin Books, 1983.

Groddeck, Georg. *The Book of the It.* New York: Random House, c1949.

Moore, W. G. *La Rochefoucauld: His Mind and Art.* Oxford: Clarendon Press, 1969.

La Rochefoucauld. *The Maxims.* Trans. L. W. Tancock. Harmondsworth, Eng.: Penguin Books, 1959.

Williams, Oscar, ed. *A Pocketbook of Modern Verse.* New York: Washington Square Press, 1954.

II

THREE ON LORENZO

D. H. Lawrence's "Spirit of Place" as Eco-monism

> " . . . it seems vital for the survival of the species that it foster an avid commitment to maintaining awareness of organic interconnectedness, since it is forever in acute peril of losing this awareness."
>
> Philip Slater, *Earthwalk*

I

If the environment provides fertile soil in the work of D. H. Lawrence, this is partly due to the complex and changing nature of Lawrence's responses to his surroundings. His responses changed because Lawrence was a visionary artist and intuitional genius searching both for physical and psychic health and renewal, and thus for personal as well as artistic reasons was extremely sensitive to the flux of life. He was searching, also, for a place that would embody his profoundly spiritual sense of the ideal community he termed Rananim. Thus his famous phrase "spirit of place" suggested an acute metaphoric formulation of the ethos of an area, of its most powerful human and historical qualities regarded as one with the physical terrain. Another way of putting this is to urge that Lawrence's "spirit of place" has both ecological and monistic facets that not only intertwine through being consonant or even identical in value or significance, but endow some of his work with a fused force or spirit that one could call eco-monism. Eco-monism can be defined as an ecological sense of human unity with nature and the earth, one in which the recognition of a crucial interdependence between humanity and nature could help to preserve nature and thus humanity. This very idea was put memorably by Justice William O. Douglas in a minority position on the 1972 Supreme

Court case Sierra Club vs. Morton (this case involved the Sierra Club's attempt to stop the Walt Disney business enterprise, an enterprise staunchly backed by the United States Forest Service, from building a huge ski resort in a remote region of the California Sierra Nevada called Mineral King):

> The critical question of 'standing' would be simplified and also put neatly in focus if we fashioned a federal rule that allowed environmental issues to be litigated before federal agencies or federal courts in the name of the inanimate object about to be despoiled, defaced, or invaded by roads and bulldozers and where injury is the subject of public outrage. Contemporary public concern for protecting nature's ecological equilibrium should lead to the conferral of standing upon environmental objects to sue for their own preservation . . . This suit would therefore be more properly labeled as *Mineral King v. Morton* (Turner p. 70).

Justice Douglas may be neither an eco-monist nor a Lawrentian, but he has put the case for nature as possessing subject status with a particular aptness for illuminating this little-acknowledged vein in Lawrence's work and sensibility. Thus, it behooves us to consider what connection eco-monism has with his "spirit of place," less to judge Lawrence's standing as a proto-ecologist than to get a general idea of how it occupies his writings.

The ambitious scope of the phrase "spirit of place" in part accounts for why Lawrence's *Studies in Classic American Literature*, for example, is so penetrating an interpretation of American literature and culture. In that work Lawrence uses a literary text as a kind of vatic unconsciousness through which to intimate the nature of the "psyche" of a place and its inhabitants, whether the place is a region or even a nation. This large enterprise involved a sense of animation or inherent life in the physical terrain culminating in a metaphysics of place, Lawrence's acute registration of the impact made by successions of individuals, communities and races upon a region, and by the region upon those humans or human communities. Thus when Lawrence writes about a restlessness or seething or hostility in a place (as he does of the American Southwest in *St. Mawr*), he is responding in part to the character of human habitation or presence as it is reflected in the mountains, hills, plains, flora and fauna of an area.

This is not to say, however, that nature in Lawrence's work lacks its own force or, perhaps, its own will. Humanity in *St. Mawr* confronts "the vast and unrelenting will of the swarming lower life, working forever against man's attempt at a higher life, a further created being" (pp. 152-153). Yet even here in this highly unromanticized opposition of humanity and nature, Lawrence slips into the animism of nature's "will." Lawrence's intensely intuitive and projective mode of observation may not conform to field observation standards of an anthropologist or sociologist or even a cultural historian. Nevertheless, it has its own distinction and validity as a visionary chronicle, the meta-impressions of place as imprinted on and recreated by the mind of one of the finest descriptive writers in English letters.

Lawrence projected upon his environment (as people usually do) what was currently moving within his soul. What is significant in Lawrence's projections is the intensity, sensitivity and intelligence of his attunements to or repulsions from a place. His reactions to his surroundings might change from time to time, even from hour to hour, but this changeableness was, willy-nilly, his typical mode of assimilating and shaping reverberations of a place upon his inner being. Anthony Burgess aptly represents the kind of conditions Lawrence (and Frieda) traveled under in Italy: "Travel was slow and painful, Mussolini had not yet taught the trains to run on time . . . The inn food was usually filthy . . . and the beds were dirty and verminous. Lawrence's journeys by post-bus or cold late train or on foot are in that great laborious tradition which produced genuine travel books—the eye slowly taking it all in, the aching feet imposing the leisure to observe the common people in the smoky inn kitchen" (Introduction to *D. H. Lawrence and Italy* p. x). From his responses to his surroundings emerge perceptions not measurable on graphs or by scholarship or in-depth familiarity with a people, but gauged instead by the aspirations and sensibility of a keen-eyed poet-visionary.

Now it seems to me that Lawrence's "spirit of place" can be regarded philosophically as a powerful interchange of not only subject and object but of subject and *subject*. Indeed, one of Lawrence's significant traits as a travel writer, poet and novelist is a philosophical monism or hylozoism, that is, an inclination to regard nature as one with the mind perceiving it. Christopher Pollnitz claims that the end of Lawrence's idea of blood consciousness "was not the identification of subject with object but a deepened sense of separateness from an ultimately unknowable object" (p. 13). However, if an object achieves what Pollnitz calls its "inextinguishable mystery" by being regarded as having an integrity of separateness, might this sort of separateness nevertheless grant the object *subject* status and thus monistic character through regarding anything (including matter) as alive or animate?

And can one take things a step further by suggesting that integrity of separateness is to some degree paradoxical and even illusionary, depending as it does on another animate force that recognizes and thus "extends" its separateness? That is, can separateness based on such an awareness as Lawrence's truly be separateness, or does Lawrence's (or anyone's) apprehension of the object bond it to the viewer so that its integrity of separateness actually rests upon its *subject-subject* relationship with its human witness? Lawrence in his poem "Fish" may not know the pike's god, but he *knows* he doesn't know that deity, and that "dark" knowledge creates a relationship of both separateness and numinous *connection* between Lawrence and the pike. He may not merge with the pike, but his sense of its separateness bonds fish and man through an integrity both creatures share, if cognitively conceived by at least one of them.

Paul Delany, in his Montpellier Lawrence Conference paper "Lawrence and Deep Ecology," intimates another problem area in Lawrence's subject-object thinking. Describing Lawrence's monistic sense of his interchange with the "Lawrence" tree on the Lawrence ranch in northern New Mexico, Delany states that "This union should not be a merging, in which man tries to appropriate nature for his own aggrandizement—as Lawrence saw it, the Wordsworth fallacy" (p. 5). Then Lawrence is quoted indicating Wordsworth as a kind of "imperialistic" anthropomorphist who would not allow (in this case) a primrose its own soul or what just above I call integrity. This merits pointing out, but it should also be made clear that Wordsworth's primrosing represents only one kind of merging. If Lawrence was hostile to epistemological possessiveness, to the subject (human) that knows and controls all, including the object status of entities like trees that can also be (and have been) regarded as subjects, he nevertheless exhibited a sort of affirmative or substantive merging often enough in his work to suggest that he indeed did not view all monism as simple or simple-minded. Lawrence *did* sometimes envision a merging of subject and object, here and there, humanity and nature, and he conveyed that unity with depth of implication and metaphoric force in more than a few important areas of his fiction, non-fiction prose and verse.

Lawrence's description of the sensibility of ancient peoples like the Etruscans or modern ones like the Native Americans (or American Indians) of the Southwest are cases in point (among others) of monism and hylozoism in his writings. (I use the pre-Socratic Greek word hylozoism to supplement the meaning of monism through its denoting no division between life and matter, a meaning not stressed in the definition of monism that all reality inheres in one element or principle.) Lawrence presents these ancient or marginal peoples as oriented by a mode of perception that endows their sense of place with a quality of close, even absolute, relating to their physical surroundings. Here, for example, is Lawrence in his vivid 1928 essay "New Mexico" describing the religious perception of both the Native Americans he had seen in the Southwest, and, on the basis of Etruscan mortuary art he had observed, a kind of unifying, monistic mind:

> It was a vast old religion, greater than anything we know.... There is no god, no conception of a god. All is god.... In the oldest religion, everything was alive, not supernaturally but naturally alive. There were only deeper and deeper streams of life, vibrations of life more and more vast. So rocks were alive, but a mountain had a deeper, vaster life . . . and it was harder for a man to bring his spirit, or his energy, into contact with the life of the mountain, and so draw strength from the mountain . . . than it was to come into contact with the rock. And he had to put forth a great religious effort. For the whole life-effort of man was to get his life into contact with the elemental life of the cosmos. . . . This effort into sheer naked contact, *without an intermediary or mediator*, is the root meaning of religion . . . (p. 187).

The depth of implication of this passage is achieved through Lawrence's ability to transfigure a mode of seeing into religious vision. And the religiousness of the vision is all the more striking for lacking a godhead, the sovereignty of deity. "Rocks were alive" is a more loaded statement than it may at first seem, for it is part of a natural order culminating in "mountain-life" or "cloud-life" or "sun-life." All the energy that gets sublimated in traditional deity religions into a Godhead possesses in Lawrence's primitivist vision a "horizontal" rather than a "vertical" direction. Thus the natural world itself is not deified, for that inclines towards pantheism, but is animated, or is even regarded as autonomous, relatively free of human projection. Humans can derive strength from the mountain by "coming into contact" with it, the very antithesis of their deriving material value from the mountain by using it technologically, that is, exploiting it. And this is intimated through Lawrence's use of "dark" in his describing the vitalization and even joy humans experience in their direct contact with the elements. Indeed, Lawrence takes his monism or hylozoism so far as to see the basis of religion as this one-to-one relation of humanity and nature *without* a divine intercessor and ruler.

Lawrence animizes the universe again in a passage of vigorous and empathetic meta-description from *Etruscan Places*:

> To the Etruscans all was alive; the whole universe lived; and the business of man was himself to live amid it all. He had to draw life into himself, out of wandering huge vitalities of the world. The cosmos was alive, like a vast creature. The whole thing breathed and stirred . . . Out of the fissures of the earth came breaths of other breathing, vapours direct from the living physical under-earth . . . The whole thing was alive, and had a great soul or *anima* . . .
>
> The cosmos was one, and its *anima* was one: but it was made up of creatures. And the greatest creature was earth, with its soul of inner fire (p. 49).

Out of this travel writing, which leads to a primitivistic religious vision, also emerges an ontology of place. Humanity, Lawrence's "philosophy" of travel implies, is what it sees its environment as or projects on it, and what it thus sees environmentally indicates its deepest nature. If humanity regards a forest as primarily a stockyard of lumber or a month's supply of *The New York Times*, this tells us much about not only the current technology, but about the character of a community's sense of place and soul—the two are interwoven, though not exactly in harmony. But if a community or a nation perceives a forest as a *subject*, an animized or even sacred place, then it will probably feel differently about its natural surroundings and perhaps act accordingly. The abusive use of place through technological and economic exploitation amounts to the objectification of an environment. This process has overtaken us today alarmingly. For example, approximately 75 acres of tropical rain forest are destroyed every minute and, according to the "geologian" Thomas Berry, it took 65 million years to grow it, and, if we destroy it—many say we are destroying it—it will never grow back—Matousek p. 33). Lawrence would have hated this devastating development. Indeed, he indicated his hatred—and terror—in a powerful passage near the end of *Twilight in Italy*:

> It is as if the whole social form were breaking down, and the human element swarmed within the disintegration, like maggots in cheese. The roads, the railways are built, the mines and quarries are excavated, but the whole organism of life, the social organism, is slowly crumbling and caving in, in a kind of process of gray rot, most terrifying to see. So that it seems as though we should be left at last with a great system of roads and railways and industries, and a world of utter chaos seething upon these fabrications: as if we had created a steel framework, and the whole body of society were crumbling and rotting in between (p. 165).

Lawrence, whose steel framework metaphor probably derives from H. G. Wells's *War of the Worlds*, is not talking here directly about a natural environment, but about a new urban growth that once *was* a natural environment. Lawrence's sensitivity to the "perfection" of form (the roads, railways and industries being built up in Italy, and elsewhere) and the disintegration of subject (humanity) exhibits an artist's preternatural responsiveness to the essential reality of the contemporary. One recalls the stunning passages in the "Industrial-Magnate" chapter in *Women in Love* in which Lawrence describes Gerald Crich's "perfection" of coal-mining technique. Such mechanistic refinement of the work process mechanizes the coal-miners to a condition of sheer inner chaos, the integrity and subtlety of their inner life warped and then destroyed. The destruction of the organic to consolidate the mechanical, the industrial, today the consumable (planting sumptuous resort hotels, even cities, in deserts) reveals technology and material culture out of touch with human proportions and the organic rhythms and limits of both nature and human nature. Lawrence didn't examine this monstrous emerging condition of modern society in the manner of a social scientist; he foresees it, and what he saw *then* in

Northern Italy and saw looming in the future has come to pass, as the rapacious commercial development is literally destroying the habitableness of the earth.

II

Place for Lawrence is usually a barometer of psyche, a definition of the deepest or strongest human drives and the configuration they reflexively acquire in being imposed on the physical surroundings. But place for Lawrence is also, as mentioned earlier, the vital autonomy or integrity of a physical environment and its response or resistance to human presence. If an individual or group is at odds with itself, or driven like *Women in Love's* Gerald Crich by an uncontrollable fury of will to dominate the natural surroundings, then the result, as in *Women in Love* or *Lady Chatterley's Lover* or the latter part of *The Rainbow*, will be a place overmastered by a human covetousness to possess that will not rest until the object is virtually annihilated. We are then confronted, as Lawrence predicted, by a devastation of place that threatens the very survival of the self-declared primary "subject"—humanity itself.

When Lawrence describes in, let us say, American Southwest fiction like *St. Mawr* or *The Princess* a quality of brooding malice or "gigantic, heavy gruesomeness" in a place, he is suggesting what nature can really be like despite or because of human modulation of an environment. Yet doom, to Lawrence, vibrates through the American forests and the seas of *Moby Dick* because Melville projects, through Ahab's crazed pursuit of the white whale, his vision of a compulsion by the American psyche to exterminate a part of its own deepest nature that it fears and cannot dominate. Or when Lawrence describes the woods in *Lady Chatterley's Lover* as shrinking between the enlarging mines and straggling company towns, he is suggesting an action and an attitude by modern society towards nature and, thus, towards itself. This attitude, as some realize today, is one that objectifies nature and that thus deprives human beings of a sustained human identity by depriving us of the crucial basis for our own most vitalized subjectness—nature, the wilds, the earth.

A monistic perspective provides another context for understanding Lawrence's frequently misunderstood and ridiculed phrase the "dark gods." In the form of the political hierophants Ramon and Cipriano in *The Plumed Serpent*, the term is certainly open to censure; the novel's literal exaltation of human beings into deity and society into elitist theocracy strikes me as very pernicious. Such "gods," in Lawrence's schema, are above normal human shortcomings. They are accordingly given a free hand to do what they want—a scope of rule and power also affirmed in *Etruscan Places, Apocalypse* and sections of *Lady Chatterley's Lover*. The resulting theory of community is obviously a politically hazardous one for the remainder of mere humanity.

But in other works (and along other dimensions in *Chatterley*) Lawrence wields the idea of dark gods with a metaphoric suppleness and variety both engaging and profound. One recalls his satiric criticisms in *Studies in Classic American Literature* of one of America's Founding Fathers—Benjamin Franklin, that insufferably rational, practical and worldly man.

> '... *the soul is immortal*.' The trite way Benjamin says it! ... The *wholeness* of a man is his soul (p. 20).

Lawrence goes on to distinguish *his* sense of order, frugality, sincerity, etc., from Franklin's arid utilitarianism ("Let all your things have their places .... avoid trifling conversation.... Avoid extremes.... Lose no time, be always employed in something useful").

Now, here are Lawrence's markedly monistic sentiments:

> ... my soul is a dark forest ...
>
> ... gods, strange gods, come forth from the forest into the clearing of my known self.
>
> ... I must have the courage to let them come and go (p. 26).

And then, continues Lawrence,

> ... I ... know why I can't stand Benjamin. He tries to take away my wholeness and my dark forest, my freedom. For how can any man be free without an illimitable background? (p. 28)

Franklin left no room for Lawrence's dark forest; he probably would leave none for Lawrence's dark gods and, I suspect, for monism or hylozoism as well. On this point we can return to the idea of the spirit of place. The "dark gods" in Lawrence's "dark" or "primitive" peoples are evoked precisely by the accessibility of these peoples to a place's spirit (or spirits), that numinous sense of a living (not necessarily human) force or presence that resides in, and in a crucial sense *is*, the natural environment. This force of life in nature, entering into instinctive or intuitive relation with Lawrence's Native Americans or Etruscans or gypsies or Midland miners, charges and recharges their lives with energy:

> When history [claims Lawrence in *Etruscan Places*] does begin, in China or India, Egypt, Babylonia, even in the Pacific and in aboriginal America, we see evidence of one underlying religious idea; the conception of vitality of the cosmos, the myriad vitalities in wild confusion . . . and man, amid all the flowing welter, adventuring, struggling, striving for one thing, life, vitality, more vitality. . . . The active religious idea was that man, by vivid attention and subtlety and exerting all his strength, could draw more life into himself, . . . more and more glistening vitality, till he became shining like the morning, blazing like a god.
> (Lawrence, *Etruscan Places*, in *D. H. Lawrence and Italy* p. 50)

In this exultant passage from *Etruscan Places*, humanity and place acquire a dynamized "subject-subject" relationship—a human being's life and sensibility crucially depend on his harmonious, even *monistic* interaction with his environment, which lives not only because nature possesses biological status but also because it inspires our human sense of on-going, ever-renewing existence through its own manifestations of life. As Wendell Berry puts it, "We do not live *on* the earth, but with and within its life. We will realize that earth is not dead, like the concept of property, but as vividly and intricately alive as a man or a woman, and that there is a delicate inter-dependence between its life and our own" (pp. 12-13).

Of course Lawrence was not primarily an ecological crusader. He was no Rachel Carson or David Brower. He was, however, a poet-seer of the organic interelatedness of humanity and the earth. Like earlier poets, philosophers and mystics,

Lawrence, dualist that he was, envisions the union of humanity and nature as virtually a sacramental relationship, and the mechanistic-industrial violation of this relationship as a sacrilege harboring a grave fate for humanity itself and the earth. He becomes apocalyptic on this score in *Sea and Sardinia*:

> The spirit of the place is a strange thing. Our mechanical age tries to override it. But it does not succeed. In the end the strange, sinister spirit of the place, so diverse and adverse in differing places, will smash our mechanical oneness into smithereens, and all that we think the real thing will go off with a pop, and we shall be left staring (p. 55).

Today it is a truism that humanity itself is smashing the earth (and thus very possibly itself) to smithereens through terrifying rates of population increase, intensified industrial and technological expansion, extirpation of natural resources and consequent multiform global pollution. Such an extreme assault on the spirit of place may not have been exactly what Lawrence had in mind, though he was impressively near the mark in the 20th-century modes of possible earthly doom that he puts in the minds of those two cunning *artistes* and futurologists, *Women in Love's* Gudrun and Loerke:

> As for the future, that they never mentioned except one laughed out some mocking dream of the destruction of the world by a ridiculous catastrophe of man's invention: a man invented such a perfect explosive that it blew the earth in two, and the two halves set off in different directions in space, to the dismay of the inhabitants: or else the people of the world divided in two halves, and each half decided *it* was perfect and right, the other half was wrong and must be destroyed; so another end of the world. Or else, Loerke's dream of fear, the world went cold, and snow fell everywhere . . . (p. 444).

Global thermonuclear devastation, globally divisive ideologies, the world going hot or cold, either through human or nature's devising—Lawrence surely deserves attention as a prophet, poet and fictionist of a 20th-century culture of ecology. Desertification or disastrous oil spills may not have been specific concerns of Lawrence, but he pondered and powerfully dramatized the kind of disordered sensibility and drive that would thrust humanity towards precipitating the world's ecological crisis.

The human gains from Lawrence's monistic outlook would hardly be manipulation of the environment to erect a "high" standard of technological living; rather, Lawrence's eco-monism implies a reverence for place that assures the evolving life of place and humanity as crucially interwoven and, accordingly, as the intense, creative and renewable experience of the human spirit. Is Lawrence's monism atavistic, simplistic, fantastical? I think not. One should keep in mind a culminating statement made by Lawrence in another Southwest piece called "Indians and an Englishman": " . . . as I look back, like memory terrible as bloodshed, the dark faces round the fire in the night, and one blood beating in me and them. But I don't want to go back to them, ah, never. I never want to deny them or break with them. But there is no going back. *Always onward. Still further* [italics added]. The great devious onward-flowing stream of conscious human blood. From them to me, and from me on" (*Selected Essays* p. 197).

The eco-monist sensibility Lawrence validates or implies in some of his significant work projects a mode of individual and social culture that, prolonging the life of earth itself, prolongs and enriches human existence. This is only part of what Lawrence means by the phrase "spirit of place," but it now appears to be and mean everything to human survival.

Works Cited

Berry, Wendell. *A Continuous Harmony: Essays Cultural and Agricultural.* New York: 1989.
Delany, Paul. "D. H. Lawrence and Deep Ecology," Paper, the D. H. Lawrence Montpellier Conference, June 23-27, 1990, p. 5.
Gutierrez, Donald. *Subject-Object Relations in Wordsworth and D. H. Lawrence.* Ann Arbor: UMI Research Press, 1987.
Lawrence, D. H. *D. H. Lawrence and Italy.* New York: Viking Press, 1972.
—. "Indians and an Englishman," *Selected Essays.* Baltimore: Penguin Books, rpt. 1976.
—. *Lady Chatterley's Lover.* New York: Bantam Books, 1971.
—. "New Mexico," *Selected Essays.* Baltimore: Penguin Books, rpt. 1976.
—. *St. Mawr* and *The Man Who Died.* New York: Random House, c1953.
—. *Studies in Classic American Literature.* New York: Doubleday, 1953.
Matousek, Mark. "Reinventing the Human," *Common Boundary.* May-June, 1990.

"Break On Through to the Other Side!":
Lawrence's "New Heaven and Earth" as Apocalyptic

> "And I saw a new heaven and a new earth: for the first heaven and the first earth were passed away..."
> *Revelation*

> "... the end of all things is inside us. Our epoch is over..."
> D. H. Lawrence, "Dies Irae," *Pansies*

> "... the loins are the place of last judgement."
> Norman O. Brown, *Love's Body*

I

Critics have in the main condemned "New Heaven and Earth," the long poem which virtually concludes D. H. Lawrence's middle-period verse collection *Look! We Have Come Through!*[1] And understandably. The poem is long-winded, occasionally obscure, repetitive, and markedly self-exhibitive and self-celebrating. Yet Kenneth Rexroth has said that "it may not be a perfect object of art, but it is a profound exhortation."[2] I hope to show that apocalyptic is the medium of that exhortation, and that it endows this underrated poem with a technical complexity and an intellectual and emotional range worthy of attention.[3] The subject of the poem, in turn, has considerable effect on the special manner in which it is expressed. The extent to which subject and manner or mode of expression are one provides a good measure of the merit of the poem. Lawrence's subject concerns a profound personal-marital experience objectified by apocalyptic conventions which are themselves modified by the revolutionary nature of Lawrence's vision.

That "New Heaven and Earth" is inadequate as dramatized

art is evident in the absence of a nay-saying realist to the mantic voice. There is no verbal or vocal "Frieda" in the poem, no *Women in Love's* Ursula to Birkin's Salvator Mundi. "Frieda," the spouse, is in the poem, but, for all purposes of creative antipodal response, she might as well not be, being asleep. Thus the poem appears one-sided, suggesting imbalance or lack of restraint. But, like Donne's "The Canonization," the poem is a paean. Both poems extol passionate love. If Donne uses "wit" both to extend and control his meanings, Lawrence uses intensity, a powerful religious convention, and confessional candor to extend and control his. Written in a different key than "The Canonization," "New Heaven and Earth" is to be heard with different expectations.

Frank Kermode has observed how immersed Lawrence was in apocalyptic thinking.[4] Lawrence describes this engrossment early in the posthumous *Apocalypse*: "From earliest years right into manhood, like any other non-conformist child I had the Bible poured every day into my helpless consciousness, till there came almost a saturation point." Portions of the Bible "become an influence which affected all the processes of emotion and thought."[5] A few pages later, Lawrence, after describing the *Book of Revelation* as "the most detestable of all these books of the Bible, taken superficially," states that "By the time I was ten, I am sure I had heard, and read that book ten times over . . . " Thus whether he loved or loathed it, apocalyptic seems to have long been a natural mold of thought for Lawrence. It can be found in a variety of forms in works like *The Rainbow*, *Women in Love*, *St. Mawr*, and *Lady Chatterley's Lover*, not to mention even very minor works such as the poems "Dies Irae" and "Dies Illa" in the late verse collection called *Pansies*. The fact that Lawrence felt ambivalently about apocalyptic is usually crucial to the artistic merit of the writings in which it appears. Without the presence of an agent of day-to-day life (Ursula in *Women in Love*, Clifford Chatterley and Mrs. Bolton— in their different ways—in *Lady Chatterley's Lover*) the eschatological energy in those works would destroy what has been called the crucial balance in Lawrence's major fictions between history and myth.[6] Yet "New Heaven and Earth" possesses force and integrity despite the absence of this important antithetical tension.

Before taking up the element of apocalyptic in "New Heaven and Earth," however, I wish first to consider the symbolic discovery central to the poem, for this embodies its revelation. The speaker declaims throughout the poem on a discovery of new regions of being which, in his estimation, are more important than those of the great discoverers of external terrain: "I touch, I feel the unknown! / I am the first comer! / Cortes, Pizarro, Columbus, Cabot, they are nothing, nothing! / . . . I am the discoverer! / I have found the other world!" (st. VI).

On one plane the poem exhibits extreme self-centeredness:

> I was so weary of the world,
> I was so sick of it,
> everything was tainted with myself,
> skies, trees, flowers, birds, water,
> people, houses, streets, vehicles, machines,
> nations, armies, war, peace-talking,
> work, recreation, governing, anarchy,
> it was all tainted with myself . . . . (st. II).

Yet this is clearly more than obsessive egotism or anti-egotism (or, for that matter, Lawrence's deep guilt as a non-combatant). Indeed the underlying point of this early passage makes the extreme self-concern unavoidable, as the theme involves a total revulsion from the past, from one's past self, and from a solipsistic mentality. This negative Whitmanian litany of ego-contempt, a "dark night" convention and phase of mystical ascension, registers the prerequisite exorcism essential, as the poem's argument has it, to achieving a new state of being. And the interweaving, here and elsewhere, of "Lawrence" and the First World War expands the scope of the detested person and self to society in the throes of violent disintegration; in a strikingly unusual association, Lawrence and modern society are temporarily one.

Nevertheless, when Lawrence says, in the very first line of the poem, that "he crosses into another world," he *means* another *world*, not only a figure of speech for his wife's body. The other world, the "new heaven and earth," is the new place created by being or becoming a new person while still, paradoxically, remaining the same person. And one becomes a new person through being liberated from self as self-consciousness, cerebrality, the illimitable and all-devouring ego. The eventual fate of the "Unliberated" in the private sphere of marital love culminates in an insanity of solipsistic misidentification:

> I shall never forget the maniacal horror of it all in the end
> when everything was me, I knew it all already, I
>   anticipated it all in my soul
> because I was the author and the result
> I was the God and the creation at once;

> creator, I looked at my creation;
> created, I looked at myself, the creator . . .
>
> I was a lover, I kissed the woman I loved,
> and, God of horror, I was kissing also myself.
> (Section III)

This is subtle and complex psychologically. To be oneself and the other is to destroy the Unknown and its life-enhancing potential. This negative merging represents a sinister omnipotence, a monstrous psychic totality of knowledge that violates finity, partiality, limit, reciprocity. It is a condition of domination by consciousness that thwarts the unconscious and cuts off its roots in the New and into the New Heaven.

The location of a New Heaven in the unconscious would be consistent with Lawrence's proclivity to invert the traditional location of the ideal—upwards, the sky, the heavens. His empyrean, his New Jerusalem, his Chthonian deities reside in "New Heaven and Earth" in the sizable if not infinite spaces of one's inner and innermost being.

Lawrence then is trying to conquer the rapacious urge to know all, which includes merging one's sensibility with the Other. The "Other" is specified as spouse particularly because marriage, with its elaborate recesses of intimacy, provides the greatest temptation to precisely the sort of merging that dissolves the self, a condition that Lawrence regarded as a large threat to personal integrity.

Thus a "maniacal horror" drives "Lawrence" to raze the structures of the known (both personal and universal) in order to emancipate the energies of the unknown. Doing so makes one "a tiger bursting into sunlight," a figure of liberation partly indebted to Blake, as in a larger sense is Lawrence's yoking of erotic experience to religious revolutionism. This unknown encompasses something larger than the unconscious or the sexually forbidden or unconventional. Not only is it "new beyond knowledge of newness," it is "living where life was never yet dreamed of" (st. V). Lawrence will not have this Rananim fenced in by any psychoanalytic or reductive associations. On occasion, he can verbally will into being the "unaccountably new," but this forcing is not a major element in the poem.

This destruction of the known also intimates the kinship of apocalyptic with revolution. Though hardly a Bakunin, Lawrence would perforce encompass social reality in his apocalyptic destructiveness. As such, the fascinating issue of the dividing line between extreme personal and social change, that is, between regeneration and revolution, is broached, as well as the important implication that both revolution and apocalyptic possess deep, and perhaps identical, eschatological roots. Lawrence might have insisted on conducting a one-man (or a man-and-woman) revolution, but this poem, as well as works ranging from *The Rainbow* and *Women in Love* to *The Man Who Died* and *Lady Chatterley's Lover*, suggests that it would have had an individualist orientation all too frequently lacking in social revolutions.

The combination of Lawrence's individualist revolution and his climactic marital experience with the vast destructiveness endemic to apocalyptic enlarges and enriches the pronounced death-and-rebirth insistence in the poem.[7] The poem was written during World War One, which provided Lawrence a central apocalyptic convention in which to set and thus magnify his death-rebirth patterns of personal experience. According to apocalyptical tradition, the "new heaven and earth" is preceded by the reign of Anti-Christ (Kaiser Wilhelm, in 1915) and universal strife.[8] Chaos and destruction comprise the unavoidable purgative events before the advent of the New Jerusalem. This aspect of apocalyptic helps to reveal the significance and complexity of a key sequence; it also allows us to test one of the more extreme manifestations of the problem of decorum or taste in the poem:

>War came, and every hand raised to murder....
>It is good, I can murder and murder, and see them fall,
>the mutilated horror-struck youths, a multitude
>one on another and then in clusters together
>smashed, all oozing with blood, and burned in heaps...
>the murdered bodies of youth and men in heaps
>till it is almost enough, till I am reduced perhaps;
>thousands and thousands of gaping, hideous foul dead
>that are youths and men and me
>being burned with oil, and consumed in corrupt thick
>   smoke that rolls
>and taints and blackens the sky, till at last it is dark, dark
>   as night, or death, or hell
>and I am dead, and trodden to nought in the smoke-
>   sodden tomb... (st. IV).

Lawrence in this hideous passage appears to be making the outrageous argument that such a mass slaughter of male populations is a good thing because it is a prerequisite to *his* resurrection.

He may suffer their fate figuratively and imaginatively, but why should they share his fate in order to implement his resurrection? First, we behold here not only Lawrence himself, but a "Lawrence" Everyman persona. Although the poem is obviously grounded in autobiographical experience, the speaker's heuristic attitude towards his experience, its suggestion of being potentially sharable, identifies him with all men in a critical phase of their life. If a gap remains between such men and this Lawrencean Everyman, the latter nonetheless proffers the body and image of his discovery of "the other world" to all men. Some might argue that Lawrence makes no exhortations at all, but surely the recorded poem itself and its cumulative impact constitute an exhortation. Ezra Pound's artist and Lawrence's explorer might be the antennae of the race, but they undergo experience common or at least available to most men.

Although this general persona still represents the extreme of individualist sovereignty over societal rights, this maneuver discloses more than merely Lawrence the alienated Englishman justifying mass carnage for a personal salvation. Moreover, the orgy of war-destructiveness metaphorically accentuates the death of "Lawrence's" old life. In this light, the battle passage is insanely vain and unethical only to the extent that the person in the poem is exclusively Lawrence, rather than a dramatized or generic individual. Furthermore, the passage is a hyperbole of "Lawrence's" self-disgust, and, by implication, of the disgust anyone saddled with too much of the "known" in himself or herself should feel. Lawrence stresses his own utter destruction, and even adds a final self-stomping: "God, but it is good to have died and been trodden out, / trodden to nought . . . absolutely to nothing . . . "

A final point about this war passage concerns its apocalyptic nature. Some of its cataclysmic violence appears to parallel that found in the *Book of Revelation*: " . . . lo, there was a great earthquake; and the sun became black as sackcloth of hair; and the moon became as blood . . . " (v. 6, p. 11. 12-17). Yet cataclysm in *Revelation* is not only cosmic in scope, but in the seven-vials sequence evinces a fury easily surpassing Lawrence's:

> . . . Go your ways, and pour out the vials of the wrath of God upon the earth.
>
> And the first went, and poured out his vial upon the earth; and there fell a noisome and grievous sore upon the men which had the mark of the beast . . . .

> And the second angel poured out his vial upon
> the sea; and it became as the blood of a dead
> man; and every living soul died in the sea.
>
> And the third angel poured out his vial upon
> the rivers and fountains of waters; and they
> became blood . . . (p. 16, 1-3).

Although both *Revelation* and "New Heaven and Earth" display intense vindictiveness, Lawrence's bloody bellicosity is primarily a hyperbole involving a symbolic individual immolation, whereas St. John's revenge, despite exegetical transformations and extenuations, is clearly (if not only) literal in its social, even cosmic scope. Nevertheless, the placement in the poem of carnage within an eschatological death-rebirth context renders the war passage, and ultimately the entire poem, distinctly apocalyptic. Lawrence in this way implies another facet in his persona here, beyond that of the millenialist martyr of the modern age in extremity. He is also the apocalyptist, a pseudonymous religious-erotic seer and revolutionary intimating the superiority of "death" not to submission to "Roman" oppressors but to his literally exploding 20th Century world.

It is pertinent to consider further what case can be made for the artistic integrity of Lawrence's personal apocalypse. In the remainder of the essay, I will examine his apocalyptic innovations, as they (and traditional apocalyptic) heighten what is distinctive and fine in the poem.

II

Regarded as eschatology, the poem harbors a somewhat complex persona. But it also contains important variations of apocalyptic which almost embody an anti-apocalyptic. Apocalyptists and millenarians often have their cake, but seldom (if ever) eat it too. Lawrence does. Indeed his innovation is related to one way of looking at the structure of the poem. This assumes the temporal form of present-past-present. In the present of stanza one, the speaker has already won his "new heaven." Then he moves into the past (st. 2-4), the time-zone of his former loathed self, to describe how awful it was and so how essential to transcend. This negative phase, a "dies irae" in the eschatological pattern, occupies more than one-third of "New Heaven and Earth." The third phase (st. 5-7) depicts past-becoming-present, and, in stanza eight, the final stanza, a celebrated "timeless" present, Lawrence's "fourth dimension" which, in extolling the new life, links the poem circularly with the joyful proclamation of stanza one.

In the final two stanzas Lawrence describes what it was that catapulted him into new being. This has to do with a new kind or sense of contact with his wife. This development, which gives the speaker the New Jerusalem *now*, also communalizes the whole experience. As, further, it is a communalizing in erotic terms, Lawrence revolutionizes apocalyptic by converting the divine sanctioning of the outer world, the customary setting for apocalypse, into a primacy upon a deeply subjective situation, a passionate and complex marriage.[9] Thus the conventions of the Johannine apocalypse become subverted by the "laws" of a conjugal eros, even if the world of Lawrence's New Jerusalem is, comparatively speaking, the size of a pearl. It takes two (occasionally three), *this* St. John is proclaiming, to make a world, perhaps most easily to make the new good world. The number of significant fictions in which Lawrence develops this idea gauges the importance to him of apocalyptic patterns. Strict apocalyptists, judging the visionary experiences of this poem, would undoubtedly demur with its innovations, finding them blasphemous or subversive of traditional usages in Last Day procedure.[10] The attachment of such people to literal apocalyptic and doctrinal imminence would on the other hand incorporate much that the here-and-now in Lawrence detested.

Lawrence's New Jerusalem, then, is not a world, a society dangled luringly in the near future, nor does it resemble the type of sophisticated availability found in such interpretations of *Revelation* as that of Hubert J. Richards: "The persecuted Christian must be convinced, not that he will soon win, but that he is now winning. The opposition he experiences from the world, and his struggle with it, is his victory."[11] It will not arrive, moreover, by heroic (or stubborn) attachment to a forbidden religion, although the suggestive ambiguity of "forbidden religion" could open a variety of routes to the New World. For Lawrence's love-community of two bears the intense purposiveness of an outlawed religious minority. It is in addition characteristic of Lawrence to explore love and lovers in terms of self and society so radically opposed as virtually to register as acute religious experience.

In apocalypse, God intervenes after humanity has maintained its integrity of resistance to societally imposed suffering. It is part of Lawrence's seldom credited humanism that in the apocalyptic world of this poem (as well as in such major works as *Women in Love*) humanity makes the Last Things occur. If in *Women in Love*, character is fate (as Mark Schorer has stated), in "New Heaven and Earth" the marital relationship creates for the lovers a new place of being.[12] Nor are the geographical metaphors recurring throughout the poem accidental; an experience this profound, this new, demands, Lawrence implies, vast figures to do it justice. Nothing short of cosmic scope will do. But more than scope is realized through apocalyptic. This religious mode provides the culminatory thrust towards what the poem is all about: the apotheosis of a marriage tumultuous in character because it symbolizes the struggle to surmount the death orientation of modern industrialized society.

The earlier poems in *Look!* dramatize the struggle, the terror and bliss, the intensified hatred and guilt and desire of illicit lovers temporarily isolated from a collapsing world. In the prose "Argument" preceding the collection, Lawrence tells us this: "The conflict of love and hate goes on between the man and the woman, and between these two and the world around them, till it reaches some sort of conclusion, they transcend into some condition of blessedness."[13] In an early poem in the series, "She Looks Back" (a title indicating the fate for such types), "Lawrence" curses his wife—and all mothers—for "devastating the vision" by her mother-love for her children by her deserted husband, Ernest Weekley. In "Mutilation" he fears Frieda will leave him, thus "mutilating" him into a fragmentary isolation. The poem "Humiliation" underscores the degradation this lover feels at realizing he cannot do without this woman ("God, that I have no choice!," he helplessly laments). But "Song of a Man Who is Not Loved" comes before "Song of a Man Who is Loved" and cheek by jowl with poems like "Mutilation" or the brief and poignant "Forsaken and Forlorn" are such verse flowerings of joyful love as "Gloire de Dijon," the pre-apocalyptic and gorgeous "I Am Like a Rose," the hushed over-mastering eroticism of "December Night" and "New Year's Eve" and another poem, "Spring Morning," that both places the lovers at the porch of the palace of apocalypse, yet looks back to the marital battlefield, possessing, as many of the best lyrics in *Look!* do, a poignant bittersweetness of past pain and present joy. The "mother" poems also complicate the picture, the symmetrical counterpart of Lawrence's semi-paralyzing past in *Look!* to Frieda's children. Such poems as "All Souls," "Everlasting Flowers: For a Dead Mother," and "Hymn to Priapus" reveal, with characteristic honesty, *Lawrence* "looking back."

Thus by the time we arrive at "Song of a Man Who Has Come Through," "New Heaven and Earth," and the jubilant but inferior "Manifesto" (in part a prosaic re-working of "New Heaven and Earth"), something has indeed been gone through, so large that only apocalyptic can contain it. "Song of a Man Who Has Come Through" and "New Heaven and Earth" celebrate the human-given "divine" reward, and Denis Donoghue's case against Lawrence as one of the "thieves of Prometheus" can obversely be viewed here (and certainly elsewhere) in a humanist, affirmative light.[14] At the end of "Song of a Man Who Has Come Through," Lawrence says one should admit the "three strange angels," but it is the finely-attuned human receptivity to "the wind that blows through me!" that ignites the apocalyptic process. So in "New Heaven and Earth," "Lawrence" passes from the stultifying and deadening past of Eastwood, his mother and father, and Professor Weekley into a vibrant new world in an adult relationship with an older married woman. No wonder he says, early in this climactic poem, "I could cry with joy."

What seems from one angle like hysteria in "New Heaven and Earth" from another begins to resemble a mystical ecstasy. Rather than resolving the troubled love relationship chronicled in *Look!*, the poem presents the aftermath of such a resolution, a phase overlooked in much love literature. It celebrates a complex marriage in terms of apocalyptic death-and-rebirth so as to universalize a deeply fulfilling relationship precisely at a time when society, in the rage of Armageddon, would most desire to annihilate such a relationship. And it presents a sensual event communicating an almost overwhelming reverence for the mysterious integrity of the spouse and thus of the marital relationship as well as of the self. In all these ways, "New Heaven and Earth" transvaluates apocalyptic. We can now briefly reconsider the sensual level of "New Heaven and Earth," as it is, even more than the war-massacre sequence, crucial in establishing our basic perspective on the poem.

The final action that dissolves the evil Old World and self and ushers in the New is the touching of the wifely flank[15]:

> It was the flank of my wife
> I touched with my hand, I clutched with my hand,
> rising, new-awakened from the tomb!
> It was the flank of my wife
> whom I married years ago

> at whose side I have lain for over a thousand nights
> and all that previous while, she was I, she was I;
> I touched her, it was I who touched and I who was
> touched . . . (Section 7)

Lawrence is distinctive for his propensity to place life, love, sex, torment and death in tight interrelation. The possible regenerations of such interrelations are intensified by an apocalyptic that is meshed by Lawrence to his preternaturally vivid sense of life and death. When "Lawrence" can newly experience through touching his wife's midbody the deepest sense of life as erotic physical relatedness and conceive it in religious terms of ends and beginnings, the convention of apocalyptic serves in his work to make the specific, concrete instances of life numinous with realized presence.

What is more graphically "there" yet taken for granted than a spouse's familiar flank ("of my wife / Whom I married years ago")? However, through the vehicle of apocalyptic and aroused sensibility it illuminates (here the sensual and sexual centrality of his wife's being), the wife's flank so blazes with reality that it translates Everyman "Lawrence" to a new world, *the* new world, of sensibility which offers a new "earth," "I," "knowledge" and "time" to the courageous sojourner. Whatever, wherever this "place," this sensibility, may be, it offers *rapture*. And who, after all, can forget that blended exultation of mind, feeling and sensation in first (or later) apprehending one's spouse as "flank," as the sacred body and being "realized" through sexual love, a sensory experience so keen and vivid, so gleaming with ineffable reality as virtually to merit being called a religious or spiritual engagement of unexcellable authority. This sort of realization I see Lawrence trying to describe here.

Further, Lawrence's New Jerusalem is (or can be) inherited by a new realization of the *related* otherness of the person closest to him. In the discovery of the full integrity and separateness of the other person, one gains one's own self (to be of course tested by the world, the flesh and the devil, and possibly even lost). Thus both together will have made a ritual passage from a former radical insufficiency to a reciprocal fulfillment.

This ideal achievement has affinities with Lawrence's idea in *Women in Love* of "stars in conjunction," but in an apocalyptic setting, it acquires a distinctive coloring. This spouse-discoverer finds the subjective equivalent of a new heaven and earth in a visionary apprehension of hitherto undiscovered regions of being: "I touched her flank and knew I was carried by the current in death / over to the new world, and was climbing out on the shore, / risen not to the old world . . . but to a new earth, a new I, a new knowledge, a new world of time" (st. 7). The vastness of the metaphor and the transpersonal nature of the transformation are repeatedly stressed by the varied, temporal, and intermingled character of the subjective and objective references (earth, I, knowledge, world of time—all "new"). Like Dylan Thomas in "The Force That Through the Green Fuse Drives the Flower," Lawrence tells us what he cannot tell us. He may strive for this paradox less compactly in this poem than Thomas does, but he is also trying to encompass an experience quite different from Thomas's, and larger too.

Part of the force of this sort of literary paradox is the accessibility of meaning interwoven with the sense of the innate difficulty in conveying that meaning: "I cannot," insists Lawrence, "tell you what it is, the new world," as Thomas is "dumb to tell the lover's tomb / How at my sheet goes the same crooked worm." The feint of inarticulateness is essential, for it indicates the problematic nature of the subject, though (of course) not necessarily the success or failure in communicating it. Lawrence's meanings in "New Heaven and Earth" are for the most part within reach. Although the poem is obscure about some areas of his experience of and with his wife, it acquires considerable clarity if seen as the keystone of *Look!*. Furthermore, part of what is obscure gains coherence and depth from the concrete imagery of the poem's climactic concluding sections (sts. 7 and 8). The literal meaning of the poem is invested in a woman's body: the figurative meaning is conveyed as terrestrial allusions (white sands, valleys, green streams, a continent, ultimately, a world). The word "world," mentioned eight times in the last two stanzas, is the pivotal figurative term binding subjective and objective realities and meanings. It indicates as well the primary verbal stress differentiating the "first," and "second" heaven and earth.

Yet this final section also contains a complicating indefiniteness. In clauses like "land that beats with a pulse," "valleys that draw close in love," and "she who is the other has strange-mounted breasts and strange sheer slopes, and white levels," Lawrence, rendering his apocalyptic vision through metaphor, universalizes his personal (or inter-personal) experience as hylozoism, the pre-Socratic philosophical conception that all matter has life or that matter and life are indivisible. But in so doing he almost reverses the literal and figurative significations just ascribed: "Frieda," the whole sexual and marital import suggests, is nearly converted into a figure for an apocalyptic religious experience cut loose from any stabilizing associations.

Lawrence is trying to convey a revolution in sensibility. The whole poem is rife with the excitement of a personally crucial experience. It centers on a symbolic enactment of an individual's rebirth, and of what he is reborn into. The enactment achieves both personal and societal significance by blending an individualist passion with an eschatological form. Thus the difficulty in, perhaps error of, assessing priorities of meaning. The point of the inseparability of meanings is not to be missed: salvation for one (or two) could be salvation for all. On the face of it, this is an outrageous (if inevitable) implication. Yet Lawrence's poem is more subtle than its salvational and dithyrambic cast would lead one to think. If he objectifies the personal substance of the poem through apocalyptic, he also disowns whatever in apocalyptic is demented by virtue of the confessional and lyrical forms of the poem. Thus the social and personal aspects of "New Heaven and Earth" qualify or contain each other. Is the poem diminished by this semantic reflexiveness and containment?

Lawrence had undergone a personally consummating yet harrowing experience in the first years of his marriage. He describes and animates it in his poem, but something is lost there, as the high intensity, the strain, even the implicit extravagance of the metaphor of apocalyptic suggest. Our ability to follow these two levels of consummation (personal and artistic), and to experience our own vicarious consummation as readers and dwellers in "the first earth," is accordingly limited. Yet this stricture is relative, for it does not indicate how much Lawrence brought back from his new world. "New Heaven and Earth" may share the fate of mystical writing in its inevitable loss of the ecstasy and splendor of the transcendence. But apocalyptic offers a paradigm and a rhetoric through which to focus and crystallize a sizable portion of a profound experience. The poem may show little restraint or composure. But in view of the growing authority of confessional poetry since Lawrence's time (not to mention Lawrence's significant place as a pioneer in this tradition), one can now respond positively to such Dionysian declamation more readily.

III

"New Heaven and Earth" embodies a poetic manifesto of an explorer discovering in his own psyche the evils of egoistic aggrandizement developed to such extremes that the roots of renewal are cut off, and a living death results, a concern informing much of Lawrence's major work. My claim that the poem is esthetically enhanced by its apocalyptic character does not contravene an excellent point made by Barbara Hardy: "Lawrence's sense of human liberation is realized when he forgets the 'he' and 'she' in a way undreamed of by Donne. This is most fully achieved in the poems, but even in the constraints of the prose fiction there emerges some sense that women and men share the same struggle."[16] Frequently the apocalyptic and anti-apocalyptic themes and motifs also reduce the sexual distinctions found throughout Lawrence's works, and offer the different rewards of Lawrence's dramatized ambivalence towards apocalypse to both sexes.

The apocalyptical interpretation also lends meaning to the last otherwise obscure stanza:

> . . . .
> The unknown, strong current of life supreme
> drowns me and sweeps me away and holds me down
> to the sources of mystery, in the depths,
> extinguishes there my risen resurrected life
> and kindles it further at the core of utter
>   mystery.

The "Unknown" extinguishing Lawrence's *second* life ("my risen resurrected life") points to the "second death" of *Revelation*—"And death and hell were cast into the lake of fire. This is the second death" (20:14)—but in Lawrence's poem it takes quite a different twist. "The unknown . . . kindles" his "second life," "further at the core of utter mystery." As one would expect in Lawrence, the resolution is individualistic, mystic, and cyclic. It is also vague. It is not so vague, however, that we should miss an important concept present in Lawrence's better work. In terms of the poem, his second life will be extinguished, but only to be renewed "at the core of utter mystery." Lawrence had nearly died several times during his life. Thus he was preternaturally sensitive to the rounds of death-and-rebirth in its myriad forms. He knew that a breakthrough experience, like all things, would sooner or later perish. But he also had faith that the consummated experience or relationship would be revivified by the ambivalent death-and-life force represented in the poem by the term "oblivion." New life through death. The New Jerusalem after the Reign of the Beast and the vast terrors of Armageddon. The authority of Lawrence's art partly issues from his gift for blending or counterpoising millenialist, pararealist traditions with an uncanny sensitivity to the here-and-now in all its zest, particularity, and transience.[17] And a certain courage resides less in the self-revelation or in the breathtaking expressiveness than in the realization that this vision of relatedness and self-culmination would pass, that it had to pass in order to immerse himself (and oneself) in "utter life," and be "drowned" and "held down" in the mysterious tides of transformation and renewal.

The "unknown, strong current of life supreme" harbors a conception that Lawrence would apotheosize differently in *Etruscan Places*, *The Man Who Died*, the late fictional fragment "The Flying Fish," the serene "Last Poems," and, despite a pronounced adherence to theocracy, in *Apocalypse* as an impersonal celebration of life. Nevertheless, the transcendent moment of two people in love assumes in "New Heaven and Earth" a compelling jubilance that little else in 20th Century literature, mirroring its Day of Wrath, would match.

Notes

[1] One exception is Barbara Hardy who, in a fine essay ("Women in D. H. Lawrence's Works." *D. H. Lawrence: Novelist, Poet, Prophet*, Stephen Spender, ed. [New York: Harper & Row, 1973]) claims that it is one of the best poems in *Look!* (p. 115). Tom Marshall, who has some good insights into the poem, offers the more customary negative appraisal: "Both 'Manifesto' and 'New Heaven and Earth' fail to achieve the kind of immediacy that is achieved in Lawrence's best poems. Poems as repetitive, abstract, and didactic as these can hardly give the reader much sense of the immediate experience" (*The Psychic Mariner: the Poems of D. H. Lawerence* [New York: Viking Press, 1970] p. 92). And Sandra Gilbert (in *Acts of Attention: the Poems of D. H. Lawrence* [Ithaca, New York: Cornell University Press, 1972]) states that "'Manifest,' and, to a lesser extent, 'New Heaven and Earth,' are in a sense mindless in their inability to find a language that can fittingly express the soul's discoveries" (p. 95).

[2] D. H. Lawrence, *Selected Poems: with an Introduction by Kenneth Rexroth* (New York: New Directions, 1947) p. 14.

[3] The presence of apocalyptic in the poem has been observed by Gilbert: "As early as *Look!* (in "New Heaven and Earth," "Manifest," and "Spring in the World") Lawrence has presented his apocalyptic vision of a personal and suprapersonal cycle of death and rebirth" (*Acts of Attention*, p. 127).

[4] See Frank Kermode, "Lawrence and the Apocalyptic Types." *D. H. Lawrence: The Rainbow and Women in Love: a Casebook*, Colin Clarke, ed. (Nashville: Aurora Publishers Inc., 1970) p. 206. It is curious that in neither this essay nor in Kermode's book on Lawrence, both oriented toward the apocalyptic in Lawrence, is any mention made of "New Heaven and Earth" as an apocalyptic work.

[5] *Apocalypse* (New York: Viking Press, 1966) p. 3.

[6] Kermode, p. 217. One exception to this generalization appears in the balance in *Sons and Lovers* between symbolic numinosity and history.

[7] Gilbert has remarked briefly on the death-rebirth pattern central to the poem (*Acts of Attention* pp. 109-110).

[8] Judging by Keith Sagar's "Chronology," the poem was possibly written sometime in the first half of the year 1915. See Keith Sagar, *The Art of D. H. Lawrence* (London: Cambridge University Press, 1966) p. 40.

[9] Lawrence, it should be stated, was not the first to present a "New Jerusalem" in erotic or marital terms. According to M. H. Abrams "The goal of the journey [i. e., the Exodus in *The Old Testament*] was usually imaged as the New Jerusalem, which is both a city and a woman; and the longing for the goal was frequently expressed, following *Revelation* 22:17, as an insistent invitation to a wedding. . . " [in *Natural Supernaturalism: Tradition and Revolution in Romantic Literature* (New York: W. W. Norton, 1973) p. 165]. Nor was Lawrence the first to internalize apocalyptic. Both Abrams in *Natural Supernaturalism* and Norman Cohn in *The Pursuit of the Millenium* (Fairlawn, New Jersey: Essential Books Inc., 1957) deal at length with this important area of social, psychological, and religious history, Abrams meticulously examining its manifestations in the 19th Century English Romantic poets and German philosophers. Lawrence, however, is distinctive in his appearing to give prime significance to an actual marriage; that he doesn't make this primacy completely unequivocal embodies a crux in the poem concerning literal and figurative meaning that is considered later in the chapter.

[10] The essential capacity of apocalyptic for sizable modification and change of its scope or goals can be seen in the following description by Abrams of secular apocalyptic in 19th Century Romantic literature: "faith in an apocalypse by revelation had been replaced by faith in an apocalypse by revolution, and this now gave way to faith in an apocalypse by imagination or cognition." (*Natural Supernaturalism* p. 334).

[11] *What the Spirit Says to the Churches: a Key to the Apocalypse of John* (New York: P. J. Kennedy and Sons, 1967) p. 136.

[12] "*Women in Love* and Death," *D. H. Lawrence: a Collection of Critical Essays*, ed. by Mark Spilka (Englewood Cliffs: Prentice-Hall, 1963) p. 50.

[13] *Collected Poems* (New York: Viking Press, 1971) p. 191.

[14] *Thieves of Prometheus* (New York: Oxford University Press, 1974) p. 112-13. Among other things, Donoghue accuses Lawrence of quarreling " . . . with life not because it refused to admit desire but because it would not tolerate the endlessness of desire" (p. 112).

[15] It certainly is possible that Lawrence is venturing on the anal sexuality to which R. E. Pritchard alludes in his *D. H. Lawrence: Body of Darkness*. A miniature critical literature has evolved in the past fifteen years to cite or contend anality in *Women in Love* and *Lady Chatterley's Lover*. But if anality in this poem is seen as the means by which "Lawrence" or the speaker has "come through," and

yet is related, as Pritchard remarks, to a way of dealing with fears of incest, one might feel the disparity between means and end to be farcically large. Even were fear of censorship or self-exposure the main motive for Lawrence's vagueness in the sexual activity involved, the vagueness, no doubt deliberate, can only help the poem. The erotic experience instigates and accentuates Lawrence's apocalyptic all the better by not being precisely described, for it expands rather than contracts all the associations and implications of the poem (sexual, marital, and apocalyptical).

Anality seems more overt in the poem following "New Heaven and Earth," entitled "Manifesto," where such passages as "I want her to touch me at last, ah, on the root and quick of my darkness. . . " and "When she has put her hand on my secret, darkest sources, the darkest outgoings. . . " (st. VII) are all the more esthetically problematic exactly because they lack the excited empyrean power of apocalyptic to sweep all before it. Kermode very briefly and inexplicitly alludes to anality in "Manifesto" in *D. H. Lawrence* (p. 80). A compact and lucid discussion of this subject in *Women in Love* and *Lady Chatterley's Lover* can be found on p. 140-43 of his book.

[16] Hardy p. 117-18.

[17] Lawrence was, for example, familiar with the medieval apocalyptist Joachim of Floris, as his history text *Movements in European History* makes clear.

Sex in Lawrence's Fiction

D. H. Lawrence once stated in a poem entitled "Sex Isn't Sin" that "Sex is not a thing you have to play with. Sex is you." One definition of the nature of his art concerns what area of "you" sexuality may be and what it may portend about the crucial centers of an individual, a society, an epoch. Such concerns give some idea of how serious Lawrence was about sexuality and its relation to human character. Insufficiently understood even today, however, is what his conception of sex was, what its relationship to or embodiment of human nature is, and how it is fleshed out in his imaginative literature. This essay will attempt to address these considerations in some of Lawrence's key works of fiction and non-fiction prose, focusing at some length on *Women in Love* and *Lady Chatterley's Lover*. The emphasis will be less on the "erotic" character of Lawrence's work than on how complex and reverberatively significant Lawrence's renderings of sexuality could be in his most famous work.

Lawrence is basically an ontological writer; he is concerned with the qualities and essences of being. This orientation, combined with the intense sensibility of a tubercular, led in his work to an involvement with the present, the *Moment*. This involvement is vividly noticeable in his verse and in his poetics (as it is in the highcharged "Preface to New Poems" essay). Lawrence approached the present in terms of the vertical inner space of what Alan Friedman has called the Underconscious (p. 24). As Lawrence's pseudonymous history text *Movements in European History* should indicate, Lawrence had a sense of history, of past, present, and future; this is further attested by the tracing of three generations in *The Rainbow* or by the autobiographical family chronicle in *Sons and Lovers*. Nevertheless, few authors have been so taken with the literary possibilities of that inner space of being. In the famous novels *Sons and Lovers, The Rainbow, Women in Love, Lady Chatterley's Lover,* in *Studies in Classic American Literature,* in verse from even the period of *Sons and Lovers* till the last poems of dying and rebirth, in the conceptual sections of *Etruscan Places,* in all of these works, he explores the inner experience of human nature so deeply as to reach the area where humanity shades into material nature.

Probings of this sort have a lot to do with Lawrence's treatment of sex. For not only do Lawrence's investigations into this inner world suggest the centrality of sex in the individual and in society but also its role as a gauge of the nature and condition of whole ranges of human being. Norman Mailer maps out some of this Lawrentian terrain in his splendid essay on Lawrence: "Lawrence's point, which he refines over and over, is that the deepest messages of sex cannot be heard by taking a stance on the side of the bank, announcing one is in love, and then proceeding to fish in the waters of love with a bread basket full of ego. No, he is saying again and again, people can win at love only when they are ready to lose everything they bring to it of ego, position, or identity . . . and men and women can survive only if they reach the depths of their own sex down within themselves" (p. 107).

Lawrence regarded the body and mind as riven by Christianity, and he took it upon himself to unite the two halves. The treatment of this dividedness recurs importantly throughout his major and minor works. Less frequent in his work but also integral to it and better known is the thesis that the real way to heal the split is to resurrect the body, which he attempts to do consummately in the phallic Christ of *The Man Who Died.* In view of the rigid sexual values of the era preceding his, it is understandable that sexuality seemed to Lawrence the most appropriate and crucial area for developing a culture of the body and mind.

But few would have imagined that anyone would have written about sex in the oblique, symbolic modes that Lawrence did in much of his better work. In the essay "Introduction to His Paintings," Lawrence makes sex into a historical prime-mover: "The terror-horror element which had entered the imagination with regard to the sexual and procreative act was at least partly responsible for the rise of Puritanism, the beheading of the King-Father Charles, and the establishment of the New England colonies" (p. 312). All this, Lawrence thinks, results from the impact of syphilis on Europe. Never one to draw back from bold speculation, Lawrence follows this statement with another which provides an essential perspective for approaching sex in Lawrence's fiction: "But deeper than this, the terror-horror element led to the crippling of the consciousness of man. Very elementary in man is his sexual and procreative being, and on his sexual and procreative being depend many of his deepest instincts and the flow of his intuitions" (pp. 312-13). "Elementary . . . procreative being," "deepest instincts," "flow of his intuitions"—all these arteries of human existence Lawrence considers embodiments of sexual nature, *and vice versa*. If a disharmony occurs, our consciousness (so exalted and emphasized in modern civilization) and our unconsciousness (so belatedly championed and sensationalized) are deeply corrupted.

The main consideration here, I feel, is not whether Lawrence's sexual hypothesis is erroneous. It embodies Lawrence's personal myth of the radical fear of sex and the body (and thus of our own instinctive life) that he felt had existed as early as the English Renaissance, and it "works" in this author's fiction as well as the mythic elements underlying the verse of Yeats or Eliot. Lawrence presents this fear as loathing and illusion in the two young, virginal sisters discussing sex in *The Virgin and the Gypsy*:

> "I suppose," said Lucille, "there's the low sort of sex, and there's the other sort, that isn't low. It's frightfully complicated, really! I *loathe* common fellows. And I never feel anything—*sexual*—" she laid a rather disgusted stress on the word— "for fellows who aren't common. Perhaps I haven't got any sex."
>
> "That's just it!" said Yvette. "Perhaps neither of us has. Perhaps we haven't really *got* any sex, to connect us with men."
>
> "How horrible it sounds: *connect us with men!*" cried Lucille, with revulsion. "Wouldn't you hate to be connected with men that way? Oh I think it's an awful pity there has to be sex!" (p. 81)

Though Lawrence is seldom as explicit and comic in his renderings of sex dialogue as he is here, it is unquestionably true that sex is regarded by some characters in his fiction as repulsive. Miriam and her mother in *Sons and Lovers*, the Princess in *The Princess*, many of the major characters in *Women in Love* at different times, Lou Witt in *St. Mawr*, Mellors in *Lady Chatterley's Lover*, Jack Ferguson in "The Horse Dealer's Daughter" all at one time or another recoil either from sex or the opposite sex.

If the sex revulsion found in more than a little of Lawrence's fiction suggests complexities about sexuality which transcend contemporary erotic hedonism, so does the difficulty of sexual relating, growth, and realization pervading his work. Few authors outdo Lawrence in revealing the hardship, tension, and dangers of courtship. One of his powerful scenes of troubled intimacy occurs in *Sons and Lovers* when Paul and Miriam make—or try to make—love. Although much attention has been given both to Paul Morel's Oedipal and other woes and to Lawrence's warping of the characterization of Miriam, it has been less noticed that in "The Test on Miriam" chapter not only does Lawrence sensitively portray Paul's sexual trials, but Miriam's, too. One night at Willey Farm the two kiss in the field. The following dialogue registers Lawrence's keen sense of the agony of dealing with sexual desire, both in Paul's frustration and in Miriam's pervasive unease and erotic ambivalence:

"Sometime you will have me?" he murmured, hiding his face on her shoulder. It was so difficult.
"Not now," she said.
His hopes and heart sunk.
. . .
"We belong to each other," he said.
"Yes."
"Then why shouldn't we belong to each other altogether?"
. . .
She hid her face in his neck with a little cry of misery.
. . .
"You are afraid?" . . .
"Yes, I am only afraid," she said (p. 283).

Shortly afterwards, Miriam in a kinesthetic image and reply, each at odds with the other, says: "'You *shall* have me,' . . . through her shut teeth." Just before saying this, Miriam, as "she gripped his [Paul's] arms around her, . . . clenched her body stiff." Her accepting words and her refusing body show what a victim of opposing forces Miriam is. She does not want what she wants; her body resists her will; what she wants to feel and what she actually feels about sex conflict. When, out of the instinct to shrink from sex, she disengaged herself from Paul, Paul soon departs with *his* fists clenched and ends up looking at the black water of a lake in an external recognition of death in himself. When sometime later they do make love, Miriam is frightened by Paul's regarding her impersonally as a woman rather than as an individual. His sexual sensibility here is one with his immersion in a sinister psychic darkness: "'I like the darkness,' he said. 'I wish it were thicker . . . '"

(p. 286). The intercourse that follows, in which, as Paul realizes, Miriam's "soul had stood apart, in a sort of horror," not only leaves Paul heavy-hearted but also feeling nihilistic: "he felt as if nothing mattered, as if his living were smeared away into the beyond" (p. 287). Then, "this strange, gently reaching-out to death was new to him." Death becomes overt in Paul, made desirable by a punitive blocking and twisting of psycho-sexual energies engendered by a combination of his upbringing and Miriam's sexual repressiveness.

Paul survives Miriam through Clara, but his closeness to death, through dangerously intertwined emotions of love and hate, suggests the psychic depths and dangers of sex and its powerful interconnections with family and parents. We find no hedonistic ease, no glamorous eroticism here or elsewhere in *Sons and Lovers*; instead, there is pain, terror, frustrated desire, embitterment, anxiety, severe guilt, dissociation and a drift towards self-annihilation.

Often Lawrence's characters encounter sexual emotions and experiences that are represented far more obliquely than those conveyed by the two sisters in *The Virgin and the Gypsy* or in the torturous courtship of Paul and Miriam seen in *Sons and Lovers*. In writing *Women in Love*, Lawrence conveys the heavy, voluptuous beauty of Gudrum Brangwen, not by creating it for the reader palpably (for instance: "Gudrun's full, round breasts, her long, full shapely legs"), but by suggesting it through Gerald Crich's acutely obsessive and dangerous desire for her. In view of the erotic sensationalism of Lawrence's reputation generally, based as it is mostly on *Lady Chatterley's Lover*, it is worth emphasizing that sexual attraction in Lawrence's works, as in the above instance from *Women in Love*, is designed for larger ends. Among other things, his serious and subtle conception and rendering of sexuality allows him, even in *Lady Chatterley's Lover*, to transcend the detailed erotic focusing that can acquire mainly a prurient appeal. It would not be easy to become sexually aroused by Lawrence's presentation of Gudrun (or Ursula), yet Lawrence movingly conveys the sexual impact of Gudrun's person on Gerald.

But Lawrence takes the sexual aspect of the Gerald-Gudrun relationship further than this. In the tight encircling of love, sex, and literal or figurative death which is found in much of his best work, Lawrence makes their relationship virtually a matter of life and death by the depths of feeling and instinct that the attraction stirs between these two central characters. And this is exactly the point: sex in Lawrence's work is often treated as an expression of non-discursive yet crucial areas of thought, emotion, and instinct which define our essential self or selves, our primary being. This is one reason why sex is so serious (perhaps at times even too serious) a matter in much of Lawrence's work. If the gamut of Lawrentian sexuality at one end and superficial frivolous sex at the other end were summed up in the two words "sexual" and "sexy," hardly any fiction is less "sexy" but more terrifyingly and perversely sexual and erotic than the chapter "Rabbit" in *Women in Love*.

"Rabbit" follows the devastating chapter "The Industrial Magnate" in which one beholds both the Victorian type and the twentieth-century type of coal industrialization and industrial governorship in the contrasting systems of Crich Senior and his son Gerald. In the "perfection" of Gerald's modern system, however, the Captain of Industry himself is left with nothing to do. As a result, Gerald is forced to confront himself. What he sees is frightening:

> Once or twice lately, when he was alone in the evening and had nothing to do, he had suddenly stood up in terror, not knowing what he was . . . He was afraid, in mortal dry fear, but he knew not what of . . . It was as if his centres of feeling were drying up . . . He would have to go in some direction, shortly, to find relief. (pp. 224, 225).

Gerald has found relief from such states by losing himself in debauchery with a desperate woman like Pussums. Pussums is partly a harbinger of Gudrun in Gerald's run of women. She does not gain the upper hand with Gerald that Gudrun finally acquires; she does, though, have in common with Gudrun a masochistic vein, and the sadism Gudrun sometimes feels towards Gerald, Pussums directs towards former lovers like the contemptible and slightly comic Halliday. Gerald's panic of emptiness, the ironic consequences of his successful modernized industrial method which has impoverished the integrity of his miners, makes him crave and thus expose himself to the willful, destructive Gudrun. This exposure lends crucial importance to the following chapter, "Rabbit," which is intimated in the complex irony and allusiveness of its title and of its first sentence: "Gudrun knew that it was a critical thing for her to go the Shortlands." As the following sentences state, it is critical because going there means she would inevitably become Gerald's lover. But, as it turns out, Gudrun's arrival at Gerald's estate is even more critical for Gerald, for his *life* hangs in the balance. "Rabbit" not only underscores a pattern of interchange between

Gerald and Gudrun that will culminated in Gerald's destruction and will lead to a death-in-life existence for Gudrun; it also intensifies earlier intimations about the present and future character of their erotic relationship.

When Gudrun appears at Shortlands, she is dressed "like a macaw," though the family is in mourning because of the drowning of Gerald's sister Diane. Gerald, we are told, is now in love with Gudrun. His admission in this state of mind that her inappropriate, defiant dress and manner please him bears deeper implications: "He felt the challenge in her very attire—she challenged the whole world" (p. 231). Indeed, the whole chapter can be regarded as a sly and grim duel between the two, centering on the rabbit Bismarck.

It is Lawrence's use of the rabbit as a medium of conveying the subterranean lust-hate drama of wills between Gudrun and Gerald that makes this chapter peculiarly memorable. Along with Gerald's sister Winifred, they go to take a look at Winifred's rabbit Bismarck. What follows is a pattern of freedom and captivity for the rabbit that will contrast starkly with the lives of Gerald and Gudrun. The rabbit's name is of course ironic in itself, but it also carries an ironic reference to Gerald who is a "Bismarck" of modern industry yet at times is as helpless as a rabbit in dealing with Gudrun. Bismarck is "free" in his cage in being removed from capturers like Gudrun and Gerald but, "let out," is both cornered by the two and subjected by them to violent, sadistic feelings that each harbors towards the other: Gudrun, trying to take hold of the rabbit, gets scratched. She

> ... stood for a moment astounded by the thunderstorm that had sprung into being in her grip. Then her colour came up, a heavy rage came over her like a cloud. She stood shaken as a house in a storm, and utterly overcome. Her heart was arrested with fury at the mindlessness and bestial stupidity of this struggle, her wrists were badly scored by the claws of the beast, a heavy cruelty welled up in her (p. 232).

Gerald notices this cruelty. He too grabs the rabbit, only in turn to be resisted by the rabbit's enormous effort to release itself. This simple and primitive energy contrasts vividly with the sinister energies triggered by the animal in the two principals. Though the rabbit is described as "demonic," it is clearly Gerald and Gudrun who are demonic in their violent feelings toward the rabbit (which Gerald savagely cuffs on the neck) and in the perversity and power in their sexual feeling for one another.

They are exposed to each other because they sense one another's lust for violence, cruelty, and willfulness. This revelation creates a mutual attraction, but considering the substance of the attraction, its "mutual hellish recognition," elements of rivalry and of domination-submission appear central to it. Gerald seems to have the upper hand in his "knowledge of her in the long red rent of her forearm, so silken and soft" (p. 238). Gerald, that is, in seeing the "inside" of Gudrun's body through her rabbit-scratched arm, also "sees" the cruelty, perversity and vulnerableness of her deeper being. This in turn strongly draws him towards "abhorrent mysteries" that develop into voluptuous, sadistic, finally murderous feelings towards each other. Gerald enters a realm of sensibility here that, "tearing the surface of his ultimate consciousness," allows the "obscene beyond" to enter: all the concomitant pornographic, annihilative sensations of torture and degradation of the other.

The sadistic, voluptuous motif and results of tearing reappear late in the book (chapter XXIX) as Gerald and Gudrun approach the climax of the deep enmity latent in their relationship from the beginning. Talking to Birkin, soon to depart for Italy with Ursula, Gerald describes Gudrun as "so beautiful, so perfect, you find her *so good*, it tears you like a silk, and every stroke and bit cuts hot . . . " (p. 430). If Gudrun's torn "silken" forearm incites Gerald's latent perversity, the sight of her wound also "tears" into his subconscious in "Rabbit" and finally emerges in chapter XXIX as a "silken" tearing of his inner being, revealing the fatal captivity of his voluptuous involvement in Gudrun's body and nature. The deadly obsessiveness of the sado-masochistic involvement (and of the imagery of tearing) is underlined shortly after when Birkin asks Gerald whether he has "'had everything now? . . . Why work on an old wound?' 'Oh,' said Gerald, 'I don't know. It's not finished'" (p. 431).

The climactic exchange of "Rabbit," sealing the "diabolic" pact between the two, appropriately follows the rabbit's sudden "burst of life" as he runs in circles around the court area where he has been temporarily released:

> 'It's mad,' said Gudrun. . . .
> . . . .
> 'I don't suppose it is rabbit-mad.'
> 'Don't you think it is?' she asked.
> 'No. That's what it is to be a rabbit.'
> There was a queer, faint obscene smile over his face.

> She looked at him and saw him, and knew that he was initiate as she was initiate. This thwarted her, and contravened her, for the moment.
> 'God be praised we aren't rabbits,' she said in a high shrill voice.
> The smile intensified a little on his face.
> 'Not rabbits,' he said, looking at her fixedly.
> Slowly her face relaxed into a smile of obscene recognition.
> 'Ah, Gerald,' she said in a strong, slow, almost manlike way. 'All that, and more.' Her eyes looked up at him with shocking nonchalance. He felt again as if she had hit him across the face—or rather as if she had torn him across the breast, dully, finally (pp. 235-36).

The obscene intimacy here, then, the "mutual hellish recognition," is all the more penetrating for suggesting warped sexual emotions which, encompassing aggressive power drives and rivalry of domination, will link sex to attempted murder. The irony about the whole sequence is that the human beings (Gerald and Gudrun) have driven the rabbit "mad." It is part of their own madness to regard the rabbit's sane, self-protective behavior as mad and to drive him "mad." Their lunacy, further, has a strong sexual character. When Gudrun, in the "high, shrill voice" that signals the emergence of her deeper, impersonal self, says "God be praised we aren't rabbits," she reveals her utter lack of naturalness as well as her and Gerald's virtual complicity in a sinister, debauched state of mind. Gerald, not understanding her, exposes himself to Gudrun's conclusive and devastating cynicism. By saying that she and Gerald are not rabbits, are not "rabbit-mad," she also ironically suggests that they are both "rabbits" in the sense of self-abandonment to brainless copulation. In the shadow of this implication, the phrase "and more" carries dreadful weight, for, in effect, Gudrun strongly implies that she and Gerald are "rabbits" with the minds of willful and brutal perverts: they are monsters. This latent but basic meaning and Gudrun's "shocking" nonchalant acceptance of it are what makes Gerald feel that he had been struck—or, in their characteristic and appropriate *sadiste* diction, torn. The "diabolic freemasonry" in deviant sexual kinship, their "hellish recognition," will by its very nature degenerate, as it does here, into a power struggle for control, domination, and finally destruction or survival.

Yet it must be remembered that both Gerald and Gudrun are attractive, intelligent, socially respected people (Gerald, in his role as an industrialist, even "a leader of the community"). Further,

Gudrun is Ursula's sister, and thus she has a blood relationship to one of the (few) life-oriented characters in this doomful novel. Gerald in turn is highly enough regarded by Birkin to be considered worthy of an offer of "blood-brotherhood," the turning-down of which is one reason for Gerald's destruction. How can these people also be brutes? That Lawrence can convincingly render them as both points up the achievement of his characterization. It points up as well that the demonic is not just latent but quite active under the persona of society leaders or highly socialized personalities, a terrifying consideration for any age or season.

It is an appropriate climax that Gerald's last "embrace" of Gudrun takes the form of his trying to choke her to death near the end of the novel:

> What a fulfillment, what a satisfaction! How good this was, oh! how good it was, what a God-given gratification at last! He was unconscious of her fighting and struggling. The struggling was her reciprocal lustful passion in the embrace (p. 463).

The key word in this passage is "lustful," linking with the network of diction in the "Rabbit" chapter involving nihilistic sexual attraction between Gudrun and Gerald. Choking Gudrun indeed seems like Gerald's most gratifying sexual experience in the entire narrative, though it means killing a woman he depends on desperately. Yet the scene is hardly erotic: it is of course horrifying. Gerald has reached the point where he cannot live with or without Gudrun, and in killing her would be killing himself, as he would if he did not kill her. Deprived of love, desire, and purpose in either the social or personal spheres of his life, Gerald can only die. In turn, Gudrun faces the disintegration of living with the sadistic artist Loerke in pre-World-War-II Germany. Daniel J. Schneider has said that "the novel's [*Women in Love*] essential power derives from the strong contrasts between the culture's dead spiritual ideals of love and benevolence and the inevitable demonic reaction from these ideals into sheer perversity and cruelty" (p. 119). That Lawrence can register this power along a sexual (and psycho-sexual) dimension suggests some of the depth and originality of sex in his work. The world of sexuality in *Women in Love* is quite a remove from Lucille's "'Perhaps I haven't got any sex.' 'That is just it,' said Yvette. 'Perhaps neither of us has.'" The two works intimate a striking variety in Lawrence's dramatized conception of sex and in the psycho-sexual sensibility of his fiction.

The Virgin and the Gypsy and *Lady Chatterley's Lover* exhibit a flattening-out or reliteralizing of Lawrence's explorations of sexual sensibility. *The Virgin*, in addition, is richly humorous about virginity and even its Dark God, while containing "doctrinal" ideas about the relationship of character development to sexual awareness and acceptance. Along with the more literal treatment of sex in *Lady Chatterley's Lover*, one encounters an allegorical dimension which encompasses both a new tenderness in Lawrence and a problematic usage of sodomy.

Lady Chatterley's Lover embodies disease, diagnosis, and cure, for the body social (incarnated in the literal bodies of the three prime characters) is what is at stake in the novel. Thus regarding Connie Chatterley as the Body of England is to make very large claims for sexuality in ways as audacious as giving Christ in *The Man Who Died* sexual desire and fulfillment.

The presentation of sex in *Lady Chatterley's Lover* is notoriously different from its handling in the earlier fiction. It is of course more literal or physical; it is also, at times, accompanied by a compelling erotic tenderness. The first sexual encounter arises directly out of Mellors's compassion for Connie's "female forlornness." Her attraction to the new life represented by the chicks the gamekeeper is raising reminds her of her own barren sexuality, and she weeps. One of the most poignant scenes of the entire novel follows:

> He glanced apprehensively at her. Her face was averted, and she was crying blindly, in all the anguish of her generation's forlornness. His heart melted suddenly, like a drop of fire, and he put out his hand and laid his fingers on her knee.
> "You shouldn't cry" he said softly.
> But then she put her hands over her face and felt that really her heart was broken and nothing mattered anymore.
> He laid his hand on her shoulder, and softly, gently, it began to travel down the curve of her back, blindly, with a blind stroking motion, of her flank, in the blind instinctive caress (pp. 122-23).

The intermingling in this passage of motifs of tenderness, unconsciousness, and desire is hardly accidental. If it represents "blind consciousness" in action, it also shows the carefully modulated character of Lawrence's sexual scenes. The "broken heart" and the "nothing mattered anymore" also represent a symbolic death which helps to make way, as will other elements and events, for the rebirth through sexual sensibility and experience of new consciousness and thus a new life.

The sexual scenes in *Lady Chatterley's Lover* are relatively mild by 1990s standards of sexual candor in literature. Yet Lawrence's modes of relatively inexplicit sexual description may prove to have more durability than has been realized. The sexual scenes in *Lady Chatterley's Lover* make an impact because their aim is not to titillate but to embody a nodal experience in the narrative. In the passage that follows, the presentation of Connie's movement towards orgasm develops meaning integral to larger significances binding the entire narrative:

> And it seemed she was like the sea, nothing but dark waves rising and heaving, . . . so that slowly her whole darkness was in motion, and was ocean rolling its dark, dumb mass. Oh, and far down inside her the deeps parted and rolled asunder, in long, far-traveling billows, and ever, at the quick of her, the depths parted and rolled asunder, from the centre of soft plunging, as the plunger went deeper and deeper, touching lower, and she was deeper and deeper disclosed, and closer and closer plunged the palpable unknown, and further and further rolled the waves of her self away from herself, leaving her, till suddenly, in soft, shuddering convulsion, the quick of all her plasm was touched, she knew herself touched, the consummation was upon her, and she was gone. She was gone, she was not, and she was born: a woman (p. 186).

Germaine Greer has objected to the vague sexual descriptiveness in scenes like this in Lawrence's work (p. 194). If we recall the immediate context, however, this extended nature-animizing simile makes good sense. The intercourse follows another sexual scene just before which had itself been preceded by Connie's admission to Mellors that she was going to Venice to give the appearance (to Clifford) of begetting an heir for Wragby. Mellors, who would be the biological father, claims he is being used. Connie's admitting this to herself does not prevent her subsequent ambivalent feelings which relate, negatively and positively (in that order), to the sequences of lovemaking shortly following the divisive topic of social fatherhood for Connie's coming child.

Thus it is no surprise that the first love-session is unsuccessful: Mellors expressing some insensitivity in "the peculiar haste of his possession" and Connie experiencing the intercourse "from the top of her head," so that "the butting of his haunches seemed ridiculous to her . . . " (p. 184). But her anguish at her sense of isolation overcomes her "mental" scorn of sex, and the two turn to each other with an apocalyptic, "primordial tenderness, such as made the world in the beginning" (p. 186).

Lawrence expands Connie's sensibility to encompass a massive region of the earth in order to show her sudden marked freedom from the constrictions of the literal imagination. But it is mind versus mind, and which one is "right"? Sexual love will always involve the "buttock-bouncing," but is Lawrence being responsible in his sea language? The metaphor is developed consistently and climactically. If "Frieda" is a land mass in Lawrence's early midperiod poem "New Heaven and Earth," Connie becomes the ocean, with its mindlessness, darkness, and depth. The depth, in particular, becomes appropriately enough the key dimension, for the sub-"mental" revelation unfolding has to do with her physical and figurative inner self being sensitively discovered, exposed, aroused into dark awareness of a sort analogous to the "sensibility" of an ocean itself. With the consummatory statement "the quick of all her plasm was touched," the animistic vehicle is dropped, and Connie is reborn a woman.

The womanly rebirth here at first seems rather facile, but the whole narrative is the proper justificatory framework for Lawrence's judgment. In the passage itself, the point about Connie's rebirth concerns the desirability of vaginal orgasm. This matter, needless to say, has been a subject of contention in contemporary thought about genuine sexual revolution for women. I do not wish to add to that dispute here more than to say that in this scene, at least, Lawrence is not patronizing Connie (his Everywoman) either by indicating this mode of orgasm as essential for her or by placing emphasis in the passage upon the non-cerebral ("dark wave," "whole darkness," "dark, dumb mass," and so on). Lawrence is not saying here (as he did, however, say, in his *Collected Letters* and frequently implied elsewhere) that "I do think a woman must yield precedence to a man . . . (p. 565). Since *Lady Chatterley's Lover* primarily depicts Connie's evolving sensibility, which is viewed mainly through her mind, it is obvious that she has a mind of her own (as the important leaders-and-the people argument that she has with Clifford in chapter 13 should also make clear). But in the first round of that sex scene in chapter 12, Connie's mind has gotten in the way, and Lawrence feels that rationality at this time—not at *all* times—is inappropriate and should be swept away, though if Lawrence had been more willing to prevent *Mellors's* mind from getting in the way, *Chatterley* might have been a better novel.

Although *Lady Chatterley's Lover* had "Tenderness" as an alternate title, the sodomy scene in chapter 16 has stood out for some critics as something despicable about the whole novel (Sparrow pp. 54-70). That controversy need not be rehashed here (except to mention Kingsley Widmer's arresting point that "Lawrence's use of taboo terms [both in chapter 16 and in the novel generally] was not only rather limited and restricted . . . but he may reasonably be criticized for not being 'obscene' enough" (p. 77). But the scene itself deserves comment. It seems naive today to regard this scene as primarily dealing with vaginal sex, considering the continuous stress in the text on shame and the need to transcend it as well as the motifs of orificial ultimacy ("the last and deepest recess of organic shame," "the bottom of her soul, fundamentally," with its double pun on buttocks and anus). But it is relevant to pursue considerations implicit in the text itself, as both Mark Spilka and H. M. Daleski have done. From this perspective, the art itself might not be less offensive than its motivation. The Mellors character is presented, especially in Frank Kermode's extravagant apocalyptic reading (pp. 28-31), as Connie's sexual hierophant, her apocalyptic initiator through a supposedly shame-killing experience into a new life. Yet this beneficial (if lordly and patronizing) role for Mellors is contradicted by the vindictive function of the scene. Mellors earlier in the novel tells Connie that he feels he is being used as a stud to put an heir in Wragby. He is perhaps jealous too that Connie is going to Italy ostensibly to find an Italian lover for begetting the new heir. Further, his realization that he would hardly be acceptable to Clifford as a "substitute breeder" must surely be a source of deep sexual and class resentment to Mellors. And the anal-sex scene occurs on the night before Connie's departure for Venice, so the "occasion" might add fuel to his anger.

Thus, there is punitive anger in his pederastic act with Connie, and it gives a dubious cast to his "necessary" role of instructing her to rise above the "deep organic shame," the "old, old physical fear which crouches in the bodily roots of us, and can only be chased away by the sensual fire" (p. 268). Whether Connie really enjoys it, an important question, is perhaps subsidiary to whether the scene can support the doctrinal role Lawrence gives it. It is an audacious sequence, to be sure, but weakened by its unresolved contradictory aspects. That these contradictions also seriously undercut the claims to tenderness as a structural value in *Chatterley*, however, is questionable. Mellors may not be one of the most attractive heroes in modern literature, but there is no reason why he should be. As an outcast rebel and a man fighting for individual survival, he should *not* be conventionally attractive, but he should be vital, iconoclastic, gentle, and selfish, and Mellors is. Still, he should not be primarily seen as a ritualistic, apocalyptic hero when he sodomizes his beloved in a mood of vindictive anger; Lawrence's thus ideologizing Mellors's bad temper is a flaw in the novel.

Although Connie is in some ways patronized in her role of sexual awakening, she is nevertheless the central character in the novel. The novel is narrated through Connie in a recessed third person point of view—*she*, not Mellors, is the primary developing, evolving sensibility of the whole story and as such looms larger than life. Accordingly, the sexual scenes, "viewed" through her eyes (and almost her body), lend considerable weight to her characterization and to her importance as a character. Though *Lady Chatterley's Lover* is at times condescending to Connie, and thus towards women, she still stands head and shoulders above Clifford's ruthless industrialization and all of the embittered or crippled male principals (including Mellors). Not merely in superficial respects does she compare with Lawrence's most vivid characters, and after all the feeble jokes about *Lady Chatterley's Lover* as a story about the romance of a vagina and a penis in love, what is left is the finely vivid sense of two people sexually in love in an age rapidly grinding down all love and life into the sensationalism, boredom, and cynicism that precede catastrophe.

Lawrence said in "Apropos of *Lady Chatterley's Lover*" that we need "a proper reverence for sex, and proper awe of the body's strange experience" (p. 333). In his four major novels, not to mention the numerous short stories, the novellas, the essays, and verse, he indicates many of the possibilities, rewards, and dangers of either facing or denying these claims. In *Sons and Lovers* one beholds sexual confrontation between young people already so burdened with family histories of bitter strife or dangerous Oedipal identifications as to make their emotional or relational development extremely difficult. *Women in Love* relates sexuality to social power and to the character of modern industrialism, and thus to the instinctual void that results from an unexamined inner life, so that the kind of person one is sexually is reflected (especially in a major character like Gerald Crich) in the way one disposes of power and, ultimately, of people in the social order. That this process is reversible, one's social being having its psycho-sexual equivalence or results, is seen in the case of all the major characters in this novel. Lawrence in *Lady Chatterley's Lover* is writing a fictional last will and testament which sharply ideologizes his sense of sex and society so that the erotic, loving couple is silhouetted against a mechanistic society that is disposed to destroy people literally. The act of sexual love in *Lady Chatterley's Lover* becomes as well an ideological ritual of life in its most concentrated and sensitive form poised against the pervasive dehumanization wrought by the modern industrial order.

Lawrence conceived of sex as a metaphor for profound expressions of being, as an invitation to psychic growth or paralysis, as a sacrament of experience, and as a medium for deadly dehumanizations. Sexual experience and value seldom come painlessly in the Lawrentian world precisely because he regarded and dramatized them as penetrating the deepest roots of our psychological and physical existence. Thus, Lawrence's continuing awareness that sex is a touchstone of the widest irradiations of our being and that it intimates our deepest inherencies of character is closely attuned to both the creativity and disaster possible in contemporary life.

Works Cited

Daleski, H. M. *The Forked Flame: A Study of D. H. Lawrence.* Evanston, IL: Northwestern University Press, 1965.
Friedman, Alan. "The Other Lawrence," *Partisan Review* XXXVII (1970): 241.
Greer, Germaine. *The Female Eunuch.* New York: Bantam Books, 1972. Greer accuses Lawrence of combining "a strong reluctance to describe what his protagonist is actually doing with the most inflated imagery of cosmic orgasm." Though she is specifically referring to *Women in Love*, the point most probably is meant to apply to *Lady Chatterley's Lover* as well.
Kermode, Frank. *Shakespeare, Spenser, Donne: Renaissance Essays.* New York: Viking Press, 1971.
Lawrence, D. H. "Apropos of *Lady Chatterley's Lover*," *Lady Chatterley's Lover*. New York: Bantam Books, 1971.
—. *The Man Who Died.* New York: Random House, 1953.
—. *The Collected Letters of D. H. Lawrence.* Ed. Harry T. Moore. NY: Viking Press, 1962.
—. *Selected Essays.* Harmondsworth, Eng.: Penguin Books, 1954.
—. *Sons and Lovers.* New York: Viking Press, 1958.
—. *The Virgin and the Gypsy.* New York: Bantam Books, 1968.

—. *Women in Love.* New York: Viking Press, 1960.

Schneider, Daniel J. *The Consciousness of D. H. Lawrence: An Intellectual Biography.* Lawrence: University Press of Kansas, 1986.

Sparrow, John. "Regina vs. Penguin Books, Ltd., "*Encounter*," XVIII. 101 (Feb. 1962): 35-43; "Critical Exchange: Or Lawrence Up-Tight: Four Tail Pieces," *Novel*, V (1971).

Spilka, Mark. "On Lawrence's Hostility to Willful Women," *Lawrence and Women.* Ed. Anne Smith (London: Vision Press, 1978). Although Professors Daleski and Spilka anticipate me in a number of key points in their discussions of chapter XVI, I feel that my extended consideration of the sodomy sequence as well as certain generalizations I make keep our arguments distinctive.

Widmer, Kingsley. *Defiant Desire: Some Dialectical Legacies of D. H. Lawrence.* Carbonsdale: Southern Illinois University Press, 1992.

III

AMERICAN PUGILISM, BRITISH ELEGANCE

The Champ of the World and the Champ of the Word: Norman Mailer's *The Fight*

> "A Heavyweight Championship is as charged as a magnetic field."   -Norman Mailer, *The Fight*

I

Prizefighting is, to some people, a brutal sport, but if there is one boxer who through consummate skills reminded us that boxing can be an art, that it can even embody a symbolic ideological activity, it is Muhammad Ali. Can the same be said for Norman Mailer's writings on boxing? Or is Mailer risking a literary knockout when he joins his own pugilism (literary or personal) to that of the pugilistic profession? Is, in other words, *The Fight*, Mailer's account of the Ali-Foreman bout in Zaire in 1974, a significant work? Such a question implies another: What does Ali *mean*, not only as a great prizefighter, but as a 20th century Black and ideologue?

Perhaps the best way to approach these questions is by identifying a context for Mailer's book found in an earlier essay called "Black Power" in his *Existential Errands* (1973):

> ... the black man, ... on the fringe of technological society, exploited by it ..., gulping prison air in the fluorescent nightmare of shabby garish electric ghettos, uprooted centuries ago from his native Africa, ... was forced to live at one and the same time in the old primitive jungle of the slums ... And ... he discovered that the culture which had saved him owed more to the wit ... of the jungle than the values ... of the West.... his music was sweeter than Shakespeare or Bach.... prison had given him a culture deeper than libraries in the grove.... The American Black had survived.... He had at any rate a vision. It was that he was black, beauti-

> ful, and secretly superior—he had therefore the potentiality to conceive and create a new culture . . . richer, wiser, deeper, more beautiful and profound than any he had seen . . . . But he would not know until he had power for himself (pp. 265-66).

One gets the scope of Mailer's definition of prizefighting in suggesting that Ali's character as a boxer is projected in *The Fight* as the pre-eminent forerunner if not present embodiment of this "richer, wiser, deeper, more beautiful and profound" Black culture. Although this might seem at first a dubious, even outlandish, proposition, one must realize that Mailer brings to it all his considerable powers of style, imagination, audacity, and ordering of material. He also brings to it his reputation as the author of "The White Negro," which offers some of the metaphysics behind his idea that Ali represents a higher level of human sensibility than does the White man. In that controversial essay, Mailer makes a case for "the American existentialist—the hipster . . . " who, living in a century overshadowed by death, must "accept the terms of death, to live with death as immediate danger, to divorce oneself from society, to exist without roots, to set out on that uncharted journey into the rebellious imperatives of the self" (*Advertisements for Myself* p. 304).

Ali does not instantly fit most people's image of a hipster, and certainly Mailer is not presenting him as one. But I would like to suggest that Ali for Mailer represents the Black male surpassing the White male in any and all facets but one (which I will broach later in this essay). Ali represents an achievement of body and mind as ego which Mailer says is "the great word of the 20th century" ("King of the Hill" p. 15). He proceeds in the same essay to pay Ali his idea of a great compliment: "He [Ali, not Mailer] is America's Greatest Ego. He is also . . . . the swiftest embodiment of human intelligence we have had yet, he is the very spirit of the 20th century . . . " (p. 15). Lest one think that Mailer's frequently bulging pugilism has routed his commitment to values of the intellect, he tries soon to justify his position: "There is no attempting to comprehend a prizefighter unless we are willing to recognize that he speaks with a command of the body which is as detailed, subtle, and comprehensive in its intelligence as any exercise of mind by such social engineers as Herman Kahn or Henry Kissinger" (p. 17).

Then Mailer makes an observation crucial to his whole position on Ali as a symbolic breakthrough in racial superiority and for his thesis of the 20th century as the Age of Ego:

> What separates the noble ego of the prizefighters from the lesser ego of authors is that the fighter goes through experiences in the ring which are occasionally immense, incommunicable except to fighters who have been as good, or to women who have gone through every minute of an anguish-filled birth, experiences which are finally mysterious (p. 17).

Beneath this powerful passage lurks the vanity that Mailer is enough of a prize-fighting adept to understand these "immense" ring experiences, merely by being aware that they exist. Mailer's acute insightfulness can be undercut sometimes by a remarkable insensitivity, as in the quotation above in which he describes childbirth as an egoistic experience analogous to some psychological events in the ring. Childbirth must be one of the great female mysteries, but this male would imagine it to be, by its very nature, the very opposite of a great egoistic event. Indeed, vanity, a department of ego, is a place and a force that Mailer is not unfamiliar with, and presents another key facet of *The Fight* that I now want to examine, as it ties into what I have urged to be a central underpinning of this book—Ali as a new level of racial achievement and excellence, a Black Nietzschean Superman, G.B.S.'s Life Force.

Nietzsche is relevant at this juncture, for, as the master of transvaluationalism, he offers a hint to part of what Mailer is about in *The Fight*—setting values upside down. Mailer takes a race of people enslaved centuries back, ruthlessly exploited in America (and elsewhere), and then, after being liberated through the American Civil War, still virtually enslaved in subtle and overt forms of racist manipulation, subordination, intimidation, and coercion, and, as a result, to add insult to injury, scorned for not being able to arise while being stomped into the ground—Mailer takes the physical prowess of this race, subtilizes and mythicizes it, and declares that it is a greatness superior to what the White race in America has achieved.

One will recognize something familiar in the conditions of this evaluation: the stress on action, on verve and endurance, on physical integrity will remind us of Hemingway, and *his* boxers, bullfighters, cowardly-courageous big-game hunters. And the cruelty or harshness behind the pivotal importance of the Test, as well as the test itself, will remind us of one of Hemingway's masters, Joseph Conrad. One might also detect a bit of D. H. Lawrence's "blood consciousness" in the implicit awareness on Mailer's part of instinctive intelligence in the "dialogue between bodies" by which Mailer defines boxing (*Existential Errands* p. 18).

This would appear to be a heavy freight of significance for an activity as disliked, even hated, by the average cultivated American, despite associations Hemingwayan, Lawrencean, Conradian, and even Nietzschean that one can (perhaps) muster to confer prestige on either Mailer or the "science of sock." But these references deserve consideration. Although Lawrence has been seen by his most hostile critics (like Bertrand Russell, a correspondent friend of Ali's, one should add) as paving the way to Auschwitz with his "blood" theory, more friendly commentators view the dramatization of Lawrence's poetics of the unconscious as the pith and root of his art's value. Hemingway usually sees the testing of guts—the famous grace under pressure—as either literally physical or as gestures of integrity or endurance (like Jake Barnes' silence about his plight and long, lonely night) that are "physical" in their intensity or ultimate reality. Certainly, there are enough situations in life where a gesture (including a fight) or physical integrity (such as resistance to bullying) embodies its own depth of meaning. And Conrad's young sea-captain's cowardly jump in *Lord Jim* from a ship after all his heroic fantasies is as memorable an instance in modern literature as any of the damning results of the body in a deeply affirmative (but here, self-destructive) action.

Thus, one can perhaps make a case through a modern literary tradition for what Mailer is trying to do in *The Fight*: offer us a symbol of physical excellence and character transvaluatively through the most oppressed and denigrated race in America.

Yet "transvaluatively" could be too strong a word here. Surely other White Americans have felt almost an inferiority complex with respect to the Black. Listen to Norman Podhoretz (in 1963): "Just as in childhood I envied Negroes for what seemed to me their superior masculinity, so I envy them today for what seems to me their superior physical grace and beauty," (quoted in Eldridge Cleaver, *Soul on Ice* p. 191). I don't think this feeling, envy, admiration, jealousy, is limited to Mailer and Podhoretz. Surely part of the attraction of American sports for American males is the extraordinary athletic abilities of Black athletes. It is all very well to be a successful lawyer or doctor with a six-figure income, a big house, chic cars, general community and professional respect, an attractive and intelligent wife, lovely children—but how Dr. White would love to soar through the air enroute to a dunk shot like James Worthy or Michael Jordan, run through tacklers like Emmet

Smith, or match Carl Lewis stride for stride streaking down the track. "I am now capable," says the once anguished Podhoretz, "of aching with all my being when I watch a Negro couple on the dance floor, or a Negro playing baseball or basketball" (p. 191). In a society in which sports achievement is as excessively celebrated, glamorized, and overrewarded as it is in America, envy and admiration of Black athletes are as American as apple pie. Mailer's admiration for Ali then is perhaps not so iconoclastic.

What is more unique or unusual is the role of ego in Mailer's hero-worshipping. The Mailer critic Philip H. Bufithis is worth quoting in this regard: "Ali seems a version of Mailer himself, which may explain Mailer's fascination with him for 15 years. If Mailer were less subtle and more loud, he would resemble Ali more than a little" (p. 122). This is an important perception. Mailer's involvement with Ali is also a disguised or symbolic self-involvement. Ali's flights of verbal and physical audacity, his terpsichorean pugilism, incorporate what Mailer himself (but surely not only Mailer) would like to accomplish.

Throughout *The Fight* Mailer gives evidence of a keen sensitivity to boxing, and of course almost everyone has heard stories of Mailer's own pugnacity, from his murderous confrontation with the American Nazi in *Armies of the Night* and his home kitchen rounds with fellow authors (reminding one of Kenneth Tynan's hilarious-ghastly "Go ahead, Norman, *Kick*-me-in-the-crotch" yarn), to his alleged amorous encounter with Germaine Greer in a New York taxi cab (perhaps *his* first Ali-Frazier bout). Whatever the arrant obnoxiousness of Mailer's bellicosity and bicep-bulging, his knowledge of boxing seems unquestionable. That in itself might not exactly be a winning proposition, but when combined with his symbolic enlargement of Ali as a new form of Higher Sensibility and his extraordinarily keen eye for the metaphysics of a prizefight as not only an intensely dramatic boxing match but a drama of polarized values, his skills as a sports journalist become impressive. Yes, impressive, for what Mailer is really up to in *The Fight* is to make himself the Muhammad Ali of prose writing. At one point, the surprisingly genial (pre-fight) Foreman tells Mailer that he's heard of the author: Mailer's the "champ among writers" (a rather handsome compliment that Mailer readily appears to tolerate). It is hardly a secret that Mailer has for well over 35 years spent much time and energy asserting (and trying to be worthy of) *that* belt. In the process of trying to win it, he has been at times little short of maniacal—so distant has the literary artist been from, say, a Rainer

Maria von Rilke as to make these two male authors seem as alike as a gorilla and a gazelle. Mailer has been annoying, offensive, even homicidal in his bids for attention and publicity. No retiring, dreamy romantic he. Yet, the plight of the artist in America being what it has been, constrained into triviality, preciousness, corruption and ultimate silence by Hollywood, TV, sports, political and other celebrities, the American artist might feel he or she has to shout to even be heard above all the din and glamour of celebrities of the Stage, Screen and Media.

This condition may not justify some of Mailer's public behavior or self-promotion but it partly explains it. What, however, Mailer cannot ever win, never achieve, no matter how hard he tries or fights or rages, is the Heavyweight Championship of the World. He may be the "Champ among Writers" (according to literary critic George Foreman), but he is not the Champ of Prizefighters, and well he knows it. Further, he is a short man in a nation that extols tall men or tallness (when has the sheriff-hero in a Western been under six feet tall?), another cross to bear. Also, although Mailer might be fairly tough, a somewhat formidable brawler (as Rojack in *An American Dream*, he cows a former prizefighter in a night club), he is in all probability no slashing halfback, no Magic Johnson of mystically perfect assists, no breath-taking sprinter. Mailer is a highly controversial writer and personality with some impressive books under his belt. But Mailer, part of his force and part of his weakness (and not just his), has wanted more, more—he has wanted to be Ali. Failing that accomplishment (as he must), he has, as mentioned earlier, tried to be the Ali of Prose. But one can pressure a metaphor only so far—its truth weakens to the extent one's imagination has to coerce the two contrasted elements together. What could result is a certain ugliness of envy that, in all gutsy honesty, Mailer confesses to early in *The Fight*: "his love affair with the Black soul, a sentimental orgy at its worst, had been given a drubbing through the seasons of Black Power. He no longer knew whether he loved Blacks or secretly disliked them . . . " (pp. 28-29). The Black Power of course hints at the news some American Blacks were dropping on White heads that indeed Blacks *were* superior, an attack that not only "masochistic" White liberals were supposedly vulnerable to but self-declared "conservative radicals" like Mailer too. But aside from this discomfort of the American 1960's and 1970's, Mailer might partly have subconsciously resented Ali (to a degree bordering on hatred) for his being a better boxer than Mailer—and being better-looking as well. Shortly before the Foreman bout, Mailer says this:

> If ever a fighter had been able to demonstrate that boxing was a 20th century art, it must be Ali. It would certainly come off as a triumph for the powers of regeneration in an artist. What could be more important to Norman? He knew some part of himself would hate Ali if the fighter lost without dignity or real effort, even as part of him could not forgive Hemingway because of the ambiguity of his suicide—if only there had been a note (p. 131).

There's the Hemingway presence but also the hatred for Ali should he lose looking bad. Clearly Mailer identifies closely with Ali, so much as to suggest on one level or another that they are doubles, and that not only part of Mailer's own mythology or ideology of self would be tarnished or threatened by an Ali defeat but some innate reservoir of vitality eroded and purpose poisoned. Ali the Champ would perhaps make Mailer the Chump of writers, but also, the harsher face we usually hide from people to whom we give our deeper affections or admiration would be revealed, as loving envy turned through humiliating defeat into a self-protecting contempt.

But we must return to ego and to its risks in a wild field of forces that Mailer defines excitingly, as I will soon depict. Let us first identify another face-off in *The Fight*—it is Norman Mailer vs. Muhammad Ali, the Writer vs. the Boxer, the Challenger who magnificently defeats the formidable Champion (Foreman) vs. the Writer who tries to match the Fighter's great art with a great prose account. Not that the literal fight itself is a second place event for Mailer. Mailer indeed makes this fight almost cosmic in its drama, and deep in its imaginative suggestiveness. And he brings to bear some of his best resources as a literary artist and critic to arrange his material to best effect. So, one beholds two towering American egos, but also two stunning personalities gifted and ready to show their stuff in their prime. But on with the Fight!

II

The book begins with a tribute to Ali's splendid physical presence: "There is always a shock in seeing him again.... Women draw an audible breath. Men look down. They are reminded of their lack of worth.... he is the Prince of Heaven—so says the silence around his body when he is luminous" (p. 2). Rather heavy stuff, is one's first reaction. "Men look down . . . . reminded of their lack of worth" seems savagely snobbish. But Mailer could well be including himself here, and he is, again, being honest about a truth not too many men will admit to—that men (like women) do make sharp judgments about each other physically. A male's physique may not be the only criterion, nor the most enduring one, of male excellence, but it certainly is one that is sometimes dominant. D. H. Lawrence would probably have given up even a few more years of his fairly short life to have had a build like Gerald Crich or even Tom Brangwen. Perhaps Mailer wishes he would have been built like some 6' 4" wide receiver, and who can blame him if he does, as hundreds of thousands of male TV viewers have probably shared that wish, even if fleetingly. Still, there is always something in Mailer of the tough or obnoxious kid who in a gang of idle youths punctures the boredom by saying "I'll take on any of you guys with one hand tied behind my back." Mailer, sensitive to other men's sense of their physical courage or cowardice (and thus cruelly mystified by Hemingway's suicide) would also feel that the average man would be abashed in Ali's presence—another one of Mailer's obnoxious truths, or half-truths.

Ali the Prince of Heaven—but even this celestial aristocrat has his off moments and days. So, like the shrewd artist he is, Mailer follows that glowing, bullying first paragraph by suddenly introducing a new key that will dominate two-thirds of his narrative. He begins by describing how Ali's skin turns "the color of coffee with milky water" when he is depressed. And that is how he appears in his Deer Lake Camp, in Pennsylvania, seven weeks before his fight with Foreman: "His sparring is spiritless. Worse. He kept getting hit with stupid punches . . . " (p. 2). Soon after, Mailer exhibits one of his best stylistic devices or "punches"— the simile or metaphor. There are many figures of speech in *The Fight*, and most of them are quite imaginative, funny, or insightful. Trying to convey the gloom in Ali's camp, he says Ali "looked bored. He showed, as he worked, all the sullen ardor of a husband obliging himself to make love to his wife in the thick of carnal indifference" (pp. 4-5). Part of the comic effect here, of course, resides in the contrast of professional boxing and training with marital love-making. Indeed, Mailer uses enough sexual or erotic analogies in the book to require a closer look.

One of the ironies of boxing, or of any hostile confrontation between males, is that their body proximity and emotional focus are similar to those of lovers. Indeed, athletes in the more physically competitive sports (perhaps supremely in boxing) are often quite warm with each other at the conclusion of the event. This need not incite theories of repressed homosexuality among athletes generally, but it does show that the bounds of physical relation and affection between human beings is not adequately delineated by the traditional psycho-physical categories of heterosexual and homosexual relating. To "stick" another boxer may mean to punch him, but Ali's trainer, Bundini Brown, uses that verb in a passage where he also describes the need of a boxer during training to maintain a "hard-on" and to be cautious "not to cum" (p. 105). Granted, Bundini is not speaking literally, but his metaphor does give one pause, and it seems probable that human beings experience, besides sublimating, sexual sensations in sports action. This might especially be the case if athletes are forced (or force themselves) to refrain from sexual intercourse during their training (at least one professional football coach had a "Tuesday" rule for his players—no sex, spousal or otherwise, in the week of a game after Tuesday). Ali in his vivid autobiography, *The Greatest: My Own Story*, puts the matter in a curiously engaging way: After a fighter in training has refrained from sex for many weeks, "Then Mother Nature takes care of him by relaxing him at night with wet dreams. When that comes, you know you're really in shape. . . . Mother Nature just took care of the overflow" (p. 441).

So Mailer begins his narrative in a minor key. But he knows his craft too well to make everything gray. Of course he is writing about one of the great prizefighters of all time, very possibly the greatest, with a professional boxing career of 14 years (as of 1974) as well as being the bearer of the world title from 1964 until it was taken from him for political reasons by the official boxing authorities in 1967, so it would not be easy for Mailer to omit a number of extremely impressive aspects of Ali's physical and psychological makeup as a pugilist. We find out, for example, that Ali's waist is as flexible as the average boxer's neck, which is one reason he could avoid punches with his arms down, an Ali trademark. We also find out about his acute intelligence in terms of various strategies, some crucial to his winning major bouts: "He invariably trained by a scenario that cast him as a fighter in deep fatigue, too tired to raise his arms in the 12th round of a 15-round fight" (p. 4). And though the typical prizefighter in training would have his sparring partners imitate their next opponent, Ali, says Mailer, would "elaborate the wit and dazzle of his own" style. Here, however, Mailer errs, for

Ali himself stated, at least for the Foreman fight, that "I've been studying George ever since Herbert [Herbert Muhammad, his brilliant Manager] arranged for the match. I've studied his record, checking out his opponents, how he beat them.... I want sparring partners who can help me work against my opponent's style so that when I get in the ring with him it won't be like the first time" (*The Greatest* p. 440).

To make this early pre-fight period even more complicated, Mailer brings in the matter of Ali's verse. Another facet of Ali's ego, Mailer makes it clear that the Prince of Heaven is no Wordsworth or William Butler Yeats (Marianne Moore, however, thought well of Ali's verse). In fact, Mailer thinks rather little of Ali's poeticizing, and one certainly has read greater verse than "I have a great one-two punch. / The one hits a lot, but the two hits a bunch." And even in what Ali describes as his own "serious" verse which ends "The law of truth is simple / On your soul you reap," (p. 101), Mailer detects evidence of plagiarism.

Yet what is curious here in Mailer's put-downs of Ali the Poet is that he makes such a to-do about Ali's physical intelligence being the equal of anyone's cerebral smarts, yet when Ali aspires to literary mentality, Mailer will have none of it. It is almost as if, despite Mailer's celebration of Black *physical* superiority, he wants to retain something of the traditional stereotype of racial polarity: White, Mind—Black, Body. Yet Ali has had a gift with words—his best "verse" is a "prose poetry" that is frequently evident: "Foreman—he just got slow punches, take a year to get there," or, Foreman's not a puncher, he "just pushes people around" (p. 12), surely irony of sizable proportions in describing the bone-crunching punches of George Foreman. Fighting Foreman, adds Ali, is "just another gym workout" (p. 62). And when told by the referee during the pre-fight instructions not to talk to Foreman, Ali asks "Where does it say [in the boxing rule book] that they [prizefighters] cannot discuss personal problems or world problems?" (*The Greatest* p. 494).

Ali's wit, egotism, and psychological pressure of abuse upon an opponent merge in a scene in Kinshasa not long before the fight. The two boxers use the same gym for workouts and their paths cross occasionally. Ali, after insulting Foreman ("Come in, chump. I ain't going to hurt you"), tells the surrounding reporters that Foreman said he didn't want to hear Ali's comment, as "George Foreman wants to keep his mind undisturbed because he's got a lot to worry about. He has to face me" (p. 50). As was often the case in

Ali's "egotism," the vanity seems partly dissolved in the audacity and wit. It also points to Ali's continual sense or tactic of psyching out an opponent. Mailer observes that boxers box partly out of vanity, to be admired: "In no sport, therefore, can you be more humiliated...." If at his best, Foreman is leonine, he is ox-like at his worst, "So the first object of training was to work on Foreman's sense of grace." Foreman has to be taught to dance, surely a great joke to a past master of that art like Ali.

Yet the minor key continues. Mailer informs us that "Ali seems more interested in talking to the press than in working. One morning he did no more than three rounds of light shadow-boxing. Then he hit the heavy bag for a few minutes" (p. 51), in vivid contrast to Foreman who, we are told just before, will throw five or six hundred heavy punches in a training session.

A picture is gradually emerging through Mailer's strategy of presenting Foreman as predictably formidable, incredibly savage and dangerous, while, in dramatic contrast, presenting Ali as unpredictable, despite his past greatness as a boxer. One of the major scenes in the entire narrative not only underlines Ali's strange ways of preparing for a crucial bout, but also suggests a large philosophical underpinning in *The Fight*. Examining both that scene and that underpinning might help us to understand something of Ali's delightfully complex, seemingly perverse and possibly magical sensibility.

III

The fight has been temporarily postponed because Foreman has received a cut over the eye in training. Mailer flies back to New York and, desiring to understand African culture more than he does, stumbles on a book by a Dutch priest entitled *Bantu Philosophy*. He is pleased to find out that Bantu philosophy resembles his own:

> Bantu philosophy.... saw humans as forces, not beings.... by such logic.... A man was not only what he contained, not only his desires, his memory, and his personality, but also the forces that came to inhabit him at any moment from all things living *and dead* [italics added—D. G.].... One did one's best to live in the pull of these forces in such a way as to increase one's own

> force ... the beginning of wisdom was to enrich oneself,
> enrich the *muntu* which was the amount of life in oneself
> ... (p. 31).

This passage (in *The Fight*) resembles part of the ontological philosophy of a fellow Westerner (of Mailer's), D. H. Lawrence. Speaking of the ancient Etruscans (and of the even more ancient Mesopotamians), Lawrence moves into one of his famed visionary exaltations:

> Behind all the [Etruscan] dancing was a ... conception of the universe and man's place in the universe which made men live to the depth of their capacity.
> To the Etruscan all was alive; the whole universe lived; and the business of man was himself to live amid it all. He had to draw life into himself, out of the wandering huge vitalities of the world. The cosmos was alive, like a vast creature (*Etruscan Places*, in *D. H. Lawrence and Italy* p. 45).

Mailer had been reading Lawrence fairly widely a few years earlier, for the Lawrence chapter of *The Prisoner of Sex*, though he may not have read such works of Lawrence as *Etruscan Places*, *Apocalypse*, or the magnificent little essay "New Mexico," all of which harbor stunning passages of this sort of rhapsodic animistic speculation. Also, the two philosophies (or three, including Muntuism) are not exactly identical. However, they do have in common a pronounced vitalism, and the primitive or primitivist belief in a universe charged with vital forces that we must be wary of (but also excited about), "So we have to be bold enough to live with all the magical forces at loose between the living and the dead" (*The Fight* p. 31).

What does all this high-charged, world- and even corpse-animating vitalism have to do with a couple of American prize-fighters? It serves Mailer as a context for the fight (being staged, after all, in Africa): "Human beings were not beings but forces. He would try to look at them [Ali and Foreman] by that light" (p. 35). Thus, Mailer attempts to exalt the fight to the dimensions of a cosmic struggle, one with two pronounced sides.

In an astute article entitled "Hot Spics Versus Cool Spades: Three Notes Towards a Cultural Definition of Prizefighting," Gerald Early makes some key points that can be used to see how Mailer further enlarges the significance of a boxing match: "racial contrast is what the male politics of boxing is all about ... " (p. 42); "Ali never really needed to fight white men to create racial contrast for a bout since, with the help of the media, he was able to make over his principle opponents into whites by virtue of their politics or their lack of politics; nearly every Ali opponent became a representation of the white establishment" (p. 43). (Early also adds that "Ali, while playing the role of the militant Muslim, denigrated his black opponents in ways that one would have expected only from a racist white, or a black ill at ease with his collective identity"— p. 44.)

If Early's points suggest a vicious side to Ali's strategy in psyching out opponents, Foreman, in this case, is glad to cooperate with Ali's baiting: "'Don't talk down the American system to me,' he says . . . . 'its rewards can be there for anybody if he will make up his mind . . . and refuse to allow anything to defeat him. I'll wave that flag in every public place I can'" (p. 83). As a Black Muslim, Ali thus needed little help from Foreman in setting up a Black-"White" polarity in this match. This gambit also assisted in making Ali hated by a clear-cut portion of the American populace—in boxing, at least, Ali was the fighter the "squares" loved to hate. Of course, Ali deliberately antagonized them which is one reason why Mailer is attracted to him. No one would call Ali an American flag-waver. Ali clearly made himself hateful to some in order to hype his fights (not that his Muslimism was insincere, of course). But some Americans would love to see him get a thrashing (or considerably worse), while others, after his loss in the first Frazier fight, would weep in the streets. Ali's striking flair for attracting publicity and the wrathful attention of White America might have served as an object lesson to Mailer, whose capacity and desire for drawing (often hostile) attention again puts the literary Champ in contention with the Ring Champ.

Some of the people who might have wept on the street after Ali's loss to Frazier were poor American Blacks who Mailer views as doubly dispossessed, first, in Africa, and then in America (p. 34). One of the most empathetic passages in Mailer's book follows:

> A poor and uneducated man was nothing without that force [basic life energy]. To the degree it lived inside him, he was full of capital, ego capital, and that was what he possessed. That was the capitalism of the poor American Black trying to accumulate more of the only wealth he could find, respect on his turf, the respect of the local flunkies for the power of his soul. . . . The establishment offered massive restraint for such massive fevers of the ego. No surprise if tribal life in America began to live among stone walls and drugs. The drug

gave magnification of the sentiment that a mighty force was still inside one, and the penitentiary restored the old idea that man was a force in a field of forces (p. 34).

It is passages such as this that make *The Fight* (and its *three* fighters) "metaphysical." Of course Ali's appeal is not only to lower-class American Blacks; it obviously crosses class and race lines. Many people, including middle and upper class Whites, admired and even loved him. Despite his "lip," his at times vicious, sometimes hilarious, tauntings, his astoundingly large and complex ego, his arrogance, Ali often made people not usually boxing fans interested in his fights in the way anti-boxing parents might be whose son had decided to pursue a prizefighting or other dangerous career. One feared he might get badly hurt, marveled when he didn't and when he even won against formidable opponents like Sonny Liston and Joe Frazier.

Mailer introduces the Congolese term for Bantu's *muntu* ("libido," for Freudians), and that word is "n'golo," which he says means force, or vital force. Ali, claims Mailer correctly, had been denied his *n'golo* by the American Boxing establishment and ultimately the American State at war in Vietnam. This deprivation more than a few Blacks would readily identify with. Of course such identification between one's racial, social, or economic status and an athlete or team goes on all the time; the joy that a large city can feel when "its" team wins the Super Bowl, World Series, or NBA championship seems, except for the most unreflective sports fan, out of proportion to its intrinsic or literal significance. But other people, not only Blacks, are hungry for *n'golo*, and few sports offer the highly concentrated symbolic charge of identification that Heavyweight Prizefighting does, and especially for Black people, in view of the way Blacks have dominated this premier category of prizefighting for the past 50 years or so.

Thus, Mailer's point that heavyweight boxers were likely to be insane, being conceivably the toughest men in the world (p. 38). As such, they certainly operated in a field of force, Bantuistic, Mailerian, Lawrencean (or Etruscan-Babylonian), and so embodied Mailer's big 20th century word, Ego. But what makes Ego worth something is when it tests itself by, as Mailer puts it in "King of the Hill," giving "us authority to declare we are sure of ourselves when we are not" (p. 15).

In the world of *muntu*, Ali thus risks his *n'golo* incredibly in a feat of daring and high comic spirits that appalls Ali's African fans (and perhaps Mailer, too), but, which Mailer doesn't point out, also

86   Breaking Through to the Other Side

indicates facets of wild humor in Ali that made him likable in surprising quarters. As boxing promoter Don King said in Zaire at that time, "Ali motivates even the dead" (p. 99), and if so, that's certainly vital force or *n'golo*.

Ali is working out with a sparring partner named Roy Williams, actually boxing, grunts Mailer, for a change. Several hundred Black Africans are present. Ali starts clowning around, going down for several knockdowns (after each of which he gives a speech). Then he *stays* down:

> The mood was awful. It was as if somebody had told an absolutely filthy joke that absolutely didn't work. A devil's fart. The air was ruined. From the floor, Ali said: 'Well, the Lip has been shut [though we notice that even in "death," Ali is far from speechless]. He's had his mouth shut for the last time. George Foreman is the greatest. Too strong,' said Ali sadly. 'He hit too hard. . . . George Foreman is undisputed champion of the world.'
> The Africans in the rear of the hall were stricken. . . . Nobody believed that Ali had been hurt—they were afraid of something worse. By way of the charade, Ali had given a tilt to the field of forces surrounding the fight (p. 59).

Shortly after, *Muntu* Mailer adds that "a man must not play with his dignity unless he is adept in the arts of transformation. Did Ali really know what he was doing? Was he foolishly trying to burn away some taint in his soul and thereby daring disaster, or was he purposefully arousing the forces working for the victory of Foreman in order to disturb them? Who could know?" (p. 59)

Thus does Mailer continually activate and intensify the vitalist world of *The Fight*. So intent is he, though, on the boldness of Ali's *n'golo* and the possible folly of his raid upon the sacral regions of *muntu*, that he overlooks or ignores the rich comedy and humanity of Ali's superb goofing-off. For any kind of boxer, not only a champion prizefighter, to pretend in front of a large hall of intense fans that he has just been totally overcome by his opponent in an upcoming bout is a comic audacity bordering on the Promethean. Mailer is surely right in his imaginative hunch at the primitivist risk that Ali is running, but just as surely a deep humor is alive in that ring that commands our awe, if comedy is the art of rebirth and renewal, whether of society or of sports champs.

Yet Mailer works his own vein of humor in *The Fight*, as well as his own *muntu*, which by testing, he, generously, hopes to add to

Ali's. Mailer goes for an early morning jog with Ali, and can't go the entire two-and-a-half miles (having overeaten some hours before), so turns back in the pitch dark to head the few miles back to Ali's camp by himself:

> Just then he [Mailer] heard a lion roar. It was no small sound, more like thunder, and it opened an unfolding wave of wrath across the sky and through the fields. Did the sound originate a mile away, or less? He had come out of the forest, but the lights of Nsele [Ali's headquarters] were also close to a mile away, and there was all of this deserted road between. He could never reach those lights before the lion would run him down. Then his next thought was that the lion, if it chose, could certainly race up on him silently, might even be on his way now (p. 74).

This would be a frightening moment for anyone, even for a Norman Mailer. It's one thing to nearly slug it out with Gore Vidal in Madison Square Garden, but quite another to take on an African lion—surely, a four-footed champion of the claw and tooth. Many are fearing Ali won't last more than three rounds against Foreman, but with this lion Mailer (or Foreman or Ali) wouldn't get far into Round 1. Indeed, he (and who would blame him?) would run right out of the ring. He has thoughts about *this* title loss: "To be eaten by a lion on the banks of the Congo—who could fail to notice that it was Hemingway's own lion waiting down these years for the flesh of Ernest until an *appropriate* [italics added] substitute had at last arrived?" (p. 75) Vain to the end, Mailer's foes might charge, missing the irony and humor beneath the conceit. And when told later back at Ali's camp that there's a zoo nearby which might have had some lions in it (but were they *all* in the zoo, one would wonder), we see an instance of how Mailer can handle vanity, not only to preen but also to deflate himself in *his* version of *The Beast in the Jungle*.

Another incident is comic perhaps more at Mailer's expense or control, and that is when he enters too overtly into the ring of *muntu* by climbing around his seven-story apartment balcony, a la Rojack in *An American Dream*, in order to test himself (while *drunk*, on this occasion) so as *somehow* (for the field of force is magical) to add his own courage to Ali's. This is vain, he says later (p. 101), as Ali hardly needed or asked for Mailer's portion of bravery or daring. Yet, Mailer adds, ominously and craftily, Ali needs all the help he can get against Foreman. Also, the upshot of the jog with Ali is another epiphany of gloom—Ali has trouble, claims *Mailer*, jogging less than 3 miles even slowly: "Norman did not see how Ali could win. Defeat was in the air Ali alone seemed to refuse to breathe" (p. 77). Clearly, it is time now to turn to the source of this terror and gloom, the slaying Heavyweight Champion George Foreman.

IV

The references to George Foreman's strength, brawn, power and unrelenting (except to breathe) brutality in the ring are frequent; they comprise one of the two dominant motifs in the book. They thus form a contrasting pattern with Ali's complex behavior—his witty taunts and jokes, his rantings, his poetry or doggerel, his supposed profound distaste (unlike Foreman's) for working out, his strong ideological allegiance and dedication. Not that Foreman is just the strong, silent type—he can even crack a good joke (as we shall see). But silence seems his medium, as words are Ali's and water is that of fish. Thus an innocent, even ostensibly Lewis-Carroll, remark to reporters like Foreman's "'Excuse me for not shaking hands with you, but you see I'm keeping my hands in my pockets'" (p. 37) seems sinister with quiet, comic menace. Mailer suggests the kinship of this silence with dangerous catatonics, and it is clear that in silence for Foreman reside abysses of possibly insatiable hunger for violence. But then Foreman's silence (which certainly detracts from his role as Ali's "white" boxer) can afford itself; for the facts can and do speak for themselves. They, through Mailer's handling, add up to a terrifying authority:

> In Caracas that night, directly before his [Mailer's] eyes, he had seen a killer. Foreman had been vicious like few men ever seen in the ring (p. 12).

As Ken Norton, who had broken Ali's jaw during a 1973 fight in San Diego, went down under Foreman's attack in the *second* round, Foreman hit him five times.

Further, in *The Fight* we are told that "Foreman had never been defeated. On the night he won the championship, he had accumulated no less than 35 knockouts, the fights stopped on an average before the third round" (p. 38). Next, we hear that even a Foreman "'punch on the arm leaves you feeling paralyzed.... Ali is a friend of mine [says Heavyweight fighter Henry Clark], and I'm afraid he's going to get hurt. George is the most punishing human being I've ever been with'" (p. 42). Mailer's description of Foreman working out on the heavy bag provides a startling mathematics and omen of pugilistic violence:

> Foreman was pounding punches into it. These were no ordinary swings. Foreman was working for the maximum of power in punch after punch round after round fifty or a hundred punches in a row without diminishing in this session, and they were probably the heaviest cumulative series of punches any boxing writer had seen. Each of these blows was enough to smash an average athlete's ribs.... One could feel the strategy. Sooner or later, there must come a time in the fight when Ali would be so tired he could not move, could only use his arms to protect himself. Then he would be like a heavy bag... his [Foreman's] fists would smash through every protection of Ali.... (p. 50).

Perhaps Archie Moore is to blame for the intrusion of not just war diction into sports writing (a long pass in football is a "bomb," two NBA playoff teams are not only having a game, but a war, etc.), a vicious enough failing among sports scribes, but for a lingo of *nuclear* battle: "Foreman not only has TNT in his mitts but *nuclearology* as well..." (p. 80). Rather than condemning such gross linguistic overkill as he should have, Mailer enters into and elaborates the terrible metaphor in three of four clever but insensitive sentences, but then returns to his own brilliant figuration, while putting one more flick of terror into the looming battle and Ali's plight: "On the night Foreman took his championship, who could forget the film of *Frazier's* [italics added] urgent legs staggering around the ring, looking for their lost leader?" (p. 80)

If all this clearly prepossessing evidence of Foreman's geniality does not fully convey the point, the following proposition might do so: "Each time Foreman knocked a man out, frustration showed on his face. Foreman looked like he still wanted to kill them [sic]" (p. 110). A final testimony of Foreman's violently merciless ring personality: "Foreman in the ring, working as an executioner, was simply not likable... he would probably win no mass popularity for continuing to hit opponents who were falling to the floor" (p. 117).

Thus, it comes as a superb cap to the motif of Foreman's frightening physical power and menace that he can also whip up a respectably good joke:

'Do you like to speak during a fight?' 'I never do get a chance to talk much in the ring. By the time I begin to know a fellow,' George remarked, 'it's all over' (p. 120).

V

The mood in Ali's entourage in the long bus-ride to the fight stadium on the morning (4 a.m.) of the fight in Zaire was "like a forest road on a wet winter day" (p. 128), nor is the mood improved by Ali's dressing room, which, all in white, "looked like an operating room" (*The Greatest* p. 479). The fact that everyone else was gloomy does not seem to daunt Ali. He says that he often "finds the dressing-room atmosphere before a fight too free" (p. 480), and usually he's the one that has to make the situation get taken more seriously. Again, one sees Ali's fine intelligence at work. But something beyond intelligence is involved in his singular and solitary high spirits before the Foreman fight, for "The odds are four to one against me in America, three to one in Europe—even three to one in Tokyo, where I'm popular" (*The Greatest* p. 480). On the other hand, he is getting telegrams and predictions of his victory from all over Africa (p. 481).

Mailer, speaking to Ali, utters these unbelievable (for Mailer) words to the imperiled Challenger: "'I think I'm more scared than you are.' . . . 'Nothing to be scared about,' said the fighter. 'It's just another day in the dramatic life of Muhammad Ali'" (p. 134). Cool enough to be humorous, Ali, then, like a philosopher, puts the Foreman confrontation in the context of more frightening events: fighting Sonny Liston the first time, enduring threats against his life after Malcolm X's murder. Such events put Foreman in perspective for Ali, though, to be sure, for no one else at that moment. Ali is the only one in the room who seems to be in full possession of his *n'golo*. As he says, but, as it turns out, means only figuratively, "'We're going to dance and dance'" (p. 138).

Ali soon enters the ring. As Challenger, he is in the ring first, and must await the Champion, a situation for some boxers of terrorizing anticipation. But this is not Ali's state of mind, and we move into one of the most beautiful sequences in Mailer's whole book:

He was all alone in the ring, the Challenger on call for the Champion, the Prince waiting for the Pretender, and

> unlike other fighters who wilt in the long minutes before the titleholder will appear, Ali seemed to be taking royal pleasure in his undisputed possession of the space. He looked unafraid and almost on the edge of happiness, as if the discipline of having carried himself through the two thousand nights of sleeping without even losing a contest . . . must have been a biblical seven years of trial through which he had come with the crucial part of his honor, his talent, and his desire for greatness still intact, and light came off him at this instant (p. 142).

Comparing this superb account with Ali's again highlights Ali's intelligence:

> I understand George's play [in making Ali wait for his appearance]. He thinks this will make me nervous . . . . But he has given me an edge I know how to take advantage of, a chance to study the crowd, to get to know their ego, their personality. Crowds exert pressure on you. Every crowd feels strange at first, no matter who they cheer for. But when I warm up, I feel their good vibrations. . . . George has given me time to test the ropes [a crucial preliminary—D. G.] and to get the feel of the distance between the center and the corner. . . . I look at the crowd from different angles. . . . I get used to the heat from the lights (*The Greatest* p. 491).

It is highly ironic that a man as intelligent as Mailer mainly projects an egoistic interpretation on another great egoist's behavior at the very moment that Ali is subordinating egotism in order to best evaluate the situation whose outcome should give him enough *muntu* and egotism for a lifetime.

Yet this is not to sizably undercut Mailer's sense of that moment (actually lasting more than ten minutes, according to Ali's trainer). The Mailer passage is a culmination of several major forces in *The Fight*. Mailer had given us sign after sign that Ali might not be ready for this fight—his distaste for training (which evokes one's sympathy, fighters who *enjoy* training suggesting barely sublimated killers), his supposedly poor performance during the Mailer jog, the possible fear of Foreman beneath his verbal assaults against the Champion, and, on the other hand, the towering image of Foreman as the Executioner of Heavyweights. Yet, by some sweet miracle, some successful magic handling of *muntu*, *n'golo*, libido, Jung's Collective Unconscious, or perhaps just some deep mystery of personal integrity (plus adequate training?), Ali is fully ready for Foreman, looking "unafraid and almost on the edge of happiness," followed by Mailer's handsome definition of *one* kind of integrity that surely lends itself as analogy or symbol to other forms of fortitude or essential wholeness.

The suggestion of a saint-like illumination emanating from Ali at this point would sound silly in most prizefight descriptions. But Mailer has earned the right to that hint of the mystical, partly through the curves of his craft. We recall that he begins *The Fight* describing Ali looking out of spirits and depressed, easily hit by "stupid punches." Now he's shining like Mailer's Prince of Heaven; it sounds almost like Lady Murasaki's Prince Genji (the "Shining One"). Thus, appropriately, his words to Foreman during the ring moment for fight instructions are startling, awesome in their self-confidence, or bluffing: "You've heard of me since you were young. You've been following me since you were a little boy. Now, you must meet me, your master!" (p. 144). Mailer has rather dressed up Ali's language here, which is cruder ("You been hearing about how bad I am since you were a little kid with mess in you pants!", *The Greatest* p. 492). Ali, during the instructions ritual, has to be warned by the referee five or six times to be quiet. It is obvious that he is abrading Foreman psychologically. But another *n'golo* is vivid for Ali here, an old ghost: He says that as Foreman glares back at him, he suddenly sees Sonny Liston ten years ago in the ring with Ali, and is reminded of the claim by critics that he could never have beaten a *young* Liston. Now a young Liston is before him.

This brief background should not reduce the audacity of Ali's pre-fight taunts here. Football fans were amazed, some enraged, when Joe Namath said his Jets would beat the seemingly invincible Baltimore Colts in the Superbowl, and that was a brag (combined with Namath's pre-game night sexual lark) to make or break an athlete's Rep. Yet Namath's boast is not really in a class with Ali's claim in authority, boldness, or ego vulnerability, or in the immediate and intense hostility of the respondent and *his* moment.

Mailer covers the ensuing fight brilliantly, and it would be an impertinence to compete with him in that endeavor. Rather, I want to stress some of the virtues of both Mailer's prose and Ali's strategy in fighting Foreman.

Ali is a genius of the unexpected, of the subtle, audacious tactic, and early in the first round, reveals one—he hits Foreman with rights to the forehead, a very dangerous punch to attempt (especially against a Champion) for reasons Mailer explains. Ali keeps throwing rights, enraging Foreman who, in charging Ali, continually gets tied up by a surprisingly strong Ali. But it is only a matter of time before Foreman's relentless power begins to control the fight. So what does Ali do? He said in his dressing room just before the fight that he would "dance," but now doesn't; instead, he uses the ropes in one of the most outrageously supple boxing tactics ever practiced. Mailer's comments here are hard to beat:

> Of course Ali had been preparing for just this hour over the last ten years. For ten years he had been practicing to fight powerful sluggers who beat on your belly while you lay on the ropes. So he took up his station with confidence, shoulders parallel to the edge of the ring. In this posture his right would have no more impact than a straight left but he could find himself in position to cover his head with both gloves, and his belly with his elbows, he could rock and sway, lean so far back Foreman must fall on him. Should Foreman pause from the fatigue of throwing punches, Ali could bounce off the ropes and sting him, jolt him, make him look clumsy, sock him, rouse his anger, which might yet wear Foreman out more than anything else. In this position, Ali could even hurt him (p. 151).

Mailer a little later says that Ali uses the ropes to absorb Foreman's bludgeoning, which makes it crucial that Angelo Dundee had loosened the turnbuckles on each post shortly before the fight, for the loosened ropes provide Ali with a decisive further dimension, for escape, for flexibility, for sudden, offensive rebounding, the irony ringing through it all that being on the ropes is proverbially the world's worst place for a boxer, as one there is usually narrowed in movement, trapped, cut off—and, if anything, Foreman has been trained to cut off Ali's movement, and thus paralyze his dancing, his rhythm, his special nuances of motion within motion. But Ali is at home on the ropes, which is where he stays for much of the fight, after realizing, during Round One (he tells us), that he is taking six steps to every three by Foreman, and that this is his chief danger, rather than being on the ropes, for he won't last fifteen rounds at a pace that is double Foreman's (*The Greatest* pp. 469, 470).

At the end of the fourth round, Foreman does catch the uncatchable Ali with a very hard punch, and, says Mailer, this makes Foreman decide he could finish Ali in the fifth round. The fifth round could go to Mailer, for it is possibly one of the greatest passages not only in boxing prose, but in all sports writing. It goes on for a full two-and-a-half pages, and shows Ali's tactic tested and stretched to its utmost tolerance. Mailer gets it off on a bad foot with some overkill diction again: "Ali got ready [on the ropes] and Foreman came on to blast him out. A shelling reminiscent of artillery battles in World War One began" (p. 159). But Mailer mainly uses his gift for rhythm, metaphor, continuity and pause to convey a boxing match as an epical event:

> Across that embattled short space Foreman threw punches in barrages of four and six and eight and nine, heavy maniacal slamming punches, heavy as the boom of oaken doors. . . .
> And Ali, gloves to his head, elbows to his ribs, stood and swayed and was rattled and banged and shaken like a grasshopper at the top of a reed when the wind whips . . . .
> All the while, he [Ali] used his eyes. They looked like stars, and he feinted Foreman out with his eyes, flashing white eyeballs of panic he did not feel which pulled Foreman through into the trick of lurching after him on a wrong move . . . (p. 159).

Near the end of the round when Foreman may have thrown 40-50 powerful punches in a minute's time, some waning in Foreman from absolute rage leads Mailer to a perceptive (and very funny) simile: "Ali reaching over the barrage would give a prod now and again like a housewife sticking a toothpick in a cake to see if it is ready" (p. 160). Ali will then come off the ropes and successfully throw "some of the hardest punches of the night" (p. 161) at the Champion. The fight is not yet over, but it has reached a climax, and that climax more than hints that Ali might well win the fight.

But I want to return to that culinary, housewife metaphor—housewife Ali—because it suggests something deeper about Ali's strategy that Mailer only intimates. Ali was attractive as a prizefighter to many people who don't usually follow or even like prizefighting. He was highly intelligent, resourceful, flexible, very innovative, and possessed a boldness, even iconoclasm, of conception and response to both boxing and life, as he experienced them as a great prizefighter and a Black that does not at all fit the customary picture, however unfair or exaggerated, of the professional boxer as a brawny, savage dummy. I've already cited Mailer's crisp definitions of boxers as acute physical intelligences. Mailer would likely admit that boxing, no matter how much of an art, can, if pursued too long, result in a brutish, pulverized (or pulverizing) sensibility. "Beautiful" hooks, "brilliant" jabs, "breathtaking" uppercuts because they have landed on someone's head or body. It is the measure of manhood of some not to focus on the pain, misery, agony of these blows, or what these blows can do (and have done) to permanently darken boxers' later lives. It has been said that prizefighters are in the ring because they want to be there. Yet a point by Gerald Early seems irrefutable: "Boxing is . . . available to a boy who cannot be a singer, a preacher, or a thief (which is really the only other job training program available to the lower class)" (pp. 55-56). It is pertinent to mention here that Ali in *The Greatest* stresses his own lower-class background, quoting (to disagree with) Mailer's assertion that Ali came from a middle-class family. Mailer perhaps is glamorizing the exigencies of Ali's early-life circumstances, suggesting that Ali had more scope for deciding what he wanted to do with his life than he really had, and thus that his decision to become a prizefighter was a "classy" gesture, rather than the result, as Early thinks, of limited options open to a lower class or minority youth. In any case, Mailer (and Hemingway before him) would exalt the sport indeed for its "Existentialist" deadliness, its threat of serious danger (people in the know really thought that Foreman might half-kill or even kill Ali in the fight)—the ring another arena (one of the few left!) where, like the Army, society could make a real man of a boy, or keep men men.

The egregious machismo of these traditional attitudes contrast vividly with an aspect of Ali as a boxer and a mentality that is seldom noticed. If a "feminine" (or just humane and genderless) perception of boxing would stress its brutal or primitive aspect, it would in Ali's case characterize a portion of the psyche of his fighting art. Housewife Ali with his toothpick feeling cake / Foreman to see if it / he is ready to eat / demolish—such are the metaphoric-literal equations in Mailer's baroque art of figuration, and beneath it, leading to Ali's grand strategy, is the most "female," "passive" technique of all pugilistic artistries—using the ropes, later called the "rope-a-dope" tactic.

Jungians would say that Ali had inducted his *anima* into the service of prizefighting. Ali leans back on the ropes—"like a woman!"—with male Foreman almost lying over him, not trying to embrace but to batter, in fact, annihilate Ali. The rope allows, as mentioned earlier, a movement beyond the ring—another whole dimension for a boxer. Usually being on the ropes meant the "new" dimension was one made by the aggressor; the ropes snared the "caught" contestant, and could render him passive and dangerously vulnerable unless he fought his way out. But Ali, with "feminine" guile, uses the ropes to avoid or soften blows, and of course to fatigue the insult-goaded Foreman.

Ali, moreover, does not believe in "manly" silence; he is famous and infamous for ragging his foes. Mailer does not repeat much of what Ali said to Foreman *during* the fight for the good reason that he could not hear much of it, but we know from the "Bomaye" chapter of Ali's autobiography that he was continually insulting, belittling, mocking the usually silent Foreman (as of course he did Liston—"You big ugly bear. . . . You gonna fall in eight," (p. 126) before their fight so as to provoke a match, again indicating Ali's craft at setting up and hyping a prizefight), and, as mentioned earlier, mouthed off so much during the pre-fight instructions that the referee threatened to call off the fight after warning Ali five times not to talk. "'I'm going to hit you [Foreman] everywhere but under the bottom of your big funky feet, Chump!'", etc. (*The Greatest* p. 493).

Ali was a master psychologist as a professional athlete, probably no one better in any sport at outthinking his opponent, and he achieved part of his splendor and triumph through a masterful combination of "male" and "female" prowess that delighted those hungry for wit and iconoclasm in a violent sport far more than it did those who looked to boxing for bruises, blood, and pain.

Let us finish the fight. After Ali's strategic, punishing counter-punching and Foreman's spending himself during his fifth-round punch-out, *Foreman*, of all people, is now on the ropes. A final punch by Ali to Foreman's head leads to one of Mailer's better similes: "He [Foreman] went over like a six-foot sixty-year-old butler who has just heard tragic news" (p. 169).

Mailer, concluding, speaks very generously about the quality of Ali's boxing: "Back in America everybody was already yelling that the fight was fixed. Yes. So was *The Night Watch* and *The Portrait of the Artist as a Young Man*" (p. 171). Ali would still not get fully credited in his own country for a stunning victory, but one important American writer would call Ali's victory an achieved work of art comparable to two other great artworks.

VI

Now let us pull back to consider a few of the larger contexts behind the fight. Although Ali projected a flamboyant egotism to increase public interest in his fights, it is clear from both *The Fight* and *The Greatest* that being a Black Muslim embodied his deepest sense of his symbolic role as a prizefighter. Mailer quotes Ali as saying after the fight, " . . . I know that beating George Foreman and conquering the world with my fists does not bring freedom to my people. I am well aware that I must go beyond all of this and prepare myself for more" (p. 182).

And sometimes during the training before the Foreman fight, this sense of a role beyond the self, his self, Ali saw in terms of a mission: "People in America . . . don't know that I'm using boxing for the sake of getting over certain points you couldn't ever get over without it. . . . I'm not doing this [boxing] . . . for the glory of fighting, but to change a lot of things" (*The Fight* p. 64).

This leads to a realization by Mailer that becomes overwhelmingly clear both in *The Fight* and *The Greatest*: "being a Black Muslim might be the core of Ali's existence and the center of his strength" (p. 187). As the autobiography persuasively shows, Ali's religion provided the strength that allowed him to sever himself from all the forces in American society that dehumanized or exploited a Black, or that made his existence dependent or conditional (beyond of course the conditionality to which all flesh is heir). Black Muslimism restored pride and ideological purpose to some Blacks, but it also offered the possibility of a new life, a new chance at personal and cultural self-definition (ritualized by the new, Moslemic names). In Ali's case, it also generated enormous pressures against him from some of the most vicious elements in our society that were offended by Ali's religion, his refusal to be drafted for the Vietnam War, and the semi-autonomy his fame bestowed on him. In a sense, Ali's Muslimism caused him to lose his World Heavyweight title, but at the same time it also inspired him with the spiritual endurance to go for years without his title, virtually to confront America at its most oppressive and, without betraying his principles, officially regain his title after defeating Foreman.

Mailer in *The Fight* envisions a great future for Ali: "The original Ali was the adopted son of the Prophet Muhammad. Now a modern Muhammad Ali might become the leader of his people. It was well for Muhammad Ali that he believed in predestination and surrender to the will of God" (p. 191). If this final salute from the "Champ among writers" seems in retrospect somewhat grandiose, there is little doubt that Ali survived and excelled during his career both inside and outside the ring in a profession more encrusted with criminal influence than most. Moreover, Ali's involvement with Black Muslimism bestowed an ideological dimension on his life and thus on that of an American Black that symbolized one means for an American Black to live with dignity and autonomy, counterweighted,to be sure, by racist hatred and even violence (Ali was shot at by men with high powered rifles while training in his isolated camp in the Georgia woods a few weeks before the fight with Jerry Quarry in Atlanta in 1970—*The Greatest*, pp. 382-87).

Finally, one is reminded of Mailer's moving passage when Ali awaits Foreman in the ring, ready after going more than five years without his title, and "his talent, his desire for greatness, still intact," his body emitting light, a mystic of the ring! The boxer's boxer? Certainly he was Mailer's boxer, his portrait of the artist as a brilliant prizefighter and strategist, as an image during his prime of physical and moral integrity that is finally just integrity, and as a goad to Mailer to transcend his occasionally venomous envy and write a book of prose worthy of the champion it creatively rivals.

Works Cited

Ali, Muhammad. *The Greatest: My Own Story*. New York: Ballantine, 1976.
Bufithis, Philip H. *Norman Mailer*. New York: Ungar, 1978.
Cleaver, Eldridge. *Soul on Ice*. New York: Dell, 1968.
Early, Gerald. "Hot Spicks Versus Cool Spades: Three Notes Towards A Cultural Definition of Prizefighting." *The Hudson Review* 34:1 (Spring 1981).
Mailer, Norman. *Advertisements for Myself*. New York: NAL, 1960.
—. "Black Power," in *Existential Errands*. New York: NAL, 1973.
—. *The Fight*. New York: Bantam, 1976.
—. "King of the Hill," in *Existential Errands*.
—. "The White Negro." San Francisco: City Lights Books, 1957. Reprinted in *Advertisements for Myself*.

The Discrimination of Elegance: Anthony Powell's
A Dance to the Music of Time

Anthony Powell's *A Dance to the Music of Time*, twelve volumes long, is clearly a major work in size. But *Dance* can lay claim to major artistic status as well. Something of its mettle can be felt in observing Powell's use of point of view and satire, his treatment of class and ideology, his distinguished novelizing of art and the artist to structure his austere world, and in scrutinizing *Dance* as a genre of fiction.

The general scope of *Dance* is impressive. The novel covers roughly five decades (from the Twenties into the Sixties). Thus, it is concerned with modern people in a context of war and peace which suggests significant correspondences between the dislocations of society and the smaller ones of individuals. The more specific ambition of *Dance* is to dramatize and analyze the dissolution of responsibility in our time by the upper class, to chart the stresses in social and private sensibility resulting from that dissolution, and to depict the pursuit of power by emergent members of the lower classes.

More of the scope of *Dance* can be observed by regarding the work generically. Is *Dance* twelve volumes, or one novel—a series novel—or both? The change of the series title from *The Music of Time* to *A Dance to the Music of Time* between *Casanova's Chinese Restaurant* and *The Kindly Ones* provides one clue.[1] A dance clearly suggests the order of pattern; the large flux of modern experience depicted in *Dance* might be regarded as an esthetic spectacle analogous to the vision of grace and harmony embracing mortal and immortal worlds in Nicolas Poussin's "A Dance to the Music of Time." But the dissimilar media and subjects in the two "portraits" also imply a large degree of irony operative in Powell's work. The disorderliness, confusion, and self-seeking in the lives of Powell's modern people convey anything but the consummate stateliness of Poussin's allegorical idyll. Furthermore, a dance is primarily a spatial event; its temporal character is minimal, whereas the dimension in a chronicle fiction is relentlessly temporal. Dance time begins and ends on a plane of esthetic satisfaction, but life time occurs subject to contingency, circumstance, character, the shock of birth and the terror of death. These underlying distinctions between dance or art time and the life-time which Powell's characters and readers must endure restrict the potentially centrifugal energies in a fiction the scale of *Dance* through irony.

Thus a question of genre (or sub-genre) relates to the structural integrity of *Dance*. If *Dance* was begun and continued as more or less discrete novels, it is difficult to explain the many links of continuation which gird the work. Individuals, families, causes, ideas, motifs and symbols recur in such an elaborate network of associations and mutually supportive material that disproving is more difficult than proving the sequency of *Dance*. Kenneth Widmerpool looms as an enlarging shadow across the entire series, great families such as the Tollands ramify into scoreless relationships with other individuals, the concept of inexorable consequences to immoral conduct imaged at the end of *Casanova's Chinese Restaurant* in the Ghost Railway, the depiction of class-climbing opportunists: all these elements, further tightened and enriched by the meditative perceptiveness of the narrator, work to unify the twelve volumes of *Dance*. Powell's large work, further unified by its sub-generic character as a *bildungsroman*, a *kunstlerroman*, a family novel, a social and historical novel, and a novel of ideas, is best regarded as a series novel. Powell might have commenced the work with no very clear idea of what its larger shape might be, and by the end of volume five (*Casanova*), have come to see that the figure of a dance provided a cohesive organization for a novel with a large pavilion of characters and a "high-class" narrative style. On the other hand, one has a reference on page two of the first volume that suggests that a dance metaphor was lurking within the work from the beginning:

> The image of Time [in Poussin's painting "A Dance to the Music of Time"] brought thoughts of mortality: of human beings, facing outward like the Season, moving hand in hand in intricate measure; stepping slowly, methodically, sometimes a trifle awkwardly, in evolutions that take recognizable shape; or breaking into seemingly meaningless gyrations, while partners disappear only to

> reappear again, one more giving pattern to the spectacle: unable to control the melody, unable, perhaps to control the steps of the dance (*Question* p. 2).

If "Time" in Powell's title is taken to mean mortality, and "Music" society (to which one "dances"), then the dancer is the individual free to create and develop himself in a society limited only by the "rules" of mortality, society, and his own character. This inverted allegorical schema posits the third term ("dance," thus "dancer") by the need of the first two ("Music" and "Time") for a third so as to comprise an order of sense. If this interpretation is tenable, then *Dance* can also be regarded as a series novel, because, besides its variety of interwoven elements, it is based on a triad of terms definitive of its nature and thus indispensable to its being. One has no "music" of "time" without a "dance." The language of Powell's central, titular metaphor projects a vision of and for the entire work, and posits all the volumes of *Dance* as an integrated fiction.

Another integrating force in *Dance* is satire. Powell satirizes people in the arts, politics, big (and shady) business, the upper class, educational institutions, Bohemia, the middle class, and the military, so that something of a cross-section of twentieth-century English society is rendered. The rendering is distinguished, further, by Powell's treating his satirized subjects as if they were real people. Widmerpool is the most heavily satirized character in the entire novel, yet his aggrandizement of power in the military, business, and politics indicates his secure footing in reality. Much has been made by critics, and rightly, of Powell's sure sense of class insignia. Yet it is possible that his capacity for blending satire with three-dimensional characterization accomplishes more for fiction than his class touch in view of the formal difficulty of introducing satire into a novel of character. What is more, Powell's people, satirized to varying degrees, are judged by ethical norms which are judged themselves.

This intricate satiric enterprise is established primarily through the adroit use of a protagonist-witness narrator named Nicholas Jenkins who, resembling Powell, is still sufficiently his own man to undergo Powell's irony. In Jenkins' case, the irony is one that all humans experience but that not all understand: the potentially instructive if harrowing discrepancies between past and present, youth and age, love and sex, all the grand polarities that a writer with speculative energy will attempt to set spinning. The new realization of attitude and self which can emerge from confronting such "classical" disparities becomes part of the "dance."

One change manipulated to invest *Dance* with form concerns Jenkins' attitudes towards the new man of power, Kenneth Widmerpool. An obnoxious "power-climber" and careerist, Widmerpool displays a character that not only reflects the instability and human inadequacy of the traditional English class structure, but also suggests insufficiencies of humanity in our normative narrator himself. Jenkins' insufficiencies do not reduce him to one of Wayne Booth's unreliable narrators. Rather they make him more human, and thus more persuasive a figure for a reader to identify with. Regarded by all his public school acquaintances, including Jenkins himself, as a boor, Widmerpool steadily makes his way in the world. Our first image of Widmerpool shows him early in *A Question of Upbringing* (volume one) jogging solitarily around the grounds of Eton in a fog. His immersion in moisture initiates the motif of Widmerpool as a subaqueous creature, and his ascent from lower to upper class surroundings is satirically analogized to the rise to land of lowly sea creatures. Thus animal caricature is one of Powell's modes of class satire. Widmerpool is continually described as possessing gills, puffing up like a fish, in short, as a monster from a medium alien to the world of Eton, Oxford, and Mayfair.

Nevertheless before the end of *A Question of Upbringing*, Widmerpool has already adopted a patronizing attitude towards Jenkins, and, by *A Buyer's Market*, is appearing at fashionable Mayfair parties. And though Widmerpool is repeatedly degraded during his relentless rise to power by such upper-class women as the debutante brat Barbara Goring and the fast, "rackety" Mildred Blaides, he is respected by important and representative middle-class characters like Peter Templer, the future diplomat Tompsitt, and Bill Truscott for his promising future in the business empire of Magnus Donners.

A scene typical of Powell's ability to merge comedy into a multi-pronged satiric weapon occurs in *A Buyer's Market* when Barbara Goring pours a castor of sugar over the persistently courting Widmerpool at a fancy Mayfair party:

> She turned to the sideboard that stood by our table, upon which plates, dishes, decanter, and bottles had been placed out of the way before removal. Among this residue stood an enormous sugar castor tipped with a heavy silver nozzle. Barbara must suddenly have conceived the idea of sprinkling a few grains of this sugar over Widmerpool, as if in literal application of her the-

ory that he 'needed sweetening,' because she picked up this receptacle and shook it over him (*Buyer's* pp. 51-52).

The description continues, exemplifying Powell's comic gift of descriptive retardation. Indeed the symmetrical low-comic parallel to the philosophic theme winding like a river through *Dance* that "all human beings . . . are at close range equally extraordinary" (*The Acceptance World* p. 85), is that most, if not all, human beings (not only Widmerpool) are ludicrous viewed in "slow motion." Nick will discover in *The Kindly Ones* that his mistress Jean Templer, two-timing her own husband Bob Duport, is simultaneously betraying Jenkins with the slobbish Brent, a man Jenkins despises. The Cham of industry, Magnus Donners, will in his senility move like a puppet. The sinister charlatan Dr. Trelawney, who exploits people with his abracadabra expertise, will in a fit of asthma be too weak to open a toilet-room door from the inside. The "kindly ones" have a way of catching up with their guilty victims in *Dance*.

The sugar-pouring episode, however, reveals much about the present. Although Widmerpool is stultified by his "libation" (partly because of a slavish reaction similar to the one he evinces earlier in *Question* when the Captain of the cricket team at Eton accidentally hits him in the face with a banana), the "sweetening" also indicates a deterioration in the conduct of upper-class girls. Furthermore, it indirectly stigmatizes Jenkins who has not declared his secret ardor for the Goring girl, and discovers, to his mortification, that Widmerpool shares his tastes in women. This continuous discovery of identification with his "dark brother" receives confirmation from Nick's unconscious when he tells Widmerpool in jest that he uses the latter's name "on clandestine weekends" (*Molly's* p. 52). Widmerpool will be rejected in *Casanova's Chinese Restaurant* by the castratory Mildred Blaides, sister of the wife of General Conyers. Again, the rejection is for a debasing reason: in a premarital trial-run at the exclusive estate Dogdene, Widmerpool manifests sexual impotence. But his arrival at the threshold of marriage into the upper class is meant to be ominous; not even the envious Jenkins has penetrated Dogdene. Nevertheless a motif of Widmerpool's humiliation by women is interwoven throughout *Dance*, and might well culminate in his relationship with his wife Pam Flitton, who stands to inherit Stringham's substantial fortune (as Widmerpool is well aware).

Widmerpool's fanatical devotion to accumulating power and prestige contrasts with two other principal characters, Stringham and the narrator Jenkins himself. Stringham symbolizes a class descent in his personal deterioration which highlights and in part explains Widmerpool's rise. If Widmerpool's track work on a drizzly day supplies an archetypal instance of his dogged persistence, Stringham's illicit smoking and suave handling of Uncle Giles' smoking in the school dorm typifies him (as, for that matter, does Peter Templer's encounter with a London prostitute about this time prefigure his ruin through women). This class ascent-descent pattern crosses near the end of *A Buyer's Market* after a disastrous Old Boys' dinner reunion in which a long, unexpected, and pretentious speech by Widmerpool on the state of finance and business in England induces a heart attack in their former teacher, La Bas, and violently changes Widmerpool's status in the class-stratified public school valuation from a figure of contempt to a coming man. The dinner is followed by a symbolic wrestling match between Widmerpool and Stringham to get a very drunk Stringham to bed. Stringham resists Widmerpool's help, and Widmerpool overpowers him in a symbolic act of class "revolution." "The two of them wrestling together were pouring with sweat, especially Widmerpool, who was the stronger. He must have been quite powerful, for Stringham was fighting like a maniac" (*Acceptance* p. 208). The broader significance of this tussle is not lost on Jenkins: "I was thinking of how strange a thing it was that I myself should have been engaged in a physical conflict designed to restrict Stringhams' movements; a conflict in which the moving spirit had been Widmerpool. That suggested a whole social upheaval: a positively cosmic change in life's system. Widmerpool, once so derided by all of us, had become in some mysterious manner, a person of authority" (*Acceptance* p. 209).

Besides representing a "class struggle," this incident exhibits our normative narrator forced into a social ambivalence descriptive of his role throughout the series. It is erroneous to interpret Jenkins solely as a defender of the upper order. His position as a novelist lends him a certain integrity and an independence of class alignment, and his moral realism compels him to chronicle and evaluate what is occurring, even if it includes upper-class moral deterioration and the success of "commoners."

From the wrestling-match incident on, Stringham will continue to plunge until *The Soldier's Art*, whereas Widmerpool is still climbing in *Books Do Furnish a Room*, now indicating political ambitions towards a Communist country in Southeastern Europe. Widmerpool's energy and ruthlessness, and, to some extent,

Powell's attitude towards political liberalism, are intimated in Widmerpool's becoming a labour M. P. by volume ten.

Widmerpool's ascent also contrasts with the less scintillant progress of the novelist-narrator, thus effecting a confrontation between, as Arthur Mizener has put it, the man of will and the man of imagination. This cold war between artist and philistine is no less basic to the structure of *Dance* than the conflict between Stringham's upper-class style and tradition and Widmerpool's egomaniacal opportunism. Not surprisingly, Widmerpool has a disapproving word about artists. In *A Question*, he weighs the merits of a literary career for one of its aspirants, Jenkins (who in a sense is the future author of *Dance*). "'To write?,' said Widmerpool. 'But that is hardly a profession. Unless you mean you want to be a journalist'" (p. 103). Even reading for non-opportunistic reasons elicits Widmerpool's censure: "'It doesn't do to read too much,' Widmerpool said. 'You get to look at life with a false perspective. By all means have some familiarity with the standard authors. . . . But it is no good clogging your mind with a lot of trash from modern novels'" (p. 104).

Yet Widmerpool's austere code for self-advancement will not prevent him from backing a left-wing literary magazine and book publishing house in *Books* when it offers channels for disseminating his political and economic views. Art for this evil Aeneas with piles possesses the one virtue of being manipulable for ideological and careerist ends. Jenkins himself is repeatedly cut down to size by the contrastive ability of a member of the lower orders like Widmerpool to scale both the class pyramid and the higher classless pyramid of modern power. Some punishment for snobbery is also dramatized here in Nick's subordination to his gross opposite (by *The Valley of Bones*, he is literally Widmerpool's subordinate, being a second lieutenant under Captain Widmerpool). Indeed, this snobbery extends to Powell himself in view of certain extremities of treatment accorded to Widmerpool and others, such as the class implications of sexual rejection by upper-class women, and Jenkins'-Powell's unrelenting use of animal and piscine imagery and of an excremental derivation to describe Widmerpool.

Nevertheless, our sympathy is with Jenkins, when, at the conclusion of *The Valley of Bones*, he hears Widmerpool tell him to "get cracking," and speculates with a disagreeable, sinking feeling within that "I was now within Widmerpool's power" (p. 192). Jenkins is fortunate to escape with nothing worse than a callous abandonment to the Infantry Training Center by the destroyer of

Templer and Stringham, when Widmerpool later has to release him: "You seem aggrieved. Let me point out there is nothing startlingly brilliant in your work—your industry and your capabilities—to make me press for a good appointment for you" (*Soldier's* pp. 192-93).

The issue of snobbery raises problems in *Dance*, for the line is a fine one that separates a valid defense of the old order in the face of ruthless enterprisers and the debâcle of modern society, from cruel dehumanization of human beings whose chief offense is to be born into a class society. Powell partly maintains artistic control by chastising Jenkins' snobbery towards Widmerpool in various ways (although Jenkins' disapproval of Widmerpool is milder than that of many other people in *Dance*) and by satirizing the upper class in the misconduct of slumming aristocrats. One thinks of Baby Wentworth and Anne Stepney, the lesbian cohabitation of Eleanor Walpole-Wilson and Norah Tolland, the ideological bumming and class irresponsibility of Erridge (Lord Warminster), and the deft vignettes of individuals like the ex-diplomat failure Walpole-Wilson, the ne'er-do-well horseman Dicky Umfraville, and the alcoholic "Alexander-Hamlet" Stringham. Although these aristocrats are satirized, they frequently emerge with some portion of dignity, revealing a capacity for redemption and self-regeneration (as do Stringham, Eleanor Walpole-Wilson, and even the rakish Umfraville). But the Widmerpudlian climbers in the broad world of business, industry, and the military, and the smaller sphere of the arts, such as the has-been novelist St. John Clarke, or the opportunist *litterateurs* Members and Quiggin, are shown little mercy, partly, it would seem, because they are ambitious within a class context: they intrude on the regnant order.

Yet no one gets off easily in *Dance*; an individual's actions catch up with him, his past germinates what he becomes. This would account for the fate of sensualists like Templer and of powerful men like Donners. And Stringham, through victimization by selfish parents, glides from an upper-class derivation to an abject alcoholism (guarded during this interval by another sinister careerist, Tuffy Weedon), rising next with the noble steadfastness of his archetypal counterpart "Childe Harold" to an almost saintly "dry" martyrdom in the army (again under *Captain* Widmerpool as *Private* Stringham, and finally to his death in the Japanese camp).

The industrial magnate Magnus Donners ("Great Giver") is an arresting case of a powerful and ominous man gradually succumbing to inner corruption. Jenkins describes his demeanor in *The*

Military Philosophers as "an animated tailor's dummy," and as "less than a human being." "Jerky movements like those of a marionette—perhaps indicating all was not absolutely well with his physical system—added to the impression of an outsize puppet that had somehow escaped from its box and begun to mix with real people, who were momentarily taken in by the extraordinary conviction of its mechanism" (pp. 206-207). By *Books*, Donners is dead, presumably from the stress of a "lifetime of weighty negotiations in the world of politics and business," but perhaps from secretive erotic vices as well. His reputation as a sadist and voyeur, if not fully substantiated, is notorious. The distinction of Donners as a characterization arises from Powell's combining a perverted sexuality with a vaguely totalitarian public image.

Sex and power, a recurrent dark harmony in *Dance*, are pitched at a key in the treatment of Donners that bears affinities with the mode of the political gothic of *Melmoth the Wanderer* and *1984*. The hallucinatory monastic dungeons in Maturin's novel and Orwell's all-seeing sadistic O'Brien are relatable to Powell's voyeur who sits on high government councils and can make or ruin small nations economically. Although we already know of his might from the Cambridge don Sillery in *Question*, the first description of Donners occurs appropriately enough at a party of the Greek-cockney fortune-hunter Milly Andriadis, whose social circle forms the demimonde into which upper class slummers, bohemians, adventurers, gays, artists true and false, and courtesans all merge: "Clean-shaven, good-looking rather than the reverse, possibly there was something odd, even a trifle disturbing, about the set of his mouth. Something that perhaps conveyed intense ferment kept in severe repression" (*Buyer's* p. 96).

When several years later (in *The Kindly Ones*) Jenkins revisits Stourwater, "a piece of monumental vulgarity, a house where something had gone very seriously wrong," Donners is even more disturbing. "Just as the last of our party crossed the threshold, one of the bookcases on the far side of the room swung forward, revealing itself as an additional door covered with the spines of dummy volumes, through which Sir Magnus Donners himself appeared to greet the guests at exactly the same moment. I wondered whether he has been watching at a peephole." He is soon after to "watch" Templer's second wife Betty disintegrate during her husband's "performance" of Lust in the Seven Vices sequence, characteristically "fiddling with the camera, smiling quietly to himself" because of, Powell tells us, Betty's crisis. Donners' fake-Arthurian castle also contains dungeons and implements of torture, which Donners enjoys showing to guests and frightening women guests with. That Donners has the air and build of an "athletic bishop or clerical Headmaster" and is possessed of "a vast capacity for imposing boredom, a sense of immensely powerful stuffiness . . . sapping every drip of vitality from weaker spirits," facilitates his transcendence of satire. So it is meant to be, for Donners is one of the dark powers in *Dance*.

The series title of Powell's novel contains a dimension of evaluation which is, as stated earlier, antipodal to such monarchs of power as Donners: the artist himself. Not only some of the worst people in *Dance* are connected with the arts, but some of the best as well. Jenkins himself is a novelist. Hugh Moreland, a serious composer and surrogate author figure, exemplifies (as does Powell himself) the dedicated, persevering artist who avoids the snares of easy artistic success. His middle-class origins and close camaraderie with Jenkins diminish some of the snobbery that flaws *Dance*. Thus, Moreland represents a model of sensibility totally at odds with the varieties of iniquitous power-seeking that animate the Quiggins, Widmerpools, and Donners.

Tortured by his troubled relations with the lovely and unstable Priscilla Tolland and the actress Matilda Wilson, Moreland realizes that he must reject the dangerous entanglements of the merging spheres of big business, the upper class, and the demimonde to survive as a creative person. The death of Maclintick, a music critic and close friend, has added more strain to Moreland's life than he can accommodate, and makes him strive to order his emotions so that he can pursue an artistic career seriously. Consequently, Moreland intimates to Nick that he is breaking off his unconsummated affair with Lady Priscilla: "The Maclintick affair has reminded me of the disagreeable possibilities of the world one inhabits; the fact that the fewer persons one involves in it the better" (*Casanova's* p. 166). This moral choice is rendered in the form of the Ghost Railway metaphor which concludes *Casanova's* with one of Powell's polished syntactical involutions animating a sense of moral terror verging on the preternatural:

> Once, at least, we [Jenkins and Moreland] had been on a Ghost Railway together at some fun fair or on a seaside pier; slowly climbing sheer gradients, sweeping with frenzied speed into inky depths, turning blind corners from which black, gibbering bogeys leapt to attack, rushing headlong towards iron-studded doors, threat-

ened by imminent collision, fingered by spectral hands, moving at last with dreadful, ever increasing momentum towards a shape that lay across the line (p. 229).

After a "career" of gross self-indulgence and self-advancement, one hurtles across a body at the end (or before the end) of the track, as do Buster Foxe and Mrs. Foxe (Stringham's mother), and Peter Templer and St. John Clark and Gypsy Jones and Widmerpool and Pam Flitton, and as would Quiggin, Deacon, Members, and others, had they the chance. Moreland elects to forego that trip.

Moreland's capacity for such renunciation reveals him as an ascetic, as it does the later Stringham, and lends force to austere philosophical observations declaimed by him from time to time and supported by "Jenkins-Powell." "That is one of the conceptions most difficult for stupid people to grasp. They always suppose some ponderable alteration will make the human condition more bearable. The only hope of survival is the realisation that no such thing could possibly happen" (*Soldier's* p. 122). Juxtapose that comment (several others can be found) with Jenkins' earlier statement in *Dance* on the deceptively centrifugal direction of the lives of the characters in this novel, and Powell's strategy of using artists to establish the commanding moral perspectives in the work become apparent:

> For reasons not always at the time explicable, there are specific occasions when events begin suddenly to take on a significance previously unsuspected so that, before we really know where we are, life seems to have begun in earnest at last, and we ourselves, scarcely aware that any change has taken place, are careering uncontrollably down the slippery avenues of eternity (*Buyer's* p. 274).

Another significant figure from the arts is the novelist and man of letters X. Trapnel. Although lacking Moreland's stature as a character in *Dance*, Trapnel dominates *Books*. Trapnel, among other things, is implemented by Powell to dramatize the intertwining of power, sex, and art in the Trapnel-Pam Flitton-Widmerpool triangle. He has written a good novel entitled *Camel Ride to the Tomb*, a metaphor for a pessimistic definition of life implicitly shared by Jenkins-Powell. An outlandish dresser who sports a walking stick with a death's-head, Trapnel is Powell's modern artist as romantic eccentric, continually on the move (around, with satiric diminution, London), cadging money to hire taxi cabs. As such, he is contrasted with Moreland, the artist as the "ordinary Englishman," whose normality conveys Powell's conviction that the artist is or can be, as Wordsworth said, a "man speaking to men: a man, it is true, endowed with more lively sensibility, more enthusiasm and tenderness, who has a greater knowledge of human nature...."

At any rate Trapnel certainly has a "more lively sensibility" than most men (including Moreland). He falls in love with the striking, stonily dissatisfied Pam Flitton, and they elope to one of the scruffier sections of London. Widmerpool is the center of several climactic scenes in *Dance*, such as his sinister dispelling of the Seven Vices "tableaux" in *The Kindly Ones* when, dressed in military uniform, he announces the commencement of World War Two to Magnus Donners' decadent guests. Widmerpool upstages his fellow egotists again in arriving at Trapnel's lair armed with briefcase and hat (which he places on top of Trapnel's manuscript of his unfinished novel), to announce his attitude toward Trapnel's parody of his writing and stealing his wife. It is a key event in *Dance* because the increasingly powerful Widmerpool easily dominates the situation, treating the ailing Trapnel's antics with contempt and (accurately) predicting the return of his wife. Widmerpool shows great poise before the potentially dangerous Trapnel, who has been taking "pills" and now menacingly parades his death's-head sword stick.

> 'Get out.'
> Trapnel did not actually threaten Widmerpool with the sword. He held the point to the ground, as if about to raise the weapon in formal salute before joining combat in a duel. It was hard to estimate where exactly his actions hovered between play-acting and loss of control. Widmerpool stood firm.
> 'No dramatics, please.'
> This calmness was to his credit. He knew little of Trapnel, but what he knew certainly gave no guarantee that a man of Trapnel's sort would not be capable of eccentric violence (*Books* pp. 202-203)

Again one is struck by the fastidious artistry in Powell's developing a grotesque youth who was the comic butt at school into a menacing man of affairs as voracious as Volpone, as ruthless as Tartuffe. One feels that decency, generosity, modesty, art, and the social order itself are menaced by the triumphal imposition of Widmerpool on his environment so near the end of the series. This is the man who, like many others, could accommodate Hitler during the thirties, who thinks that German anti-semitism would be dropped "when matters get straightened out a bit. After all, it is sometimes forgotten that the Nationalist Socialists are not only 'national,' they are also 'socialist'.... They believe in planning" (*Molly's* pp. 54-55). But Widmerpool can extend himself in any direction politically and by *Books* and the post World War Two years, he is referring to "Marshal" Stalin as a "great man." Nor does the Katyn massacre, in which some ten to 15,000 Polish officers taken prisoner by the Soviet Army in 1939 were executed, ruffle his broadmindedness. Paying lip service to the effect that Russians "behaved in such a very regrettable manner," Widmerpool lets them off with language that should bring Orwell back to life: "How can we approach our second most powerful ally about something which ... is almost certainly ... the consequence of administrative inadequacy, rather than willful indifference to human life and the dictates of compassion" (*Military* p. 107). This might sound like the generosity of a man who would put old school acquaintances to death for expedience, and so it is. Still, if in the continuing battle between the men of power and the men of sensibility in *Dance*, Widmerpool seems to overcome Trapnel, he will fail to overcome Jenkins, one tough veteran.

The third member of the Trapnel-Widmerpool triad, the vindictive nymphomaniac Pam Flitton Widmerpool, is clearly one of Powell's Furies (she helps to ruin Trapnel's life by walking out on him and destroying his novel manuscript with brutal contempt). An important revelation (if true) about Pam's origins is disclosed in *Books* which bolsters the structural integrity of *Dance*. Dicky Umfraville hints to Jenkins that as Flavia Stringham's lover he is Pam's biological father. Thus an ethical principle suddenly seems to fall into place in the shape of the cause-effect essence of immoral conduct. Pam, as an illegitimate child of an important and delinquent member of the upper-class hierarchy in *Dance*, will plague all but especially bad and irresponsible men. In this role she resembles the "kindly one" Widmerpool who announces the war to the irresponsible upper and upper-middle classes. Pam tells the swaggering Odo Stevens that he is a washout in bed; she, as well as Widmerpool, drive Templar to his death in an attempt to be worthy of her, and she is a continual goad in Widmerpool's fat side.

Fortunately for the integrity of *Dance*, it is not Pam that "resolves" Widmerpool, but the youthful, sinister Murtlock, thus gainfully deflecting the marked tendency of Powell's novel from being satiric *class* warfare (*Dance* upper class once again scoring off class climbers).

Other characters Powell is content to lash. He and his fictional half-self, Jenkins, sustain a running battle with left wing ideology and ideologists, and it is not surprising to find such people as Quiggin, St. John Clarke, the homosexual ex-painter Deacon, and even Widmerpool (not to mention the art tarts, Gypsy Jones, and her upper-class double, Anne Stepney), associated with radical values and causes, which in turn associates radicalism with opportunism. Radical ideology, in its discontent with the social hierarchy and its apocalyptic promises and pretentions, serves as one of the principal objects of Powell's satire. It represents to Powell a rationalization for rejecting life as, for better or worse, it is. Powell extends this satire of ideology vertically, ridiculing upper as well as middle class characters. "Comrade Erry," Lord Warminster, the oldest son in the large Tolland family, is the type of telescopic philanthropist like Mrs. Jellyby in *Bleak House* who bleeds for the distant downtrodden, but shows little interest in the plight of one's immediate family. A *muzhik* aristocrat, he opts for a classless society in which he will still be boss, as his middle-class radical double Quiggin snidely implies in *At Lady Molly's* when pointing out to Nick that Erridge will allow Quiggin and Quiggin's mistress Mona to live on his estate " . . . until the whole thing is turned into a collective farm with himself at the head of it." Significantly, the upper-class Erridge had died by *Books*, whereas the lower-class power seekers remain alive and formidable.

Quiggin himself, a self-styled Northman of Plain tongue, wields his bad manners to insinuate himself into the good graces of powerful upper-class people by the novelty of his effrontery and incessant moroseness. Competing with his equally self-promoting public school chum and rival Mark Members for employment as Clarke's personal secretary, he soon goes on to bigger game, trying to exploit Erridge's dubious social consciousness. Quiggin, however, loses his mistress, the tooth-paste model Mona, Templer's ex-wife, to Erridge who is not above exercising "droits du seigneur" on his comrade-vassals.

Powell's conservatism has its disturbing aspects. Though ideology deserves satirizing in an age as given as ours to total "solutions," we suspect advice to accept a reality in which the advisors are so comfortably situated (Jenkins and Powell come from old county families, and though not affluent, they are of the upper class, with all the possibilities of access, prestige, and general security rendered by that status). Animalization is a standard device in satire, but when the animals are all middle and lower class people, while upper-class figures like General Conyers are compared to Michelangelo's Jehovah and to the Homeric gods, we realize that the game is class warfare, not only social satire. Yet a Widmerpool, by the very magnificence of his conception, substantially transcends charges against Powell's satiric characterizations. Severely abused by Powell, he is one of the significant comic figures in modern fiction, surely recognizable in his Stakhanovist ethic as a pernicious type found wherever power beckons. He also embodies Powell's gift for integrating the comic and the ridiculous with the sinister, as in the tableau sequence in *The Kindly Ones* where Widmerpool announces the war in a military uniform that makes him look like a hermaphrodite.

Any attempt to interpret *Dance* as a comic work cannot ignore the increasingly sinister character of the novel in the final or "Winter" triad. There is the ubiquitous sexual allure and destructiveness of Pam Flitton, which are related to the death or degradation of a number of major male characters (such as Kenneth Widmerpool, Peter Templer, Odo Stevens, and X. Trapnel), Widmerpool's increasing immorality (including his primary role in the deaths of both Templer and Charles Stringham) and public power, and the appearance in volume twelve of Scorpio Murtlock, who not only destroys Widmerpool but can perhaps be seen as the heir in *Dance* to Widmerpool's power quest in the contemporary form of totalitarian occultism (one knowledgeable character, near the end of the final volume of the series, claims that Murtlock "might go anywhere") (p. 262). *Dance*, furthermore, does not end in the communal restoration of traditional comedy. On the contrary, the last line of the twelfth volume, *Hearing Secret Harmonies*, almost appears to annul the authority of Powell's commanding and complex art-and-life metaphor, and suspend the work between life and death. Indeed, that final sentence, "Even the formal measures of the Seasons seemed suspended in the wintry silence," also suspends *Dance* between volume twelve and volume one. The reader is confronted with an implicit circular action which suggests that in Powell's realist comedy the lessons of life, of how to live, must be re-experienced if not learned the first time through. The "lessons" of course might not necessarily be the same, but they could be even harder or more dangerous the next time, and failing them could imperil ourselves, society, and life itself, given the degree of power accessible today and the kinds of people who want it.

The series title articulates the fundamental artistic context of *Dance*. It presents a philosophic stance as well as a metaphor for projecting one means by which humanity can come to grips with the mysteries of human nature and society. The use of terms of art to encase his novelistic world implies an order by which to measure the shortcomings of his characters, and offers a contrast to the anomie of modern life. Powell is not intimating that life should or could possess the perfection of a work of art, nor that all people should be artists. Rather, the life of the serious artist and the microcosm of order that his creations represent symbolize a civilized existence possible for people who try to live with imagination and control. Thus the acceptance of life is projected in *Dance* as spheres of insufficiently congruous sociality and solitude, as aging, but also as a dry grace inaccessible to Widmerpool's totalitarian rationality. If this acceptance does not culminate in the conception behind Poussin's painting wherein human limitation is affirmed by allegorical figures of time and deity in a radiant dance scene, it is as much as a sophisticated novelist can affirm in our harrowed age.

Note

[1] Anthony Powell, *A Dance to the Music of Time*. London: Heinemann, 1951-1975.

Spring	v. 1 - *A Question of Upbringing* v. 2 - *A Buyer's Market* v. 3 - *The Acceptance World*
Summer	v. 4 - *At Lady Molly's* v. 5 - *Casanova's Chinese Restaurant* v. 6 - *The Kindly Ones*
Autumn	v. 7 - *The Valley of Bones* v. 8 - *The Soldier's Art* v. 9 - *The Military Philosophers*
Winter	v. 10 - *Books Do Furnish a Room* v. 11 - *Temporary Kings* v. 12 - *Hearing Secret Harmonies*

A paperback edition of *Dance* is also available in a four-volume paper-bound set (New York: Popular Library, 1976). The series is also available as separate novels for each volume.

IV

TWO SAN FRANCISCO POETS

"The Holiness of the Real":
The Short Poems of Kenneth Rexroth

> "The holiness of the real
> Is always there, accessible
> In total immanence."
>
> Kenneth Rexroth,
> "Time Is the Mercy of Eternity"

I

Kenneth Rexroth, who was born in 1905 and died in 1982, was a major American poet. He wrote poetry for over sixty years, and though he had some recognition during his lifetime, it was far less than his work (particularly his verse) deserved. A bohemian, an astute social critic and radical, a mountain climber (he wrote an unpublished book about how to climb mountains), an acute transvaluational thinker and wit, a "confabulator," a translator of poetry from a half dozen languages, Rexroth failed to gain the recognition during his lifetime that he deserved as a poet in part because American literary politics and literary critical orientations did not work in his favor during a sizable part of his career. Ironically, much of his best verse was written from the 1930s to the mid-1950s, a period when academic, literary, and political tastes prevailed that were alien to many of the social, philosophical, and artistic values for which Rexroth's art and life stood.

Rexroth's view of poetry as communication, as heightened speech between persons, was violently at odds with the New Criticism and its idea of a poem as a self-referential text to be demystified by exhaustive analysis and interpretation. His attachment to a world-wide avant-garde and to the political left wing alienated him from such influential, politically and esthetically conservative critic-poets as John Crowe Ransom and Allen Tate and their journal *Kenyon Review*, not to mention the politically radical, but anti-West-Coast New York intelligentsia represented in the 1940s and 1950s (and afterwards) by *Partisan Review*. Rexroth's libertarian, Anarchist, Asian-culture interests were not only anathema to the Philip-Rahv, Mary-McCarthy, Delmore-Schwartz circle, but to American English Departments in general; the impression at even a "Pacific-Rim" university like the University of California at Berkeley was that Rexroth was a kind of literary charlatan, a literary poser who along with Henry Miller, Kenneth Patchen and other such literary loonies could be ridiculed or ignored. This arrogant and erroneous attitude overlooked the fact that Rexroth had been part of a vigorous artistic vanguard centered in San Francisco since the 1930s which had intercultural relations with the political left wing (mainly Anarchist) as well as with the Beat Renaissance of the mid-1950s which he publicized and championed. Further, as Clayton Eshleman has pointed out, Rexroth "was either the source of or a participant in every poetic movement of any worth here [in California] throughout the '40s, '50s, and '60s" (*The Los Angeles Times Book Review* p. 1).

In addition, Rexroth's philosophical anarchism put him at odds with American Communists from the 1930s through the 1950s. Rexroth's bitter contempt for and attacks against the "Stalinists" everywhere was even keener than his enmity towards the New Critics (who he was fond of calling "Corn belt Metaphysicians"). Also, being (falsely) associated with the sexual theories of Wilhelm Reich and with the mystique of Asian religion and philosophy further damaged Rexroth's reputation, as of course did his living in San Francisco rather than in the art, publishing and publicity capital of the country, New York City.

In particular, Rexroth's brief 1950s affiliation with the Beat writers—Ginsberg, Corso, Kerouac—though typical of his generous support of young artists, stigmatized him as merely a "Daddy of the Beats" (as East-Coast critic Alfred Kazin impudently dubbed Rexroth). This association merely confirmed the image of Rexroth in some influential quarters of American literary opinion-making as a West-Coast literary buccaneer. It was only in the last fifteen years or so of his life that Rexroth's translations of Asian verse gained him some recognition (although he had some broad if fleeting publicity during the mid-1950s from reading poetry to jazz accompaniment in San Francisco nightclubs, even getting included in *Life Magazine* on one occasion). Even as recently as the early 1990s, one could walk into good bookstores in America and find only books of his verse translations (and, occasionally, of his lively, perspicacious essays, like *Bird in the Bush* and *Classics Revisited*), and nothing of his own verse.

This is a great shame, for, as I hope to show, Rexroth is an important poet. He wrote a large number of first-rate poems, long and short. Yet, as Lee Bartlett has urged, "Rexroth is arguably the most undervalued American poet and essayist of this century" (*American Poetry* p. 95). *The Phoenix and the Tortoise*, a mid-period book of verse (1940), was once described by Thomas Parkinson as commensurate in worth to Eliot's *The Four Quartets* (*Ohio Review* p. 66). Rexroth wrote a number of significant long poems, such as Part I of *The Phoenix and the Tortoise*, the book-length *The Dragon and the Unicorn*, and the two relatively long works written in Japan in the 1960s and 1970s, respectively, entitled *The Heart's Garden, The Garden's Heart* and *The Love Poems of Marichiko*. However, he also wrote a good number of short poems that in themselves should accord him high stature as a poet.

Thus, I want to look at some short poems by Rexroth written over roughly two-thirds of his life, from the 1920s to the 1970s. The only long poem I will discuss is *Marichiko*, a remarkable work. Two primary subject categories in Rexroth's verse of love and nature include many of Rexroth's best poems such as "When We With Sappho," "Lyell's Hypothesis Again," "The Signature of All Things," the three Andrée-Rexroth elegies, "Time Is the Mercy of Eternity," "Yugao," "Falling Leaves and Early Snow," "For a Masseuse and Prostitute," "Towards An Organic Philosophy," "Another Spring," the broadly political poem "August 22, 1939," and the seven "Marthe" poems. Most of these poems deserve to be as well known as "Sunday Morning" or "The Love Song of J. Alfred Prufrock" or "Snake" or "September 1, 1939" or "Crazy Jane Talks With The Bishop" or "By the Road to the Contagious Hospital" or "Skunk Hour" or "Howl."

One of the best passages in one of Rexroth's best poems, "Time Is the Mercy of Eternity," runs as follows:

> The holiness of the real
> Is always there, accessible
> In total immanence. The nodes
> Of transcendence coagulate
> In you, the experiencer,
> And in the other, the lover (*CSP* p. 248).

The first three lines especially strike me as providing a golden thread through significant, representative Rexroth poems. It suggests first a spiritual dimension present in much of Rexroth's better work, but, importantly, projected in terms of the everyday and the "everywhere." The last three + lines above amplify the first idea and make it more specific—if the holiness of the real can include more than love, it reaches an apex in love, and, by implication of the figure latent in the passage, suggests a gamut between which all experience and phenomena stream in Rexroth's superior poems. I will suggest this transcendent character in selected poems, for one of Rexroth's most distinctive qualities in his verse is the hint of the supernatural in the natural. Often, however, it is a supernatural that is immanent or indwelling rather than celestial or religious in the customary sense, and can be as ordinary as an oak tree or a cow, but *fully* seen and experienced as if for the first time.

II

Rexroth is a memorable poet of reminiscence (let alone reverie), recalling his mother Delia (in "Delia Rexroth"), his first wife Andrée Dutcher ("Your ashes / Were scattered in this place. Here / I wrote you a farewell poem"), his entranced childhood in "Un Bel di Vedremo" (" . . . that other / World before the War," a world of Debs and Huneker, of lace evening gowns and Japanese prints), the grisly scene of the Chicago stockyards in 1917 on his first visit to Chicago (narrated movingly in the 1950s poem "The Bad Old Days"). He likes to reminisce because he feels, usually convincingly, that he is recalling objects, people, values, events worth re-evoking, but he also draws attention through reminiscence to the transience of life and thus to the need to crystallize value amidst the flux of existence. Also memorable is Rexroth's capacity to project a passion so consuming even in reminiscence that it almost obliterates past and present, suggesting in matters of love the hopelessly arbitrary character of such time divisions.

A painful poem of reminiscence appears in the 1940 volume of verse entitled *In What Hour?*. A book with a large number of political poems (and some Cubist ones as well), this volume contains the brief, moving "Northhampton, 1922 - San Francisco, 1939":

> All night rain falls through fog.
> I lie awake, restless on a twisted pillow.
> Fog horns cry over the desolate water.

> How long ago was it,
> That night with the pear blossoms
> Quivering in the pulsating moonlight?
> I am startled from sleep
> By the acrid fleshy odor of pear blossoms.
>
> Somewhere in the world, I suppose,
> You are still living, a middle-aged matron,
> With children on the verge of youth (*CSP* p. 129).

A reminiscence need not include a present (though it of course implies one), but it certainly does a past; Rexroth often uses the two time frames effectively to evoke poignancy. In the present, alone in San Francisco, he thinks of Northhampton, Massachusetts seventeen years ago, and of the woman (a girl friend, according to Rexroth's literary executor, Bradford Morrow, named Shirley Johnson, who also figures centrally in "When We With Sappho") who made that past memorable. In the present, he is alone in bed, rain and fog outside, fog horns intensifying the mood of the present, making even the adjacent Pacific Ocean "desolate." The present, further, is desolate through contrast with the moonlit and ecstatic Northhampton past, full as it was of quivering and pulsating lovers. The triggering agent associating (and contrasting) present and past is, again, pear blossoms with their "acrid fleshy odor" and thus their reminder of sharply sensual love. He wonders (perhaps a little bitterly) about the nameless beloved in the present—a middle-aged "matron" probably with children. She is alive somewhere, no longer young, and somewhere else. That is all, but, with a few evocative images, a contrast of time present and past, Rexroth conjures up a whole dimension of experience, past opulence of love and present miserable loneliness (lying awake "on a twisted pillow"). Both that "twisted pillow" (wrung with longing, perhaps loneliness or despair—"desolate" water, but also the poem's speaker) and the use of pear blossoms in past and present tie the two times together, yet contrast them too, the quivering in the past suggesting the image of sexual love, the twisted pillow in the present a lonely lover's "object" of displaced passion. Not a major poem, "Northhampton" crystallizes a poignant moment (and night) of reminiscence of love and its loss.

The Phoenix and the Tortoise, which contains some of Rexroth's greatest verse, also includes probably his greatest love-reminiscence poem, "When We With Sappho." "Sappho" is too long a poem to analyze at length here, but I would like to quote the first stanza in order to exhibit the poem's felicitous naturalness of expression and lyricism which in part result from Rexroth's 7-9 deft syllabic meter and his deceptively simple diction:

> We lie here in the bee filled, ruinous
> Orchard of a decayed New England farm,
> Summer in our hair, and the smell
> Of summer in our twined bodies,
> Summer in our mouths, and summer
> In the luminous, fragmentary words
> Of this dead Greek woman.
> Stop reading. Lean back. Give me your mouth.
> Your grace is as beautiful as sleep.
> You move against me like a wave
> That moves in sleep.
> Your body spreads across my brain
> Like a bird-filled summer;
> Not like a body, not like a separate thing,
> But like a nimbus that hovers
> Over every other thing in all the world.
> Lean back. You are beautiful,
> As beautiful as the folding
> Of your hands in sleep (*CSP* p. 139).

Here, sexual love and intercourse are compared to organic human occurrences like sleep and hands folding in sleep. But the comparison moves towards metaphor, for sex, sleep and nature ("bird-filled summer," and ocean wave) are so blended as almost to render nature and human nature as one. Sexual love is presented as an activity and action as natural as the elements, but then a commanding perspective in Rexroth's verse is the congruence of human existence with the phenomena of nature. His love and nature verse is full of this concentricity and even of blended identification, whether in the stunning "Lyell's Hypothesis Again," climaxing (again, in a love setting) in its "immortal / Hydrocarbons of flesh and stone" or in the exquisite post-organic quietude of the poem "Still on Water," in which "Solitude closes down around us / As we lie passive and exhausted / Solitude clamps us softly in its warm hand" (*CSPKR* p. 157).

In Wordsworth's poetry, nature and human nature are also congruent, but Wordsworth sometimes strains for a moral resolution. In the 1850 version of *The Prelude*, this tendency goes so far as to compel him to grant the prize to mind as Deity in the grand relationship, tension and concentricity he establishes between humans and nature. The mind, for Wordsworth god-like, must dominate and reign supreme. D. H. Lawrence shows more respect for the "otherness" and integrity of nature (most fully in his *Birds, Beasts and Flowers*) by perceiving in flora and fauna a mystery of being beyond human sensibility ("I didn't know his gods," he says of the fish he has just caught and killed but whose world of instinct and sensations he would never comprehend). At the end of "Snake," after allowing his "education" to impel him to throw a log at the retreating reptile, he says, in admitted shame and confusion, "I have a pettiness to expiate." Rexroth's love verse, in turn, describes both nature and the act of sexual love with a naturalness and poise that dramatize human passions embodying a world of sensibility far removed from that of Christian guilt or the urge to dominate nature or Freudian self-consciousness. Nature in Rexroth's verse is not assigned a moral and ultimately a subordinate role. Closer to Lawrence and to Asian verse, Rexroth suggests that nature *is*, and that humans inhabit the world analogously to fish in water.

The accomplishment of "Sappho" is in part its recording and mediating experiences of love, time and process through reverie as poetic art. The poem doesn't depend on the facile appeal of vivid eroticism or voyeurism, or of dissatisfaction as sensationalized longing. If there is a consciousness in the poem, it is one so arching through time and transience as to resemble Nicolas Berdyaev's beautiful term the superconscious. The lovers try to sustain the almost supernatural vividness and clarity of Sappho's sensibility, under "Gold colossal domes of cumulus cloud / [which] Lift over the undulant, sibilant forest." The poem offers the golden core of a love encounter that the poet-lover knows must end yet reconciles himself to through an almost mystical state. Nearly nothing is left in the way of longing, ineffectuality, or the ineffable, and even the drift of the lovers ("with" Sappho) towards death is assuaged by the peak of love reverie reached in the poem. The final five lines of "Sappho" moves into a quiescence of post-orgasmic serenity unified with nature's sure being:

> Your body moves in my arms
> On the verge of sleep;
> And it is as though I held
> In my arms the bird filled
> Evening sky of summer (*CSP* p. 142).

That "as though" divides natural and supernatural realization by a hair's width. In doing so it implies in "Sappho" a sense of human limits accepted while crucially suggesting as well that such limits enclose more than enough to content one deeply. Both limits and a contentment that almost challenges limits are conveyed through the natural entities and phenomena of this world and earth—summer, naked bodies, grass, talk, silence, copulation, clouds, sky, evening. The natural is almost supernatural in the sheer accessibility of its "total immanence." As love, it becomes "the nodes of transcendence," and, conveyed in a poem, becomes, to Rexroth, a sacramentalizing of experience. Or as he puts it at the end of the poem "A Letter to William Carlos Williams," a poet "creates / Sacramental relationships / That last always."

The profound contentment present in "Sappho" is also present in a much simpler poem, "An Easy Song" (from the later 1960s sequence "Air and Angels" in Rexroth's *Natural Numbers*, 1964):

> It's rained every day since you
> Went away. I've been lonely.
> Lonely, empty, tenderness—
> Longing to kiss the corners
> Of your mouth as you smile
> Your special, inward, sensual,
> And ironic smile I love
> Because I know it means you
> Are *content*—content in French—
> A special, inward, sensual,
> And ironic state of bliss.
> Tu es contente, ma cherie?
> I am, even if lonely,
> Because I can call to mind
> Your body in a warm room,
> In the rainy winter night,
> A rose on the hearth of winter,
> A rose standing naked,
> In the perfume of your flesh.
> Moi aussi, je suis content (p. 115).

The tonal authority here is conveyed through the casual, relaxed air Rexroth achieves in the poem, embodied in such touches as the "you" at the end of line 1 (and throughout the poem), which effects both informality and subtly suave rhythmic movement. The "I've" in line 2 adds to this strategy of the informal, which, combined with such intimate references as kissing the corners of the beloved's smiling mouth, links informality to love intimacy, all culminating in the beautiful French sense of the word "content"—a "special, inward, sensual, / And ironic state of bliss." In this poem, the corners of the woman's mouth serve as one of those little pockets of intensified reality so central to Rexroth's "holiness of the real."

III

Rexroth wrote poems about love in more than a few of its myriad permutations. If, accordingly, he could write memorably of love as realization of self and other, of each through each other (as in the "Marthe" poem "Growing"), he could also speak of the ineffable poignancy of love's, like nature's, transience, as he does in the 1940s poem "Another Spring":

> The seasons revolve and the years change
> With no assistance or supervision.
> The moon, without taking thought,
> Moves in its cycle, full, crescent, and full.
>
> The white moon enters the heart of the river;
> The air is drugged with azalea blossoms;
> Deep in the night a pine cone falls;
> Our campfire dies out in the empty mountains.
>
> The sharp stars flicker in the tremulous branches;
> The lake is black, bottomless in the crystalline night;
> High in the sky the Northern Crown
> Is cut in half by the dim summit of a snow peak.
>
> O heart, heart, so singularly
> Intransigent and corruptible,
> Here we lie entranced by the starlit water,
> And moments that should each last forever
>
> Slide unconsciously by us like water (*CSP* p. 145).

The poignancy of the knowledge that the great moments of human experience will end can be so sharp that at times anguish seems bearable only by vividly voicing the grief it causes. Rexroth, like poets from the ancient Greeks on, takes his turn with this old lament, and "Another Spring" is one of the more impressive results. The word "heart" in fact designates the crucial pivot of the poem; put another way, it releases all the hovering meaning of the nature description that accumulates in the verse, which, striking as it is, needs and points to a resolving force.

Even a scant gaze at the nature description in the poem should reveal that something more than description is in play. The two segments of semantic action in the first stanza intimate an attitude towards nature. That attitude is that nature "behaves" or occurs—as one might expect—naturally (without "assistance" or "taking thought"). Nature doesn't even "behave," which suggests human choice—it simply (or complexly) *is*.

If stanza one implies a meaning to or behind the nature description, stanza two submerges us in nature through an ostensible presentativeness that is one of Rexroth's subtlest representational achievements as a poet (as he put in his "Introduction" to D. H. Lawrence's *Selected Poems*: "The clarity of purposively realized objectivity is the most supernatural of all visions," p. 11). The lines, here and in other poems, effect a preternatural directness and authenticity, rather like an unexpected caress or a sudden cool breeze on a hot day. Indeed, such naturalness almost seems to overcome the ineluctable artifice of art:

> The white moon enters the heart of the river;
> The air is drugged with azalea blossoms
> Deep in the night a pine cone falls;
> Our campfire dies out in the empty mountains.

There is a human presence in the poem here—*our* campfire suggests the presence of another person. A human agency is of course also implied by the word "heart." These small human references, true, contribute also to mobilizing meaning in the poem, which parallels the movements of the seasons started in the first stanza and underlies the entire poem. Stanza three moves even more deeply than stanza two into presentational immediacy, with no sign of human presence beyond that implied by the observation of the scene. The images here, as in stanza two, are (as in all of Rexroth's better nature poems) sharply recorded, lucid, and exact: "tremulous branches," the black lake, the Northern Crown only half seen because of the "dim summit."

With the climactic stanza four and the final fifth line, the poem dramatically changes tone, pulling the reader up short with its vivid address to that old epicenter of passions, the heart. Why is the heart intransigent and corruptible? Seemingly contradictory, these two qualities are relatable through irony, for they describe the human vulnerability to change and transience that is like nature's in its inevitability, but unlike nature's in its human meaning (thus "singularly"), which is the human capacity to both experience beauty, serenity, joy, yet know that these special states will end. Nature of course can be beautiful, and though it requires a human presence to experience such beauty, nature doesn't need such an observer. The fate of the observer is that he experiences through nature's beauty and naturalness his own "unnaturalness" both in the form of a fickle or changeable heart and of a mind that knows that beauty and thus itself perish.

If this is so, the poem urges more than Seize The Day. "Another Spring" reaches further by intimating an insuperable human entrapment and our need to make what we can of that limitation, a predicament partly resolved by esthetic embodiment and experiencing.

A sharper grief than that in "Another Spring" resides in all three of the Andrée-Rexroth elegies, Rexroth's tribute to his first wife Andrée Dutcher who died in 1940 and who, like Rexroth, was a vanguard artist. Here is the first two-thirds and more "objective" part of the second elegy:

> Purple and green, blue and white,
> The Oregon river mouths
> Slide into thick smoky darkness
> As the turning cup of the day
> Slips from the whirling hemisphere.
> And all that white long beach gleams
>
> In white twilight as the lights
> Come on in the lonely hamlets;
> And voices of men emerge;
> And dogs barking, as the wind stills.
> Those August evenings are
> Sixteen years old tonight and I
> Am sixteen years older too— (*CSP* p. 166).

The simplest of the three elegies, this one is moving in its progression from these sensitively recorded details of place sixteen years earlier when Andrée was last seen alive to a present without Andrée, in which Rexroth remains

> Lonely, caught in the midst of life,
> In the chaos of the world;
> And all the years that we were young
> Are gone, and every atom
> Of your learned and disordered
> Flesh is utterly consumed.

This elegy does not exhibit self-pity, despite the "lonely"; generally, the feelings in the poem are banked low by only being implied. Nevertheless, the poem would not be acceptable by the standards of an impersonalist esthetic, according to which any competent, self-controlled poet sublimates or otherwise conceals his "real" or personal feelings. Rexroth always insisted that T. S. Eliot's esthetic impersonalism concealed an intensely, even embarrassingly, personal poetry (an opinion also found in Douglas Bush's biography on Eliot). Conversely, I feel that Rexroth's own verse is considerably less personal than his own personalist poetics would indicate, a point implied by Thomas Parkinson who put it as follows: " . . . the curious thing is that this poet who speaks so frequently of personality as necessary to poetry . . . should himself become in these poems [*The Phoenix and the Tortoise*] more type than person" (p. 608).

This elegy to Andrée acquires a certain impersonality by in the main relying on direct objective statement by which to register its pathos, not only in the irremediable passage of time when they were together, but in the final immutability of the loss of Andrée, herself inexorably gone. This statement is not so much impersonal as distanced. Even the very personalness of the poem, the intensity of relationship, serves to keep the reader removed from ready identification. Despite the deeply anguished awareness of the utter finality of the loss, no consolation is offered, short of the dubious one of the resultant testamentary poem itself.

IV

Rexroth in the mid-1950s wrote a series of seven (perhaps eight) poems to his third wife Marthe Larsen in an attempt to win her back during a rocky period of their marriage. He ultimately failed to do so, and it is significant that in his *Collected Short Poems* (1966), Marthe's name was removed from the original series as it had appeared in *Poetry Magazine* in the early 1950s (Gibson, *Kenneth Rexroth* p. 90). William Carlos Williams in an otherwise favorable review of *In Defense of the Earth* arbitrarily dismissed the "Marthe" poems as merely "private." The poems are not private; they are personal in a way that elicits universal identification. Rexroth wrote poetry that is to some extent personal without, on the one hand, being embarrassingly or clinically private, or, on the other, being so universal or vague as to abort any personal response in the reader. And though he championed a personalist poetics, his verse, as urged earlier, is less personal than one might expect.

One of the attractions of the "Marthe" poems is the quality of their language. Generally, the language is fairly plain, even simple.

This is especially true of "Loneliness," the fourth poem in the series. The attitude behind this poem is that the force and authenticity of the experience Rexroth wants to communicate can be conveyed *only* by using the most lean language possible. It is as if any figure of speech, any extravagance of language, would be as discordant as the bray of a trumpet during the slow movement of a Mozart string quartet. There are a few "big" words—"corpuscle," "surcharged," "resonant," "penitent," but generally, the language here, as in most of the series poems, consists of simple monosyllabic words: thin, hear, voice, say, full, word, lost, black, flesh, night, day, and so on. Lyrics of course usually exhibit a simple or lucid diction. Rexroth's generally simple diction, however, is all the more commanding in "Loneliness" because all of it revolves around a single word, the central word of the poem and its title:

> To think of you surcharged with
> Loneliness. To hear your voice
> Over the recorder say,
> "Loneliness." The word, the voice,
> So full of it, and I, with
> You away, so lost in it—
> Lost in loneliness and pain (*CSP* p. 230).

As part of the former "Marthe" series, this loneliness concerns that of a loving husband and wife who are alienated from each other. If my reading of a preceding "Marthe" poem, "She Is Away," is correct, sexual infidelity was likely, as Rexroth long had a reputation for a wandering eye. More than one San Francisco Bay Area witness claimed that Rexroth struck at any female who moved. The "Marthe" series could be regarded as an extended expiation for some serious marital impropriety and as a recommittment to love.

Whatever caused the break and the loneliness in "Loneliness," the consequences are conveyed with a sense of sorrow and misery moving to behold. The force of the grief hangs in the poem like flayed skin. The pain of the loneliness is accentuated by Rexroth's apparently living alone—it would seem that "Marthe" or the beloved has left him. A separation has occurred, although, judging by the earlier, #2 poem, "She Is Away," "Marthe" appears to be with him still, though perhaps soon to depart ("This night might be the last one of all"). This poem, then, like the rest of the series, is a celebration of their love designed to win "Marthe" back in spirit or in the flesh, or both. But if the "Marthe" poems are a celebration with ulterior motives, "Loneliness" is a poem definitely, but not entirely, in a minor key.

Rexroth is consumed with loneliness. With "Marthe" away, he is "lost in loneliness and pain, / Black and unendurable." (It was common knowledge in the San Francisco Bay-Area arts community that Marthe had left Rexroth for Robert Creeley. According to Linda Hamalian in her absorbing biography of Rexroth, "Rexroth's condition [during Marthe's absence] deteriorated to the point where his friends actually feared for his life" [p. 265]). But to rise above the appearance of grieving for his own pain of loss, he imagines "Marthe's" loneliness, too. Indeed, the poem, altruistically, begins with *her* loneliness: "To think of you surcharged with / Loneliness . . . . " This sense or awareness of "Marthe," of the Other, already indicates the turning of the spirit that will move Rexroth from alienated closeness to a new openness towards his wife and beloved. The movement from one to the other in fact is the development of the poem. But what begins the turnabout is Rexroth's emphatic sense of the other person's misery, or loneliness, a sensitivity running throughout the series, and manifest in the fundamental self-searching and defining of his being in the elementalities of the universe found in the first poem of the series, "The Reflecting Trees of Being and Not Being." There is a significant sense in which the "Marthe" poems are a discovery and consolidation of self through a re-adjustment and, hopes Rexroth, rejuvenation of relationship with the Other embodied in "Marthe," his mystic bride.

The intensities of the passion of anguished loss and yearning in "Loneliness" are extraordinary:

> Black and unendurable,
> Thinking of you with every
> Corpuscle of my flesh, in
> Every instant of night
> And day. O, my love, the times
> We have forgotten love, and
> Sat lonely besides each other.
> We have eaten together,
> Lonely behind our plates, we
> Have hidden behind children,
> We have slept together in
> A lonely bed (*CSP* p. 230).

This ends the first or negative phase of the poem. Not only is the diction direct or simple, but the situations are ordinary, everyday domestic moments—at the dinner table, with the children, in bed.

Behind all this simplicity of language and experience concerning a marital rift resides the attitude that only by reducing experience and language to their basic components will the reformation occur that could heal the wounds of marital alienation. Another consequence of the lucid, simple diction and emotional directness of "Loneliness" is that they universalize the experience in the poem; anyone could well have gone through the blackly unhappy events in the poem in which spouses lie miles apart in the same bed. Such intense loneliness represents a death in life ironically rendered all the more poignant and painful by the depth of shared love.

The second, affirmative phase of the poem, vivified by being in the present tense, is initiated by the religious diction of the changing, renewal, and ascendance of the soul in penitence:

> Now my heart
> Turns towards you, awake at last,
> Penitent, lost in the last
> Loneliness. Speak to me. Talk
> To me. Break the black silence.
> Speak of a tree full of leaves,
> Of a flying bird, the new
> Moon in the sunset, a poem,
> A book, a person—all the
> Casual healing speech
> Of your resonant, quiet voice.
> The word freedom. The word peace.

The heart turns, "awake at last." Loneliness is a kind of darkness, and is particularly dark when it results from discord between people who love each other and share much of each other's company. In this passage one hears of a "black silence." Rexroth is also "Lost in the last / Loneliness...." All the sullenness and coldness and self-conscious, heavily strained silence of husband and wife, lovers, not speaking to each other is like a kind of drugged, unrestful sleep, even a protracted nightmare. But the turning, the gradual and blind moving of the soul from the dark to the full-moon phase of its life, its repulsion and attraction, begins (as already mentioned) earlier. The writing of the poem and the written poem represent the turning; the process and the accomplished poem recreate the progression from lostness to the light of the waking of a new urge to relate in love, but the initial turning itself precedes the poem, as it must.

Thus the poem celebrates the hope of, the desire for,

reconciliation. The hope is full of an appeal to words from the beloved, words about simple, natural things, a leafy tree, a bird in flight, the new moon, or about elements of culture, poems, books, social relations. These things mentioned in the special voice of the beloved would not really be referential; they would not really be about birds and books and the moon. They would reach to something deeper, something the very opposite of loneliness; they would transcend themselves, be made exquisitely real, even sacred, through the speaking mouth and reconciled mind of the beloved wife. When loneliness is ended, when hatred or coldness turns back into love and relation, all the simple or precious phenomena of life, so shared, so given by loving spouse to spouse, *become* freedom, *become* peace, as much states of mind, not just words, as the dominating loneliness in the poem was never just a word.

"Quietly," another poem like "Loneliness," from *In Defense of the Earth* (1956), is regarded by Morgan Gibson as part of the "Marthe" series. Whether or not it is, "Quietly" could serve as an ideal conclusion to this moving set of poems about the crises and blissful renewal of marital life and love.

"Quietly" may not be one of Rexroth's major love poems, yet it is a good example of slender material well realized:

> Lying here quietly beside you,
> My cheek against your firm, quiet thighs,
> The calm music of Boccherini
> Washing over us in the quiet,
> As the sun leaves the housetops and goes
> Out over the Pacific, quiet—
> So quiet the sun moves beyond us,
> So quiet as the sun always goes,
> So quiet, our bodies, worn with the
> Times and the penances of love, our
> Brains curled, quiet in their shells, dormant,
> Our hearts slow, quiet, reliable
> In their interlocked rhythms, the pulse
> In your thigh caressing my cheek. Quiet. (*CSP* p. 243)

The title word embodies the basic mood of the poem. In the context of what appears to be post-orgasmic love and rest, everything is transformed into quietness—the woman's "firm, quiet thighs," Boccherini's "calm" music "washing over us in the quiet," the quiet movement of the sun westward over the Pacific, the quietness of the lovers' bodies, of their brains " . . . curled, quiet in their shells," their hearts " . . . Quiet, reliable / In their interlocked rhythms. . . ."

As in other Rexroth nature poems, the state of human being is related to the eternal natural verities—the quiet movement of the sun, the enriched and rested silence of human minds after lovemaking, the sense of the bodies' tranquillity after the sexual exertions, tensions, and climaxes of loving. The choice of the music of Boccherini is deft and typical, for Rexroth, with his orientation towards Mediterranean culture, the cultures of Southern France and Italy, would regard the 18th century Italian composer's music as the essence of the sophisticated emotion and civilized calm he would aspire to achieve in his own work and, as a humanist radical, bring about in modern society. "Our bodies, worn with the / Times and the penances of love" suggests the griefs and strife as well as the joys and pleasure of the marriage. This marital complexity, again, implies a lyric poet of mature love experience.

Music operates in the poem in several ways. Beyond the exquisite tranquillity of Boccherini, Rexroth's prosody has its own subtle and suave musicality in its syntax, its use of repetition, and its skill in imaging quietness. All of this projects a striking experience of contented love as a quietness which does not occlude the earth in all its quietnesses, but, rather, includes them in such a way as to relate sexual love, the pulsing flow of the blood, and marital harmony, to human culture (Boccherini) and the natural activity of the skies (the sun).

"Quietly" is virtually one sentence, and not a grammatically complete sentence at that. By extending prepositional and adverbial phrases, and by seeming to render an entire phase of a special experience, using the repetition of the word "quiet" ten times to describe both bodies and minds and a heavenly body, Rexroth creates his own music. Each phrasal or rhythmic unit seems, feels, sounds like the stroke of a bow on a cello, and thus the ordered expectancies of a normal syntax and the syntactical closure of a grammatically complete sentence would be out of place. Lyric poems comprised of syntactic fragments or bravura extensions of phrases and closures are nothing new. What counts is that some form of control exists. In "Quietly" this control resides in the repetition of the word "quiet," in the mood of quietness as serenity pervading the poem, and, finally, in the residual sense that whatever else happens in life to these two people or to other human beings, the post-sexual tranquillity conveyed in this poem embodies a completeness and fulfillment of experience that borders on the holy.

V

The Love Poems of Marichiko represents an order of love verse strikingly different in some ways from all Rexroth's other love verse and remarkable for a man in his late sixties. *Marichiko* is a sequential verse narrative of sixty short verses (supposedly written by a Japanese "poetess" named Marichiko) that Rexroth claims to have translated in Japan during the 1970s. Actually, Rexroth did not translate the poems; he *wrote* them. I have considered at length elsewhere why Rexroth perpetrated this curious ruse. Let it suffice to say here that the poems constitute an unforgettable union of passion and poignancy, crystallized by a context of love bliss and almost unbearable forlornness. In short, the series comprises a mini-tragedy of being loved and left. Thus the deeper thematic elements in the poem provide its searing eroticism with a process of tragic realism that is a high achievement in American love verse.

The set of poems is too long to scrutinize in its entirety here, but a quotation sketch of the work will convey its flavor and some of its force:

> I sit at my desk.
> What can I write to you?
> Sick with love,
> I long to see you in the flesh.
> I can write only,
> 'I love you. I love you. I love you.'
> Love cuts through my heart
> And scars my vitals.
> Spasms of longing suffocate me
> And will not stop (#1).

This intensity is typical of the poem and of its dramatic desperation and anguish. Apt metaphors communicate the power of the passions running through this love. Says "Marichiko,"

> Making love with you
> Is like drinking sea water.
> The more I drink
> The thirstier I become,
> Until nothing can slake my thirst
> But to drink the entire sea (#7).

With such an unquenchable appetite for love, we are subtly prepared for some strong erotic episodes, and soon get one:

> You wake me,
> Part my thighs, and kiss me.
> I give you the dew
> Of the first morning of the world (#9),

in which the cunnilingual sex is partly sublimated by an apocalyptic content suggesting through poetic license the extremity of passion of this love experience. A far sharper, almost terrifying sensuality emerges some poems later:

> I scream as you bite
> My nipples, and orgasm
> Drains my body, as if I
> Had been cut in two (#24).

This love is so obsessive and overwhelming to "Marichiko" that even daytime, the major phase of our conscious lives and strivings, is subordinated to night and dreams of love and lover:

> Because I dream
> Of you every night,
> My lonely days
> Are only dreams (#15).

One could notice here how much effect Rexroth is getting out of concise, spare diction, short verse lines, and almost no metaphors, qualities found in some of his best love and nature poems. In the "Marichiko" poems, these traits are so condensed, so tautened as to lead through a paradoxical process of inversion to a considerable expansiveness of emotion and reference. There are just a few words and two to two-and-a-half foot verse lines, but the words are chosen with utter precision of meaning and emotion to make a powerful impact. The verse sentences of this series poem, chiseled to quintessential expression, embody a core of realized experience, evoking again Rexroth's mystical immanence of "the holiness of the real."

The poem sequence achieves a witty grammatical and semantic bliss that is as moving as it is illusionary (and it is both) in #20:

> Who is there? Me.
> Me who? I am me. You are you.
> You take my pronoun,
> And we are us.

This pronomial "jeu d'esprit" will late in the sequence imply bitter irony for the narrator, who, in merging herself with her beloved, will lose herself disastrously, for, when "us" dissolves, "me" and "I" seem, so violently disunited, selfless and virtually dead.

Relations subtly, mysteriously change, and by #38, after a few quiet hints in two or three preceding poems, we get *this*:

> I waited all night.
> By midnight I was on fire.
> In the dawn, hoping
> To find a dream of you,
> I laid my weary head
> On my folded arms,
> But the songs of the waking
> Birds tormented me.

which is followed five poems later by

> . . . .
> Crickets sing all night in the pine tree.
> At midnight the temple bell rings,
> Wild geese cry overhead
> Nothing else (#43).

and

> . . . .
> My hollow eyes and gaunt cheeks
> Are your fault (#44).

Clearly, another, sinister phase of the relationship has evolved. Little reason is given for its occurrence ("Our love was dimmed by / Forces which came from without,") we are told (#46), but that explanation is vague at best, and leads us to think that the cause of the end of love is less important than its occurrence, which (for some people) is inevitable, like the succession of the seasons, or death.

The final poems in the sequence are as fraught with grief, misery and bitterness as the earlier ones were radiant with joy and ecstasy:

> . . . .
> My heart flares with this agony.
> Do you understand?
> My life is going out.
> Do you understand?
> My life.

The final poem in the sequence implies death of life for the woman, in these concluding lines:

> I hate the sight of coming day
> Since that morning when
> Your insensitive gaze turned me to ice
> Like the pale moon in the dawn (#60).

Thus the series does not end sensationally, on a flourish of melodrama or violence. Rather, it ends the way such matters often enough end in life, in rejection, estrangement, bitterness, one's desire to live ebbing into a darkening grayness. "Chilled through, I wake up with the first light," she says in the same poem. Life is now monotonal, dominated by the dark side of the moon of love that shone lustrously earlier in the poem sequence.

One could possibly squeeze a moral from the "Marichiko" poems, but that would falsify the pith of this verse, for the real integrity of the sequence (Rexroth's most coherent, tight-knit one) does not arise from some facile, causal explanation or moral judgment. Rather, like the Scandinavian sagas in which blood feuds erupt from either mysterious or trivial causes and move relentlessly towards doom like Fall towards Winter, the "Marichiko" poems suggest that love begins, grows, wanes and sometimes ends. One can't always explain it, love can be like that. It *does* end, and that is as much a part of the actual trajectory of life (if less palatable to our basic ideals or fantasies) as unending love or marital fidelity. Aside from such bony realism, the "Marichiko" poems are remarkable for so utterly blending romance and realism that the extremities of ecstatic love become inextricably part of the same world of experience as the acrid horror of abandonment. They are especially remarkable, though, for being so free of moral pronouncement and for the narrative they frame, which allows Rexroth's capacity for an impersonal poetics even more scope than do most of his love lyrics.

VI

Rexroth's prosody, which has received little critical commentary, accords distinction to his poetry. This contention applies particularly to the seven-nine syllable line in which much of his finest verse (both short and long) is written. Affirming Rexroth's syllabic line, Lawrence Lipton has said that a line length indicates "a formal notation of the verse. There is more opportunity here [in Rexroth's syllabic line] for the alternating legato with staccato passages than the longer, flowing lines of poetic prose permit" ("The Poetry of Kenneth Rexroth," *Poetry* XC, 3 [June 1957], p. 177). A few lines from "Inversely, As the Square of Their Distances Apart" (from *The Phoenix and the Tortoise*) will demonstrate Rexroth's suppleness with syllabic verse:

> I lie alone in an alien
> Bed in a strange house and morning
> More cruel than any midnight
> Pours its brightness through the window (*CSP* p. 149).

The syllabic count here varies from seven to nine per line, but that count is governed, as it should be, by semantic stress as well as by sound values. The first line ending with "alien" emphasizes the condition of forced or dismal solitude, in contrast to a preceding three stanzas of being with the beloved in a blissful solitude of natural surroundings at night. "Bed" in line two presents a harsh contrast to the nature "bed" on which the speaker as an unalienated lover previously lay with his beloved. Line two ending with "morning" also stresses that word contrastively with the context in the three preceding poems of "Inversely" of a fusion of night and darkness, love and nature. The irony of a daylight that is "crucial" because it reveals, indeed, illuminates, one's love-loneliness is accentuated by what could be called the "strong" positioning of "More cruel" in line three and "Pours" in line four, places in the lines where climax of meaning result from visibility of position.

Beyond such an indication of the semantic-prosodic craft within Rexroth's syllabic verse, one notices that his line also exhibits a fine ease and grace of movement (which is especially evident when correctly read aloud). It might at first appear that a seven-to-nine syllable line could be constricting, or read or scanned unnaturally. With Rexroth's line, the very opposite seems true. His verse often achieves the quality of impassioned speech, of common (but heightened) discourse. Rexroth claims he wanted to write poetry the way he talks. His Hoosier accent aside, he seems to me to have brought that aim off.

Another example of Rexroth's syllabic verse illustrating a point about his prosody can be found in the opening lines of "A Sword in a Cloud of Light" from the six-poem series for his daughter Mary called "The Lights in the Sky Are Stars" (in *In Defense of the Earth*):

>Your hand in mine, we walk out
>To watch the Christmas Eve crowd
>On Fillmore Street, the Negro
>District. The night is thick with
>Frost. The people hurry, wreathed
>In their smoky breaths. Before
>The shop windows the children
>Jump up and down with spangled
>Eyes. Santa Clauses ring bells.
>Loud speakers on the lampposts
>Sing carols, on juke boxes.
>In the bars Louis Armstrong
>Plays White Christmas ... (*CSP* p. 239).

One can observe the witty irony studding this passage (Santa Clau*ses*, *Louis Armstrong* playing "*White* Christmas") or the sharp descriptive eye for the combination of holiday festivity with blatant commercialism and stress. A basic prosodic feature, moreover, is that the short syllabic line generates a high-charged speed that contributes to the sense of jangled energy, joy, and excitement indicative of a typical modern city Christmas and of modern city life. The diction consists of simple, short words which help in creating a brisk pace which in turn adds to the discordant holiday energy of the poem.

If the prosody often seems to possess an effortless felicity, the diction of some of Rexroth's "New Poems" in *Natural Numbers* (1964) is slack and even sentimental (as in the poem "Coming"— "Rushing ... / Down the California coast / to your curving lips and your / Ivory thighs"). And even in the verse from the powerful middle period the language once in a while sinks below Rexroth's usually energized use of the colloquial, and becomes flat or pale (and, on the other hand, it can sometimes become inflated or pretentious, as in the early Cubist poems, or in some passages of philosophical exposition in the otherwise impressive and underrated *The Dragon and the Unicorn*).

At its best, in poems like "The Signature of All Things" or

"Yugao" or "Lyell's Hypothesis Again" or the "Andree-Rexroth" elegies, Rexroth's poetry does not even seem like poetry in the sense of being a "verbal construct" or a convention of artful words and syntactic and rhythmic strategies—rather, it seems like an exalted experience undergone through words which have been rendered so clear, so "artless" and "right" as to take on a kind of numinous transparency revealing the heart of the poem's life itself. This intense limpidity, when it occurs in Rexroth's verse, can make his poems distinctly crystalline, a mystical image and quality he himself frequently invoked.

VII

The words "crystal" and "crystalline" provide a metaphorically apt link to the last aspect of Rexroth's verse that I will discuss: contemplation. Rexroth ends one of his finest poems, "Time Is the Mercy of Eternity," with these words:

>   Suspended
> In absolutely transparent time, I
> Take on a kind of crystalline
> Being. In this translucent
> Immense here and now, if ever,
> The form of the person should be
> Visible, its geometry,
> Its crystallography, and
> Its astronomy. The good
> And evil of my history
> Go by. I can see them and
> Weigh them. They go first, with all
> The other personal facts,
> And sensations, and desires.
> At last there is nothing left
> But knowledge, itself a vast
> Crystal encompassing the
> Limitless crystal of air
> And rock and water. And the
> Two crystals are perfectly
> Silent. There is nothing to
> Say about them. Nothing at all (*CSP* p. 251).

It is hard to ignore the word "crystal" which in one form or another is mentioned five times in these last 23 lines. This pivotal word and image relate to a few of Rexroth's ideas about contemplation, and informs us too about the purpose of contemplation in Rexroth's verse generally. The point I would like to emphasize is the significance of Rexroth's definition of the poet and of poetry as a person and an activity relatable to contemplation. He puts this relationship vividly in an essay called "The Visionary Painting of Morris Graves":

> Civilization endures as long as, somewhere, they [contemplatives] can hold life in total vision. The function of the contemplative is contemplation. The function of the artist is the revelation of reality in process, permanence in change, the place of value in a world of facts. His duty is to keep open the channels of contemplation and to discover new ones. His role is purely revelatory. He can bring men to the springs of the good, the true, and the beautiful, but he cannot make them drink. The activities of men endure and have meaning as long as they emanate from a core of transcendental calm. The contemplative, the mystic, assuming moral responsibility for the distracted, tries to keep his gaze fixed on that core. The artist uses the materials of the world to direct men's attention back to it. When it is lost sight of, society perishes (*Bird in the Bush: Obvious Essays* p. 57).

Although Rexroth regards the roles of the artist, contemplator, and mystic as overlapping, in the passage above he significantly differentiates them. If the contemplator and the mystic have their attention riveted on the "core of transcendental calm," the artist "uses the materials of the world to direct men's attention back to it." (It is hard to excuse a libertarian like Rexroth not being more sensitive to the male-chauvinist use of the term "men" here and elsewhere in his work.) Then follows this emphatic sentiment: "When it is lost sight of, society perishes."

This august definition of the artist's (and contemplator's and mystic's) role in society is also one that ennobles art enormously. One hears often enough the trite pieties intoned about the humanities: that they are one of the brightest gems of civilization, that engaging them will enrich and broaden one's imagination, and so on. But for a poet to urge that poetry (and thus art) as contemplation constitutes the webbing that keeps society from disintegrating or from destroying itself is a startlingly forceful claim. It is a perception easy enough to vulgarize by insisting it means that verse or contemplation is concerned with the "deeper things" in life.

However, by dramatizing in "Time Is The Mercy Of Eternity" the contemplative, mystical process through imagery of the crystal which by its very nature reduces physical reality to its basic structure (thus accentuating the "mystical" qualities of transparency, clarity, heightened visibility), one provides a kind of direct, "phenomenal" authority for words asserting the primacy of contemplation as vision. Vision is intensified, even exalted, seeing. But contemplation and vision go beyond that, for, as in "Time" or in a slighter, monistic poem by Rexroth called "The Heart of Herakles" (from "The-Lights-in-the-Sky-Are-Stars" series), one crosses the traditional and arbitrary line between subject (the "I") and object (the "it," Other, World) and, becoming part of one's surroundings, transcends their and one's own partialness towards an exalted clarity ("I take on a kind of crystalline being"). What follows resembles the Buddhist transcendence of all worldly ties and associations represented as Nirvana (the good and evil of one's history going by, as well as "personal facts, sensations, desires"). One is left in this mystical denudation in a state of mind—again, crystalline—that Rexroth mentions frequently and which can be summed up in lines from his long 1967 poem *The Heart's Garden, the Garden's Heart*: "He who lives without grasping / Lives always in the experience / Of the immediate as the Ultimate."

Again what Rexroth is doing with his crystal figure, so symbolically climactic to his entire poem and, considering the definition from *Heart's Garden*, to his work itself, is imaging or symbolizing the contemplative state. Rexroth urges in a long and fascinating essay on Martin Buber (in *Bird in the Bush*) that the artist has a better grasp of reality than the mystic (and contemplator, by implication), for art—at its best—lacks the metaphysical greed of mysticism, and connects or identifies the everyday world with the transcendent one. Mystical contemplation, at least as a dimension of the religious mind, stresses an absoluteness about human existence that art (*some* art) does not accept (*Bird in the Bush* p. 139).

Rexroth's artist would insist that life is transient, fluxional, conditional. Samuel Johnson's kicked stone is in itself "ineluctably" real, but an undeniable part of its reality is that it too will decay and finally disappear. The truth latent in this kind of reality is, according to Rexroth, the only absolute that exists, and on such a realization rests responsible vision. There is no absolute in the traditional religious sense even in "Time"'s two crystals of self and world, unless one wishes to say that they are "absolutely" real or reside at the center of reality. But one need not decide on this absoluteness, need not even *say* and thus think anything about them. Perhaps that constitutes some of the meaning of the last three-and-a-half lines of the poem: "And the / Two crystals are perfectly / Silent. There is nothing to / Say about them. Nothing at all." The silence beyond words and thoughts (let alone "facts, sensations, and desires") is conceivably a mystical aural facet of the crystalline vision climaxing "Time," and as such offers a summit of tranquillity from which to contemplate newly how time is the mercy of eternity.

When James Wright wrote in 1980 that "Over the years I have learned that I am far from being alone in being so grateful to Rexroth, and I believe he has saved many poets from imaginative death," (*Sagetrieb* p. 113), he was in part alluding to Rexroth's essays and translations, but even more to Rexroth's love verse. But I would guess that what poets like Wright and many others—poets and non-poets—essentially prized about Rexroth's work was that he seemed to have a great knack for clearing away the rant, pretentions and chicanery in society concealing reality. When he turned his keen sense of the real away from organized society, which he described as held together by the Social Lie, and focused (especially) on love and nature subjects, a particular lucidity, vividness and intensity emerged in his verse that one could call the natural supernatural. Speaking of D. H. Lawrence's *Look! We Have Come Through!*, Rexroth says "reality is totally valued . . . The clarity of purposively realized objectivity is the most supernatural of all visions." This applies perfectly to Rexroth's own verse as well, and is another way of indicating that numinous glow on and *within* the natural and the ordinary that his best work gives off—the holiness of the real.

Kenneth Rexroth was one of the significant American poets of the 20th century, and a better poet than many who get included in anthology after anthology and in sensationally tragic biography after biography. Rexroth, whatever his pretentions, infidelities, lies and arrogance, lived out his life and set his poetry and prose and erudition and radicalism so firmly within it that we overlook what dedication and integrity it took to achieve this work in an age that never adequately acknowledged his worth as a *poet*—and is only now beginning to do so.

Works Cited

The Contemporary Writer: Interviews with Sixteen Novelists and Poets. Ed. L. S. Dembo and Cyrena N. Pondrom. Madison: University of Wisconsin Press, 1972.

Eshleman, Clayton. "Selected Poems of Kenneth Rexroth." *Los Angeles Times Book Review* 31 March 1983.

Gibson, Morgan. *Kenneth Rexroth.* New York: Twayne, c1972.

—. "'Poetry is Vision'—'Vision is Love': Kenneth Rexroth's Philosophy of Literature." *Sagetrieb, Special Issue-Kenneth Rexroth* 2:3(Winter 1983).

Gutierrez, Donald. "Kenneth Rexroth's *The Love Poems of Marichiko*." *The San Francisco Review of Books* 12:1(Spring 1987). See also *American Poetry* (1990) for a longer version of the same essay.

—. "Kenneth Rexroth's 'When We With Sappho' as Reverie." *American Poetry* 4:1(Fall 1986).

Hamalian, Linda. *A Life of Kenneth Rexroth.* New York: Norton, 1991.

Lawrence, D. H. *Selected Poems*, ed. by Kenneth Rexroth. NY: New Directions, 1947.

Parkinson, Thomas. "Kenneth Rexroth, Poet." *The Ohio Review* 17:2(Winter 1976).

Rexroth, Kenneth. *Assays.* New York: New Directions, 1961.

—. *An Autobiographical Novel.* Garden City: Doubleday, 1964.

—. *Bird in the Bush: Obvious Essays.* New York: New Directions, 1959.

—. *The Collected Shorter Poems of Kenneth Rexroth.* New York: New Directions, 1966.

—. *The Heart's Garden, The Garden's Heart.* Cambridge: Pym-Randall Press,1967.

—. "The Love Poems of Marichiko." *The Morning Star.* New York: New Directions, 1979.

—. *Natural Numbers: New and Selected Poems.* New York: New Directions, 1963.

—. *Selected Poems.* Ed. Bradford Morrow. New York: New Directions, 1984.

—. *Sagetrieb, Special Issue, Kenneth Rexroth* 2:3(Winter 1983).

The Beautiful Place in the Mind: Robert Duncan's "Often I Am Permitted To Return To A Meadow"

> I have a dream. It is the best dream a human being can have. Alas, it comes all too infrequently. I am in a place that is very special. It has no particular name. Although it is some geographic location—the countryside, the city, a house or a building—it does not resemble any place on another planet, it is that unfamiliar and strange. And yet, unlike strange places in ordinary dreams that may evoke uneasiness and fear, this place, by its very dissimilarity from everyday places, becomes the ideal place to be in. For in it there is no fear, no anxiety or apprehension, no pain, guilt, sin, or remorse, and no concern for the consequences of one's actions (Zusne p. 21).

Thus begins a description of what has been described as the ideal enclave and *beau lieu* or beautiful place. According to Leonard Zusne, it is an "experience of an integrated personality . . . a symbol of an archetype of the self" (p. 22). This site is distinguished by Carl Jung from the *tenemos*, a sacred or protected area of antiquity which, if also symbolic of the self, has "more of the character of a refuge, a re-doubt, and a place of rest than a good, beautiful, and ideal place to be active and to have experiences in" (p. 22). After discussing the presence of the beautiful place in Jung, various myths, and literature, Zusne concludes:

> The land of the ideal enclave is not to be found to the east or west of any point on earth. But neither is it an empyrean of lofty ideals or a Nirvana. It is an island solidly anchored in the human psyche, reachable after a long and arduous journey (p. 29).

This final point allows me to approach both my subject and my critical perspective in discussing Robert Duncan's poem from his book *The Opening of the Field* entitled "Often I Am Permitted to Return to a Meadow." This poem is indeed concerned with the psychic archetype that Zusne presents above. Duncan's poeticization of that archetype, however, is based on a complex reflexiveness. This treatment begins with the traditional epistemological polarity of subject and object, or, respectively, mind and place, and inverts it monistically into a unity held, it is implied, by the poet's vision, so that place is mind and mind is place, or almost are. This fluid translatableness of subject and object, found in any number of audacious artists, Wordsworth, Cezanne, D. H. Lawrence, is the metaphoric pivot on which "Meadow" revolves.

I have suggested that the poem can be regarded as a performance in monistic epistemology, and that at the core of this subject-object fusion or reversibility is a visionary sense of an ideal enclave. However, this vision and super-rational commingling take on considerable complexity in the course of the poem, as one basic image reference merges into another. The reader begins with place in the first-line title which in line one proper of the poem is related as simile to the mind. In lines 2-6, the fluctuations between mind and place are so fleet and involuted that the traditional rationalist split between the two is broken down. Thus from this "derangement of the senses" we are prepared for the next turn, the metaphor of architecture. If a place can exist in the mind, it is not a large step to include buildings, built places, something more cultural than meadows or pastures, but like the latter a subdivision of place, though a place in the mind.

The opening lines deserve a closer look. First, we are told that the meadow to which the poet or speaker is allowed to return is not a mentally constructed place, and thus is not his. Yet, the poem states next, the meadow is a "made place," and in this different sense does belong to the poet. So how can a place, Duncan's meadow, both be and not be part of the mind? The implication is that this sense of a special Place, though not a constituent of the poet's personality or character, is part of a deeper, more impersonal, inheritance, something perhaps akin to a visitation from Jung's Collective Unconscious. Such an image would not be the poet's, yet, once experienced and assimilated, becomes his (and the reader's) because it is "so near the heart."

This archetypal activity in the mind readily leads from pasture to hall, allowing "architectures" to extend their own figurative facets so as to include another basic and monistic feature of the poem, the archetypal female. Duncan refers in the fourth and fifth stanzas to three grand-sounding women, the First Beloved, the Lady, and a Queen Under the Hill. These are all prototypical ladies, suggestive of one's mother ("First Beloved"), the Virgin Mary (the "Lady"), and a primeval Earth Mother or pre-Christian Mediterranean matriarch as well as a dead female personage. A key monistic transference in the poem, then, is that "architectures," part of the structure of those beautiful places from which, with the polished ease of a pleasant dream, one situation or context merges into and becomes another, have become archetypal women with broad cultural associations (Mother, Christianity, Graeco-Roman and Mediterranean myth). This transference is not surprising. Woman is traditionally associated with the most Beautiful Places; in more than just romantic contexts she is often even the heart and center of them.

Thus we have three changes that can be varyingly stated: place—mind—architecture—women, *or*, mind—place—architecture—women. I have already alluded to the philosophical and esthetic implications of whether mind or place should come first (or either), a consideration I will try to resolve later. Let us instead consider the fact that another mirror or word follows these four key terms and figures: "words." The words in a rudimentary sense are the foundation of the poem; without them, none of the other basic contexts or shifting images would exist. This is obvious, as is the fact that this symbolic treatment of words represents a poet's tribute to the medium of his art. But it is also implied that the shifting imagery, the Cocteauesque montage, had its life, its ultimate being, in words. Does this mean then that words, language, constitute the essence of the poem? Were this so, the subtlety of the poem would be limited. On the contrary, the poem seems to me to transcend this delimiting homage by making even words subordinate not merely to place again, but to a special place: *le beau lieu*. All this and more is crystallized in stanza five, which I read as the climax of the poem:

> She is Queen Under the Hill
> whose hosts are a disturbance of words within words
> that is a folded field

I feel that the stanza represents a climax because the five key terms of the poem are either mentioned or implied, and are mentioned in a manner that gives them the form of final meaning, like figures in a frieze. As Queen Under the Hill, the dead (but also living) Goddess, one's Mother (who *lives* in one's mind), whether dead or living, or mortal or immortal female force, this "Triple Goddess" harbors hosts. A richly connotative word, "hosts" refers us back to the "hall" and "architecture" that grew out of the pastoral of the mind. It also suggests in this context that words are hosts to readers as guests, and that thus we too, through poetry's words, have access to the "eternal pasture" that is "so near the heart." But "hosts" also suggest a large number or multitude, and if one recalls the earlier etymology of the word "guest," the latent meaning of a guest being a captive to one's host means here also that one is a captive to this primal woman, as a poet is captive to the creative imperatives of the Muse. And the reader is also a "guest" to these associations as they may apply; more directly, he is captive to the "disturbance of words within words," and to their ultimate and transcendent conversion into the "field folded," that is, the Beautiful Place. Thus the reader, through the poet, the artist, is captive in the ideal enclave made by the subject-object fusing of the poet's visionary exaltation.

What, however, is to be made of stanzas 7 and 8 which appear to belittle the preceding rhapsody of vision? "It is only a dream," we are told, a dream

> ... of the grass blowing
> east against the source of the sun
> in an hour before the sun's going down ...

"Dream" here at first seems negative in its diminishment of visionary experience; the whole event is reduced to an image of natural energy, wind moving against grass towards the center and symbol of prime energy. This directional source of energy, the East, contains a secret when connected with the lines "whose secret we see in a children's game / of ring a round of roses told." The lyrics for that children's game are

> Ring a round of roses,
> Pockets full of posies,
> Ashes, ashes
> All fall down.

The "secret" of the source of the sun told in this game is death, but it is also "magic" protection against death in the form of the creative flow of nature that represents absolute beauty, and, by association, art. The source of the sun, the East, is a symbol of birth, rebirth, and new life, the very opposite of the West with its traditional associations with death. Like a child, the artist, the poet, knows the secret of the sun, of sources of energy. The "secret" is that what is generated by energy also perishes. But the remaining part of this secret is that energy is eternal, and that if the sun goes down, it also comes up again. Energy is Eternal Delight, said Blake. Energy, implies Duncan, is recurrent light, and recurrent inspiration. Thus, the dream encompasses Duncan's meadow vision rather than negating it; it enriches the meaning of his visionary meadow by providing a fundamental source to the Beautiful Place.

That these two stanzas do not basically undercut the poem is further suggested by the affirmative character of the final stanzas of the poem:

> Often I am permitted to return to a meadow
> as if it were a given property of the mind
> that certain bounds hold against chaos,
>
> that is a place of first permission,
> everlasting omen of what is.

Duncan makes the connection between meadow and mind in terms of a simile, thus suggesting a certain poignancy in the gap created by the subject-object (or subject-subject) differentiation. Whether or not that separation is essential, too much distance between mind and meadow would make life excessively abstract, bleak, and cold. If, on the other hand, meadow and mind were one, and in some senses they perhaps can be, such an identification would last only briefly, analogous as it otherwise could be to several straight hours of joy or terror. The union of meadow and mind is best temporary. It makes return, and thus regeneration, possible, and perhaps is all of the *Beau Lieu* needed to retain these "bounds" against chaos. And a Beautiful Place would lose its beauty if experienced too much.

The "place of first permission" is, then, a visionary haunt, a special place. What permits this return, this special, archetypal visitation? Clearly it is the mind itself as self-creation; it is the mind in its first realization of its creative, artistic character, a kind of heightened self-consciousness. Permission to this type of person is self-endowed. In this sense, the artist, to vary Wordsworth, is father of the artistic man. Beyond this oblique signal of artistic autonomy, we have a gesture of the supreme reality of the artistic imagination. This mind-place, haunt of creative sources and fertility, is also the "omen" of not only what is important, but of what will be important in the future.

Thus Duncan's poem is a celebration of the powers of art and artist through a symbolic presentation of the preserves of art, the special "meadows" and agents of inspiration which evokes the "architectures," Lawrencean flaming flowers, and interfolding pastures and thought basic at least to a certain kind of poetry. The first five lines of the poem (including the title) imply the resolution of the mind-and-surroundings problem concerning whether the beautiful place is "out there" or internal: surely, it's both. The scene is not originally the poet's, but he *makes* it his through imaginational reshaping (a "*folded* field"), and also by "placing" it near his heart, by giving it, that is, emotional force and substance. Once this internal consolidation of the external occurs, the "real" location of the meadow becomes insignificant. The significant thing—the highest reality, the "everlasting omen"—is what the poetic mind makes of its creative sources, and that regeneration occurs, for poet, for all.

Works Cited

Duncan, Robert. *The Opening of the Field*. New York: New Directions, 1960.
Zusne, Leonard. "A Cartography of the Uncharted Lands of the Mind." *Essays in Arts and Sciences* 10:1(May 1981).

V

CULTURE CRITICISM

The Mass-Media Celebrity: Big Star, Little Fan

"The rich man is a . . . thief."
St. John Chrystostom, *Homilies*

"Unfortunately in America today either you're a star or you're nobody."
Michael Bennett,
Director, *Dreamgirls*

The early 1990s triumphant proclamations of the collapse of world Communism by Capitalist America should be more modestly spoken by a nation that has an inexcusably huge deficit, ongoing and serious racism, Reaganism's brutal indifference to the poor and outrageous generosity to the rich, and crises in education, marital life, drug and alcohol consumption, sexual disease, public violence and so on. A subtler problem endemic to triumphalist American Capitalism, and expressed in its pernicious symptom of money as the maker and marker of human importance, is its cult of the mass-media celebrity.

A celebrity is defined as a famous or well-known person. Such a definition, however broad, still implies that the famed individual has done something important or valuable to deserve his or her scintillant reputation. While this is sometimes the case, all too often manipulative media techniques rather than numinous human talent underlie the contemporary phenomena of celebrity. And the end, as well as the means, of such media-derived fame, is the generation of billions of dollars, milked from the masses and fed to the overprivileged few who are superstars in the advertisement, sports and corporate worlds.

Any critique or stricture of mass-media celebrities could well be driven by more than a little outrage. Indeed, in view of the extravagant rewards accompanying media celebrity, it is a wonder that *more* people are not outraged by or seriously critical of those gilded deities. When a Michael Jackson grosses $125,000,000.00 in two years or a Jack Nicholson $50,000,000.00 (including residuals) for Joker in the movie *Batman*, the belittlement of the average person is the dark underside of such magnification. Thus the passive acceptance by or virtual endorsement of most Americans of astoundingly high salaries awarded to a small number of media-made stars is worth pondering.

Richard Schickel has some insightful observations to make accounting for our American passivity towards or even acceptance of both celebrities and their salaries. In his *Intimate Stranger*, he claims that celebrity is "a-possibly-*the*-most vital shaping (that is to say, distorting) force in our society" (p. 10), and that it "is singularly a subject that reaches into everyone's brain in strange and irrational ways" (p. 65). Schickel then suggests the dynamics of this interpretation of specifically but not exclusively film stars: " . . . the films . . . began to be perceived (albeit unconsciously) not as ends in themselves, discrete creations, but as incidents in a larger and more compelling drama—the drama of the star's life and career, the shaping and reshaping of the image of him or her that we carry in our minds" (p. 36). A character from literature, Joyce's Stephen Dedalus, Woolf's Mrs. Dalloway possibly makes a deep impression on a reader, but that impression or influence remains within the boundaries of the esthetic experience of a significant novel. Only a fatuous reader would so exalt Thomas Hardy's Tess Durberville as to wonder what Tess would think if one married for economic stability rather than for passion or would consider copying Jay Gatsby's particular strategy to win a Daisy Buchanan. Something about literary art develops or can develop a crucial sense of distance between even an attractive literary character and an influenceable reader, and that margin, traditionally called esthetic distance, is an important sign of a reader's ability to integrate and order the worlds of imagination with his own sense of reality (even the young reader in particular can sometimes derive inspiration or ideals from a first contact with great literature that could well lead to an enlarging sense of self-fulfillment or life possibility).

Although identification with a movie star might also generate strong ideals or ambitions in the fan, the disparity between the life circumstances of star and fan are often so extreme that the ideal is generally a foolish if not dangerous one to emulate. Schickel's thesis, central to his absorbing book, is that contemporary mass media have created an extreme distance between star and fan while simultaneously giving the fan the illusion through the potency of and simulated nearness produced by the media that star and fan are close. This widespread illusion can lead to dangerous extremes. As Schickel points out, "Violence . . . is a last despairing attempt to get the loved object to acknowledged the lunatic's fantasy of intimacy as a reality" (pp. 5-6). Most fans (the millions of them), if not driven to such extremes, nevertheless experience subtler corruption of their ideals by making gods and goddesses of mass-media celebrities and thus making some portion of their own lives and sensibilities spurious.

Film stars in particular, because of the deliberately exaggerated fluidity between their movie roles and publicized lives and the intense glamour encompassing and permeating both spheres, pervade the deepest reaches of sensibility of the influenceable fan. Considering, further, that the level of character or professional excellence embodied in some film stars does not appear to be particularly high, the influence of such stars on the young or upon other impressionable individuals can be quite pernicious. The point would not be to eliminate ideals or dreams or images of inspiring celebrities but to relate them to individuals and goals in ways that are more sensible and ennobling. Star fans not protesting superstar salaries not only undercut their own value or "price" but in effect affirm the right of the star to the monstrously swollen salary (such as Michael Jordan's $6,000,000.00 in 1990 for *non*-salary income alone).

Professional athletes, rock and movie stars, TV commentators, CEOs, investment bankers simply—or complexly—receive far too much money for their work or play. I am not urging a gray society of uniformly identical salaries in suggesting that the people who exhibit high skills in sports, who act, who perform popular music, who run corporations or present commentary (or simply news) on television should *not* be earning six digit annual salaries (let alone seven digit ones). Simple decency and social concord demand that a nation examine the propriety of paying a cleaning woman $6,000.00 for a year's hard work and a movie actor (or financier) millions for a single movie (or deal).

American society is fixated in an adoration of a small minority of individuals; it is an adoration that doubly—and unjustly—profits a few at the expense (in more ways than one) of the many. And the deep irony is that these stars make huge earnings on the basis of explicit and implicit standards that, as urged above, belittle those who "pay in" and, often, exalt those who receive both the vast pay and the massive publicity and dizzying fame. The commercial use of athletes to push sportswear or media stars to promote other products compounds the evil of the celebrity commercial subculture, for it puts additional millions of dollars in the pockets of celebrities already making millions a year. This not only further mischannels huge sums of money that could have been directed to better ends, but also increases the disparity of incomes in America. Thus, magnification and diminution of human beings are tautly intertwined aspects of media-celebrity culture.

Celebrity can confer god-like status on an individual. Indeed, "status" is too pale a word for the charged field that a "celeb" supposedly generates. He or she seems possessed of more than human force or energy or attraction, and the old meaning of the religiously luminous words—glory, splendor, radiance—appears to live again in the dazzle of celebrity. Surely this preternatural light, this electricity of great being, is genuine in some cases—artists as different, as say, Mark Rothko, Thelonious Monk, Stravinsky, Meryl Streep, Jean Renoir, Louise Nevelson, Marcel Proust, Ford Madox Ford, William Butler Yeats are (or were) magically gifted in their powers of creativity, performance or imagination. Society, civilization benefits from them enormously, and, indeed, some of the greatest of these artists, a Mozart, a Baudelaire, a Cezanne hardly received their due while alive. Unfortunately and very significantly, the insufficiently acknowledged greatness of a living Cezanne is all too much overbalanced by the excessive rewarding of even a *second*-string professional athlete, of a Barry Manilow, of an Elizabeth Taylor (the high point of whose acting career, according to Pauline Kael, occurred in the movie *National Velvet*, when Taylor was twelve).

That romance, once literary and chivalric, has in our century become a medium for Hollywood glamour and star cults, is of course nothing new today, with the contemporary barrage of mass media "impacting" the public from every direction with images of overrated or inflated celebrities. (The recent rise of such star-oriented media magazines as *People* and *Self* only intensifies the glittering presence of media celebrities in the public's mind.) But a grave side effect of the romance of the media "superstar," besides threatening the ego limits and even the sanity or life of the celebrity, is, again, the significant diminution of the worshippers. One may or may not be conscious of such belittlement, yet it can have much to do with how a person basically feels about himself.

However, the opposite sort of identification with a star can lead to an equally unhealthy self-inflation, or to the kind of fantasy involvements of intimacy between fans and stars that can result in a John Hinckley-Jodie Foster "relationship." This extreme identification can, as we know, have deadly results. As Schickel puts it, "Murder is the ultimate intimacy" (p. 180). Schickel elaborates these points earlier in his book: "violence . . . is a last despairing attempt to get the loved object to acknowledge the lunatic's fantasy of intimacy as a reality" (pp. 5-6). Granted, the case here concerns lunacy in the mind of the beholder, yet one must ask to what extent the star and the entertainment industry are to blame for this insane identification. They certainly bear more than a little responsibility, as they do for the extreme pervasion and *invasive* corruption of (particularly young) people's minds.

Schickel is well worth quoting at length on this last point: "many of us . . . are in daily spiritual communion with our celebrity favorites. At a certain point of overexposure to the endlessly transmitted, symbolically weighted images of famous people, these figures take up permanent residence in many inner lives as well, become, in fact, omnipresent functionaries in their reveries and fantasies, guides to action, to sexuality, to ambition" (p. 266). As a result, fans (and not just young ones) begin to falsify their own nature or character potential by assimilating romanticized, undesirable or unrealistic traits or ideals from celebrities some of who themselves are living schizophrenic lives or lies (as many intimate star biographies, from Humphrey Bogart and Joan Crawford to Rock Hudson and the once seemingly seamless Cary Grant, make clear). The subtly grave result is a character or personality formation (or deformation) based all too often on a fantasy or fake stellar personality.

Schickel suggests another force behind the glamour and idolizing of mass-media stars which he traces back to the 1920s: "the new celebrities had . . . plugged into the most basic of American fantasies, the dream of reward without apparent effort, the dream of being uplifted overnight" (p. 39). It is a fundamental irony of American culture that it contains both the go-getter, hard-working, self-made-man ideal on the one hand, and the alluring fantasy of overnight success or fame on the other. Societies can survive such ironies and paradoxes, but they are not necessarily beneficial. If the Horatio Alger myth nurtures the delusion that Americans are autonomous agents who can get along without one another, that all that counts is sufficient red-blooded American drive, know-how and desire (or greed), it seems down the generations to have evoked its "shadow" side, that Americans deserved a miracle no matter how limited their minds or talents if they simply had enough desire or luck to be awarded what they had not earned (of which the huge sweepstake-awards programs that litter society today like Biblical locusts are a telling example).

The glamour of celebrity fits into this cultural syndrome of the Instant Fortune all too well. In more ways than one, the film celebrity is often a not particularly exceptional person who is lucky (or unlucky) enough to be spotted by the film studios. That the Lucky One (Ava Gardner, Kim Novak, Ronald Reagan) often can't act any better than the average person on the street is besides the point, for all Americans are deserving (if some more than others). Yet, ironically, once one is swept up among the stars, dwelling in the stratosphere of exotic resorts, pearl-gray stretch limos, select parties in Bel-Air and Palm Springs, then the principle of exclusion begins, and what becomes paramount about the mass-media celebrity is not his or her likeness to the rest of us, but a deity status leading, among other things, to such maxims of distancing from the hoi polloi as Esther Williams' celebrity-survival etiquette: "Walk fast. Don't stop and shake hands. You touch them, they don't touch you . . . You also learn to avoid eye contact" (Schickel p. 5).

An individual's self-esteem in relation to media celebrities is, I feel, subtly and dangerously linked to American attitudes about success and failure. Money remains widely accepted as the primary gauge of the worth or at least the "success" of Americans. We very probably talk about nothing (not even sports) as much as we do about money. People might get angered by the outrageous salaries of top professional athletes, movie or TV stars, pop or rock performers, corporation heads or lawyers (not to mention that of an investment banker named David-Weill who, according to Ralph Nader, earned $50,000,000.00 in 1983—[p. 205]). Nevertheless, we Americans more or less accept the fact of stunningly large salaries (let alone inherited wealth, Paul Fussell's "Top Out-of-Sight" class such as the Rockfellers and the Duponts) partly out of resignation due to feeling helpless to curb them, and partly because huge salaries reside or originate in business and private enterprise, a supposedly sacrosanct domain in the American mental geography. A person deserves, the argument goes, whatever the market will bear or offer, though not enough is said about the serious *public* loss of monies in this system of aggrandizing massive private and corporate wealth, especially in the unethical form of gigantic and inadequately socialized corporate gains and power.

Little is said as well, strikingly ironic in a self-declared Christian nation, about the immoral character of making as much money as the "system" will allow—and more than it will allow, if possible (while many people are just getting by, and many aren't). Americans get conditioned to feel that the sky is the limit when it comes to profits; underlying that edifying ideal is the credo that America is great because it is a country where a man—but, traditionally, not a woman—can make his fortune.

The dark side of this ideal is that such uncontrolled pursuit of wealth has a seriously subversive effect both on economic stability (as distinct from economic prosperity) and on the realization of community in America. Such community means an acceptance of one's dependence on or connectiveness to either other individuals and groups or to a spiritually energizing ideal beyond the ego. The communal idea of human interdependence in turn suggests a limit on personal material aspiration. It also suggests something crudely unethical about the Rags-to-Riches dream, not because it is illusionary (Mike Tyson is cited by *Forbes* as making over $28 million dollars in 1990) but because it is "rugged individualism" burned down to its core of ruthless selfishness and unbridled self-advancement. If there is anything disturbing about the characteristic policies of the Reagan decade, it resides in their intense exalting of the rich and punishing of the poor. Indeed, the plethora of TV programs like "Lifestyles of The Rich and Famous," of magazines like *Unique Homes*, of publicity material about countless expensive ways of spending lots of money attests to the increase of wealthy people today with a corresponding increase of the homeless and destitute. Such a marked justification and celebration of wealth virtually revives Thorstein Veblen's gold-crusted phrase "Conspicuous Consumption" as the logos of the age. One message beneath this wealth worship is that if one cannot be a mass-media celebrity, he or she can try to ape a "celeb's" "lifestyle." Secular and even religious conceptions of honorable poverty become utterly unsustainable under the pressure of such gilded avarice, selfishness and display.

While private fortunes continue rising like the skyscrapers which all too crudely symbolize both corporate and private wealth, streets, bridges, job opportunities, schools, families and family life deteriorate; air, water and soil become polluted possibly irreversibly, through the excesses of industrial and consumption technology; and people more and more hype themselves all through the day and night on alcohol, drugs and life-threatening pills. All the uncompromising Biblical injunctions against greed are conveniently and continually overlooked in our society (and, of course, elsewhere—one need only recall the extreme disparity of wealth in many Latin American countries). Further, America rationalizes the predatory ruthlessness of some of its citizens (leading, ironically, to corporate concentration of financial and political power subversive of a free enterprise) by asserting the very questionable equation that Free Enterprise=Democracy, and by exhibiting versions of a plutocratic trickle-down process.

What can be done about the mental and social pathology of celebrity worship is hard to say. Human beings need numinous images, models, or experience to intensify and renew life and values. However, a critical shortcoming of modern mass societies like ours is that the sense of the holy has been vitiated by the mass-media commercialization of all values and experience. Twentieth-Century Americans are engulfed in what Norman Mailer long ago called "commercial totalitarianism." To expect education to solve or resolve the crises of an excessively high-pressured, uncontemplative society like ours is either naive or malicious, considering the formidable persuasive powers of the mass media, the extreme power of big business and government to manipulate American society and the willingness of educational institutions to comply in effect with the pressures exerted by such powers. Moreover, there are simply too many people today discontent with their lives, jobs, marriages, or social life, and too alienated from their own potential creativity or personal force, to tolerate life without the thrill or allure of media celebrities. If American society demands too much from the schools (including conformity to consumption values), it demands *far* too little from our vastly powerful business corporations and our national political and military institutions in the way of exemplifying noble standards of behavior and a morally compelling vision of reality.

As long as people can avail themselves of the glittering images of fraudulent celebrity so easily through television or VCRs, they will continue to fill their emptiness, discontent, or anxiety with the antics of these meretricious phantoms. This will go on as long as money and big money-making itself are over-esteemed. Vulgar, childish or gross taste is not so much innate as nurtured and stimulated socially. If the stimulation could be impeded by a non-authoritarian just cap on financial earnings to dim the lure of big-star careers and instant fortunes, it would change the spirit and structure of our society considerably and beneficially. The claim that such a ceiling would be communistic is correct if the implicit societal context is very early Christian rather than Soviet. However, a sane and decent salary and money culture is far off as long as the dollar remains our God and the Holy Spirit the green light to worship that god without restraint or scruple. If, as Thomas Carlyle held, "Society is founded on hero worship," and if our mass-media celebrities are our heroes, it is time for a revolution in sensibility.

Works Cited

Kael, Pauline. *Kiss Kiss Bang Bang*. New York: Bantam, 1969.
Nader, Ralph. *The Big Boys: Power and Position in American Business*. New York: Pantheon, 1986.
Schickel, Richard. *Intimate Strangers: The Culture of Celebrity*. New York: Doubleday, 1988.

Wanted: An American Intelligentsia

> "In [Matthew Arnold's] *Culture and Anarchy, Friendship's Garland,* and *Essays in Criticism,* ideas are crucial because they are the only instruments of social redemption. A society in which ideas are not found alive and vivid is doomed."
>
> Denis Donoghue, *England, Their England*

One of the major if quieter problems besetting America today is its lack of an adequate intelligentsia. Many organizations or groups fill a part of the need for one, but none fully functions as one. There are people in our society who mainly use their minds intellectually, that is, to generate, develop, savor, and evaluate ideas, trends, perceptions, emotions. These people are found in the editorial departments of publishing houses, in special research and funding institutes, libraries, newspaper and magazine staffs, academic and anti-academic journals and reviews, museums, high schools and other places.

Yet all these signs of intellectuals do not comprise an intelligentsia. Very important among the factors that could account for the inadequacy or even virtual non-existence of an American intelligentsia is the absence of a genuine or stable tradition of one, which is in no little part due to a long-standing American hostility towards or suspicion of intellectuals (described by Richard Hofstadter in his *Anti-Intellectualism in American Life*). In France, the concept of an intelligentsia is rooted in the early modern history of the country. Connected with the emergence of a middle class, the intelligentsia in France has long been literary and philosophical, its representatives not only philosophers, but novelists, satirists, essayists, poets. With the 19th-century cleavage between the intellectuals and the middle class, the bent of the French intelligentsia (in its bohemian aspect) changed to one of shocking the Bourgeoisie, indicating a severance from society or its normative class which in the 20th century many have unfortunately come to see as basic and eternal.

The art historian Arnold Hauser, discussing the rise of the intelligentsia in England historically, also intimates some problems endemic to an intelligentsia regarded socially: "It is not until the beginning of the mid-Victorian period that the intelligentsia comes forward in England as a group without ties, 'socially unattached,' 'beyond all class distinctions' 'mediating' between the classes" (v. 4, p. 132). Hauser extends the point about the developing alienation of the 19th-century European intelligentsia:

> The intelligentsia's apparent independence of the middle class, and consequently, of all social ties, is in accordance with the illusion, cherished by both the bourgeoisie and the intelligentsia, that the things of the mind live in a realm beyond the distinctions of class. The intellectuals try to believe in the absoluteness of truth and beauty, because that makes them seem the representatives of a 'higher' reality and because it compensates for their lack of influence in society . . . (p. 134).

Hauser's points are indeed applicable to American intellectuals today, who, whether on college campuses or not, are alienated by the absence of intellectual (as distinct from professional) community, and by living in a society that has little understanding of and use for them. Further, some intellectuals (described by Andrew Ross as "rentier" intellectuals), create their own isolation by either their disapproval of the larger, popular culture which surrounds them ("mass culture"), or by a defensive haughtiness toward the less literary or cultivated. If the wealthy person owns stocks, bonds, Rolls Royce and yachts, the intellectual has *his* Joyce, *his* Foucault, *his* Hugo Wolf, *his* Miró to show that his culture, being immaterial, is *his* wealth. To expect normal humility from intellectuals in a society that doesn't understand or care for their achievements in understanding or in synthesizing ideas is probably asking too much. Intellectuals, on the other hand, need to become more sensitive to the fear people generally have of an elite; recalling their own fear or resentment of other experts should remind them of the threat they could pose to the less cultivated, intellectual or intelligent.

Furthermore, intellectuals, by reducing some of the ego in their intellectual pursuits, make themselves more open to other people and to the larger culture (though trying to avoid being corrupted by it is no mean feat). Ross describes the traditional elitist or rentier intellectual (he cites Dwight McDonald) as being "unwilling to perceive the popularity of the native culture as a site of contestation" (p. 62). Yet what does this stricture really mean? Should the admirer of Rilke's or Thomas Pynchon's work also love country music or demolition derbies or pro ice hockey, or does Ross mean that the "Rilkean," armed with *The Duino Elegies*, should (somehow) mediate Rilke and Nashville? If so, how? One can certainly perceive Nashville or an NFL game as popular or mass spectacles but how that perception can lead to the use of such events as contestations of what used to be called "high" and "low" culture is not readily discernible.

Perhaps the advantage of a consciously alienated and *activated* intelligentsia is that it can function with a clear knowledge of its social role in society—its weight could be pivoted more effectively if its "classlessness" were sharpened into a critical stance, astutely conscious and thus purposive as a significant group in a society in need of a higher civilized purpose. Historically, such an intelligentsia could be revolutionary or at least pre-revolutionary as a result of being alienated, its class impotence or dissociation generating an ideology of social upheaval or renewal through adversity with or hostility towards the old order.

It is more likely, however, that such alienation and lack of connection with power or social responsibility can deprive intellectuals and artists of the crucial sense of the limits of reality, and can breed as well an arrogance or resentment towards centers of power or society itself that simply deepens the alienation perceived by Hauser and likely to occur anyway in complex and class-ridden mass societies. Thus isolated, the intellectual or artist comes to feel that he or she alone has a grasp of Reality or Truth, and comes to sadly enjoy this exclusive possessorship, pleased yet unhappy that the crowd worships brazen idols. Intellectuals have generally not exerted or experienced large-scale power in American society. According to David Riesman, "The New Deal and World War II gave many intellectuals and academic people a pleasant feeling of being close to the seats of power, of being in on big doings. To some extent, this feeling was delusive—an aspect of the amiable come-on Franklin Roosevelt practiced with many different groups . . ." (pp. 108-09). The administration of John F. Kennedy has also been regarded as a period when intellectuals were (or hoped to be) close to the throne of power, but Kennedy's tenure was too short to allow for significant acquisition of social and political power by intellectuals. In any case, intellectuals in positions of sizable social or political power probably would not behave better (consider Henry Kissinger under the Nixon administration) or worse than anyone else.

Perhaps there is something to be gained by some degree of distancing between an intelligentsia on the one hand, and the power centers of society at large on the other, as long as the gap is not too great. Some degree of social distancing could be essential for Utopian thinking, a valuable imaginative activity in modern secular societies, as someone has to keep conceptualizing and imaging ideals and alternative possibilities for better social organization and individual possibility. However, this distancing and *being* distanced probably does more harm than good, for it puts intellectuals out of touch with the everyday world and its quotidian outlook, corrupted or pedestrian as some intellectuals may consider them. Ross has put this point significantly: "Today, a code of intellectual activism which is not grounded in the vernacular of information technology and the discourse and images of popular, commercial culture will have as much leverage over the new nomination of modern social movements as the spells of medieval witches . . ." (p. 212).

The liberating imagination of the intelligentsia explains why intellectuals are often among the first sectors of a society that a regime, when it turns tyrannical, attempts to terrorize into silence. Autocrats realize the threat of the free, critical intellect and imagination, and move to stifle them instantly and often brutally.

Academic intellectuals do occupy a crucial area of power as influence (as well as a central place among contemporary intellectuals), and that of course is primary access to the minds and emotions of the young, some of whom will one day be running or at least shaping society. The "practical" men of power in the outside world realize and often distort this danger and periodically try to stigmatize the more bold or stimulating academics as Commies, pinkos, weirdos, atheists, "humanists" (unintentionally complimentary!), what have you. As long, however, as American intellectuals do not combine their considerable potential, businessmen, politicians, militarists and others will continue to impoverish and endanger our society by belittling the great need of society for ideas, dissent, intellectual exploration, and the deepening of sensibility, and by exaggerating the importance of money, commodities, material acquisition and national defense.

II

An intelligentsia might be regarded as a loose-knit yet identifiable community or association of intellectuals. An intellectual is an individual concerned primarily with ideas, but, crucially (or ideally), with values as well. An intellectual might or might not be an ideologist (for example, a Marxist, a Jungian), but usually has organized a system or at least a personal constellation of ideas, insight, beliefs, values and emotions by which he or she more or less structures the otherwise overwhelming phenomena of major modern events, natural and social disasters (earthquakes, wars, depressions), books, essays, films, developments in the arts and sciences, social and political currents, and so on.

Essential in a definition of an intellectual is a background or context of values in thinking and sensibility. Values designate standards, principles, ideas or ideals by which we determine the worth or nature of something—a work of art, person, apple, social movement, anything. If one can say that values embody an individual's set or constellation of esthetic, moral, philosophical criteria for deciding on the essential nature and *worth* of something, they as such involve evaluation, "valuing" or testing the essence of a movie, political candidate, novel, wine.

The idea of an intelligentsia might to some sound pretentious, outlandish, even suspect in the land of McDonald's, IBM, and Exxon, Hell's Angels, Jerry Falwell, Donald Trump, the Dallas Cowboys and, consummately, Ronald Reagan and George Bush. Yet it is the very existence of these peculiarly American phenomena that makes America desperately in need of an intelligentsia. Just as bad money and bad art drive out good, so bad taste and bad ideas and manipulated ignorance or prejudice or greed drive out the beauty, intensity and completeness of thought and feeling made possible by finer standards. Americans, for example, sorely need to become better educated or more sophisticated about political ideologies. The average person in our country assumes that everyone left of a Democrat is communistic, that a Socialist is a Communist (and vice versa), an Anarchist is only a terrorist or Bomb-thrower, and a Fascist is someone right-wing or racist or simply very conservative or oppressive. Some educating about different political ideologies might help to allay the virulent political hysteria in America particularly towards anything left-wing. This in turn could create for our nation a less hidebound reputation in world opinion. Also, a higher political culture in the average American might make it harder for our political and economic leaders to support right-wing regimes, as they so relentlessly have since World War Two because of the self-serving resistance of the latter to communism, as well as for conservative or reactionary politicians to stifle freedom of expression by labeling liberal or left-wing views "Communistic."

I pursue this extended definition of intellectuals to lead to the proposition that intellectuals are necessary, even crucially valuable people in any society, and that our society (not to mention others) is imperiled by its lack of an adequately responsive (and responded to), effectively unified intelligentsia. Some would scoff at this. We have, they might claim, college professors, advanced-research institutes, curators, journalists, librarians, educators, engineers, editors, poets, writers, artists, philosophers, scientists, among others—surely, they comprise an intelligentsia, a group of people with intellect. They might, but, as I see it, in our country they do not do so sufficiently. A country with intellectuals can be one thing, one with an intelligentsia something else. If there is a basic reason for this distinction with reference to the United States, it would seem that it has to do with the increased institutionalization of American society since World War Two. Individuals with highly developed minds, creativity, or erudition have been more and more orienting themselves vocationally towards such places as universities, corporations, law firms, and management posts.

Ever since the Second World War, universities have undergone enormous growth in student enrollments, faculty, administration, funding, research, athletic programs and physical plants. This development is not necessarily a cause for rejoicing; it has not exactly produced the universal improvement or individuation of the minds and feelings of all or most people. Russell Jacoby underlines the movement towards academe by American intellectuals and scholars: "By the 1960s the universities virtually monopolized intellectual work; an intellectual life outside the campuses seemed quixotic. After the smoke lifted, many young intellectuals had never left school; others discovered there was nowhere else to go. They became radical sociologists, Marxist historians, feminist theorists, but not quite public intellectuals" (p. 8).

Jacoby then tries to account for this drift towards the universities (which he feels leads to the "eclipse of *general* intellectuals" (p. 155): "Nor was the possibility of intellectual life outside the university enticing for the post-1940s intellectuals . . . to live from selling book reviews and articles ceased to be difficult: it became impossible. The number of serious magazines and newspapers steadily declined (and the pay scale of those remaining hardly increased), leaving few avenues; the signs all pointed towards the colleges" (p. 19).

To make matters worse for the growth of a vital or simply viable American intelligentsia, universities are in some basic ways hierarchic, regimented institutions. They certainly are not the ideal location for stimulating an avant-garde or for developing public intellectuals or bohemians. This would not be so bad if our society still provided low-rent neighborhoods with communal interchange in which bohemians, intellectuals, and artists could subsist and thus work and create (such as North Beach in San Francisco or Greenwich Village in New York before they became fashionable and thus too expensive for the very people who had made them attractive areas to live in). Academic tenure may provide bold, speculative or radical thinkers with some protection from community, special-interest, political or college-administration reprisal, but just the routine of teaching and researching often settles academics into grooves of specialization which can reduce the urgency of other concerns, including societal crises, like the universal and increasingly apocalyptical pollution, military-arms buildup, the plight of the poor, the homeless, the elderly. Why be deeply bothered about such crises when there is research to pursue about the influence of John Donne on early 20th-century American poets or the history of the concept of the social contract from Hobbes to Rousseau or the changing conceptions of geology since Lyell or evolution since Darwin? Further, university academics often are inclined or pressured by their departments to publish in periodicals that will advance their careers or insure academic celebrity rather than in places where they would have a larger or "lay" audience (one example of an academic who has striven for the widest possible audience is the astronomer Carl Sagan, whose essays in the mass-circulation weekly *Parade Magazine* on subjects like Nuclear Winter and American-Soviet-Union relations represent a significant achievement in popular academic journalism).

There can be of course something corrupting, sterilizing about permanent academic residence for artists and intellectuals. Aside from the customary "philistine" charges about the unreality of the university world, it can cramp the rich interchange, the flux and variety of events and experience that city life outside of academe provides. How many New York Abstract Expressionists would have gone on painting significantly had they taught *regularly* or full-time? Granted, some of them killed themselves slowly or quickly under the ruthless (but also invigorating) pressures of New York and its art world, but being artists *and* regular, full-time teachers would for many of these artists not have been a viable alternative.

Many poets have since World War Two been especially attracted to academe for obvious reasons. That a number of poets in the past did not have the stability to make much or anything of their academic posts is something that is less easy to assign blame for than at first appears. The desperation and general intemperateness of a Delmore Schwartz or a John Berryman perhaps results in part from family or personal psychopathology, but also reflect the virtual ostracism that any sensitive person (let alone an artist) feels living in a country in which the Business of America is Business. Being a poet or intellectual (however gifted or brilliant) in such a culture is brutally difficult. Public indifference to artists also has driven them into the universities.

For artists and intellectuals less heralded than Delmore Schwartz, the going is not easier, even if some are less prone to Schwartz's maniacal self-immolation. Working full time (on a newspaper, in an office or museum or library) drains creative energy, and teaching full time, with its particularly subtle dangers, can thwart or re-direct an artist's or intellectual's energies (despite occasional course releases, leaves or grants). Furthermore, Americans live in a far-flung, fast-paced society with many urban centers, which makes a national or even regional congregating by American intellectuals difficult. And the mass media are generally not receptive to subversive or bold ideas, Minority Reports, the visions of artists or the conceptualizations of intellectuals. On the other hand, academe offers a better environment for airing and pursuing ideas, theories and concepts than does, say, a bank or and insurance company. And those anti-academicians, from politicians and businessmen to anti-academic intellectuals, who propagate the platitude that academe is not the real world, simply don't know what reality or academe is if they assume that reality includes evil.

Some have felt that the closest America came to harboring an intelligentsia was centered in New York around a famous intellectual periodical. Whatever its flaws, *Partisan Review* from the late 1930s to the 1950s represented a voice and cultural and ideological distinctiveness impossible to find since (although some, including myself, found Dwight MacDonald's 1940s journal *Politics* more personable and humane). Discussing some of the individuals associated with *Partisan*, Irving Howe partly explains why that voice and distinctiveness existed:

> These New York writers constituted the first intelligentsia in American history—which is a shade different from a group of intellectuals. The figures near Emerson formed a community of intellectuals but not an intelligentsia—not, at least, as defined by Renato Poggioli: 'An intellectual order *from the lower ranks* . . . an intellectual order whose function was not so much cultural as political.' Poggioli had in mind the Russian writers of the late nineteenth century, but one can find points of similarity with the New York writers. We too came mostly from 'the lower ranks' (later composing rhapsodies about the immigrant parents from whom we instantly fled). We too wrote with polemical ferocity. We too stressed 'critical thinking' and opposition to established power. We too flaunted claims to alienation.

Shortly after, Howe also refers to the institutionalization of intellectuals: "In the early fifties, as jobs opened up in the universities, all this changed and the *Partisan-Review* group ceased being an intelligentsia—indeed, ceased being a group" (p. 140).

Of course it is tempting to idealize and glamorize the *Partisan* "crowd." Although some of these intellectuals and artists were friends, often enough they were in substantial and even violent disagreement with one another, again the result of the tendency of intellectuals to place intellectual integrity (also fueled by egoism, jealousy and obstinacy) above everything else. But however "fraternal" or divided such people as the Trillings or Mary McCarthy or Sidney Hook or Dwight Macdonald or Lionel Abel or Edmund Wilson or Clement Greenberg (to name just a few) have been over the past 40-50 years, the fact remains that even at their most concerted, the New York intelligentsia haven't had much impact either on mass American society or on the centers of social, economic and political power where the crucial decisions are usually made. Not only Ronald Reagan but probably even the far more informed and intelligent Jimmy Carter has no idea who Meyer Schapiro or Joseph Frank or Pauline Kael or Mark Rothko is (or was), and that ignorance, I feel, points to a crucial gap in our culture between art/intellect and power, and between art and society as well.

The New York intellectual world, engaged, bristling, vanguard as it traditionally has been for intellectuals throughout the country, has not amounted to or induced a national and thus a significantly authoritative intelligentsia. How could it have, given, again, the breadth and complexity and diversity of America? Further, this intelligentsia, at least as represented by *Partisan Review*, has been mainly oriented in its cultural enthusiasms towards Europe (Proust, Mann, Kafka, Joyce, Picasso, and so on). Yet if we look at San Francisco, we see a strikingly different cultural orientation that, with some tolerance for generality, could be termed Asian. Certainly some of the most important writers and artists long associated either with San Francisco or the West Coast—Kenneth Rexroth, Gary Snyder, Mark Tobey, Richard Diebenkorn, Morris Graves, to mention a few, have been more influenced by Chinese and Japanese culture than they have been by *Partisan Review's* European cultural idols. According to Rexroth,

> People in the rest of the United States . . . have difficulty in adjusting to the fact that the Pacific Coast of America faces the Far East, culturally as well as geographically. There is nothing cultish about this. . . . The residents of California, Oregon, and Washington are as likely to travel across the Pacific as across the continent and the Atlantic. Knowledge of the Oriental languages is fairly widespread. The museums of the region all have extensive collections of Chinese, Japanese, and Indian art. Vendantist and Buddhist temples are to be seen in the coast cities. And of course there are large Chinese and Japanese colonies in every city . . . besides the direct influence of the Orient on them, the Seattle painters, Graves, Tobey, and Callahan, the Portland painter Price, the San Francisco abstract expressionists, have all avoided the architectural limited-space painting characteristic of western Europe from the Renaissance to Cubism . . . (*Bird in the Bush, Obvious Essays* pp. 47-48).

And though the picture became complicated when East came West in the form of Allen Ginsberg, Gregory Corso, Jack Kerouac, and Lawrence Ferlinghetti, to *help* bring off the San Francisco Renaissance, the fact remains that it was out West that "Howl" and the Beat writers first exploded.

San Francisco was in part receptive to the Beats because it had already had a significant art culture for at least two decades, beginning with the arrival of Kenneth Rexroth and his first wife Andrée Dutcher from Chicago in 1927. In the 1940s poets like Robert Duncan, William Everson (Brother Antoninus), Jack Spicer, Weldon Kees, Philip Whalen and others began either to emerge locally or arrive from other places in the West (some arriving, like Everson, at the end of the war from the Waldport, Oregon detention center for Conscientious Objectors). Further, the California School of Fine Arts, located in North Beach in San Francisco, had artist-teachers like Clifford Still on its faculty and students like Ernest Briggs, and artists like Richard Diebenkorn, David Park and Elmer Bischoff resided in the Bay Area. Rexroth, well before becoming the "Librarian" to the Beats and serving as a significant mentor to Duncan and other literary youngsters, had been active in Bay Area Anarchist discussion circles, creating a lively format thereby for new ideas about art, culture, politics and society, an activity extended by George Leite's magazine *Circle*, located in Berkeley. Thus, it is erroneous to regard the Beats as coming to San Francisco to "make" the San Francisco Renaissance. They were a significant later phase of a vital cultural scene that had existed for years before their arrival, and without which they might not have received as much attention as they did.

The New York scene is one—though a great one indeed—among many cultural centers (another one being Los Angeles from the 1930s on in the literary arts, and from the 1970s on in the increasingly active visual-arts scene). Further, the tendency of such separations and multiplicities of cultural centers, rather than signifying a healthy pluralism, suggests a division and thus dilution of force which, if somehow more centered and concentrated, could perhaps add up to an *American* intelligentsia of range and proportions that would command attention and respect from either or both the nation and the "Power Elite" itself.

The old *Partisan Review's* distinctive stance of high-brow (if ungenteel), ideological, vanguard engagement certainly is not identifiable in most serious contemporary periodicals, many of whose contributors are academics and not located in big cities. *Partisan* did possess a consistent tone, esthetic, and ideological orientation for many years under Philip Rahv, William Phillips and William Barrett, on whose banners Marx, Freud, Kafka, Eliot, Mann, Proust were, among others, battle-cry names indeed. No current journal or review that I can think of quite pulls together a "class" or group of intellectuals or artists with a sufficient identity of values and culture and social-philosophical outlook to form a kind of intellectual consensus, conscience and even a community of sorts. Given the diversity, breadth and complexity of American society, perhaps such a publication is not possible. Perhaps all one can expect is the multiple groups of coincident interests and values created by the good general and specialized periodicals we already have. Such a variety of periodicals are crucial in forming what Robert A. Nisbet (and Peter Kropotkin before him) described as intermediary communities to protect the individual from the direct pressure of the state and diversify and enrich his or her range of social outlets and networks. Serving as more than media for expression of significant views, such media also permit people to identify a community of values they can align themselves with.

Yet a periodical that is even exclusively devoted to forming or aligning an intellectual community, an intelligentsia, is what, among other things, is needed today, hard as it may be to subsidize, and free as it should be of academic or corporation sponsorship or control. Ezra Pound once said that the poet is the antennae of the race. I would urge a variation of that van-guard maxim: The intellectual and the artist are—or could and should be—the moral, emotional and perceptual consciousness and conscience of a country. When it became known in the mid-1950s that France, a nation that had stood for high European civilization for centuries, was torturing "its" Algerians, it was the intellectuals (Jean-Paul Sartre and others) who raised a cry of protest, and whose protest registered a dramatic impact on an entire nation. When Alfred Dreyfus was framed for treason in the 1890s by a complex of violently reactionary forces, it was another intellectual (*and* literary artist), Émile Zola, whose words—"j'accuse!"—rang memorably in protest against the right-wing, anti-Semitic attempts to crucify the French-Jewish military officer. Henry David Thoreau's spending a night in jail for not paying war taxes is overly famous in our own culture, at least compared to the under-publicized anti-war activists in our era held for multi-*year* sentences in American prisons for "assaulting" nuclear war installations with hammers and crowbars (such as the Reverend Carl Kabat, who spent *seven years* in a Federal penitentiary in Sandstone, Minnesota), but Thoreau's is undeniably a symbolic gesture of moral protest by an intellectual. The Sacco-Vanzetti trial and execution evoked an enormous resistance in the 1920s among intellectuals, artists, radicals and others, and Kenneth Rexroth was surely right when he claimed that that execution represented a major and dark watershed in the 20th century American life. (And in the early 1990s the Salmon Rushdie case has rallied and united literary intellectuals internationally in a manner hard to excel probably in large part because of the literal terrorization by the "censors.") The Sacco-Vanzetti Case did arouse something in America resembling an intelligentsia, as did the Vietnam War (though that war certainly aroused other important sectors of the population too). Further, New York City writers and artists in particular have occasionally bonded together (especially P. E. N.) to protest the serious abuse of artists and intellectuals by repressive regimes throughout the world, a manifestation of sorts of an American intelligentsia.

III

Given such responses among intellectuals and others to critical social events, can one say that nothing is really inadequate about our intelligentsia, and, indeed, that America *has* an intelligentsia? That when it's needed, it's there, and thus must exist? But the Sacco-Vanzetti trial did lead to the execution and Vietnam did last long enough to become in different ways a shattering experience for both nations (but especially for Vietnam). Speculation that a fully mobilized or more cohesive intelligentsia might have either prevented or at least shortened that war overlooks the fact that many intellectuals supported the war up to 1969 or so. The inaction or nihilism of the German intelligentsia during the 1920s, Thomas Mann intimates in *Dr. Faustus*, helped smooth the way for Hitler.

Sartre, in his *public* response to his country's Nazi-derived torturings of a colonial people, aroused a nation (though one should also recall that Sartre supported Stalinist Communism into the 1950s). Over 50,000 people, including Yves Montand and Simone Signoret, attended Sartre's funeral. How many Americans would attend the funeral of, say, Harold Bloom, or even that of a more overtly political American intellectual like Noam Chomsky or Irving Howe? To be sure, France, with its one great, centralizing city, is a far smaller country than the United States, which makes an organized, effective community of intellectuals easier to achieve. It is also a country that respects, even reveres, its artists and intellectuals. As Ernst Robert Curtius says in *The Civilization of France*, "In France, and in France alone can literature be regarded as the nation's most representative form of expression. . . . All the national ideals of France are colored and shaped by literary form. In France if a man wishes to be regarded as a politician he must be able to express himself in some form of literature. If he desires to exert influence as a speaker he must have a thorough knowledge of the collective literary treasure of the nation" ([1962] p. 91). Imagine

George Bush, Bill Clinton or Ross Perot quoting Hart Crane or Thomas Pynchon to make a hit with the American people during a campaign speech. This is not to say that every Frenchman can quote Racine or loves Baudelaire's verse; many (according to Theodore Zeldin) don't even know who these writers are or even read newspapers. Yet respect for artists and intellect resides at the center of French culture while it exists only on the circumference of the American culture. Admiration of artists and intellectuals is not a noticeable trait in American culture (except for the odd superstar), and that has significance for a viable American intelligentsia.

Academics were often effective in mobilizing ideas and people against the Vietnam War and in bringing speakers to campuses where forums, lectures, speeches and demonstrations made a strong impact on a key area of a society at war, its youth. This experience suggests the obvious and crucial fact—that academic intellectuals, despite their extreme unpopularity among some sectors of American Society, *can* occupy a vital role in helping develop or organize an intelligentsia around a key national issue or crisis. But generally, elaborating an intelligentsia through the colleges has not occurred and probably won't, all things considered. Professors are in part hobbled by the routinizing curb of classes to teach, and perhaps even more by an understandably obsessive involvement in research either to gain tenure or to keep abreast of scholarship. As a result, academics tend to become temperamentally conservative and disinclined to function as *public* intellectuals. Conceivably, one way out of such hermeticism would be genuine college encouragement of faculty to take part in significant academic-related public service. Even this could be problematic, however, for if a public-minded or activist professor feels it is in the public interest to openly criticize the pollution record of a nearby corporation or factory, and if the school receives funds from the polluting organization, the green flow (or subtler fluxes) towards the college might soon cease. Today academe's being morally compromised by its relations with powerful social-economic interests tends to sizably limit university support of committed academic public intellectuals.

What could be an outlet from this impasse and rewarding and far-reaching in consequence is a community of intellectuals and artists consisting of *both* academics and non-academics, of professors, high-school teachers, writers, artists, magazine, newspaper and book-publishing editors, lawyers, business people, priests, rabbis and ministers, librarians, actors, carpenters, engineers, bankers, doctors, architects, dentists and others. The non-academics could give the professors more of a sense of how the "real" or "outside" world operates, and the academics could instill in their non-cloistered associates more respect for disciplined conceptualizing and researched support of generalizations, perceptions, and judgments. Some academics could be helped either to see or develop interest in issues beyond the theoretical or hypothetical by interaction with the non-academics in city forums, symposia, town-hall meetings and the like (some academics of course do directly interact professionally with society), and non-academic intellectuals could gain by sharing of or confrontation on ideas with teacher-scholars who generally have more time for study and abstract thinking than they have. Not all academics are intellectuals (let alone *public* intellectuals), as their range of intellect or originality with ideas is not sufficiently broad or probing, nor do they often appear to have a sense of themselves as the premier moral, esthetic, or intellectual authority of their nation, a role, as suggested earlier, hardly acknowledged by American society.

Non-academic professionals and skilled workers, for their part, are not always intellectuals, but often enough are or could be. But an intelligentsia is not, or need not be, an elitist club of some sort (though intellectuals are as prone to snobbery—"Oh, you haven't read Proust in *French*?!"—as any group). The major "criteria" should be a moral, esthetic, or philosophic passion for ideas, learning, or values, and a drive to relate them to a sense of the major issues, crises, evils, virtues or trends of a given time. Certainly anyone from a chaired Professor at Harvard to a carpenter's apprentice can aspire to this noble calling of relating thought and value to social reality. Academics, because of their professional environment and specialized training, tend to be elitist in good and bad senses of the word; non-academics, on their side, can be as philistine or smug as denizens of the "real" world. But these are only tendencies in either sphere. If everyone had to be a saint before he or she could aspire to a significant realization of intellect or values, far less would be achieved in permeating the world with culture than has been.

Jacoby addresses the crucial need in America to extend (or recruit) an intelligentsia *beyond* academe:

> To identify intellectuals with academics and their fate almost capitulates to the historical juggernaut; it implies that to be an intellectual requires a campus address. Others are barred. Why? Even apart from plumbers or carpenters who might be intellectuals, some professions

> would seem to possess at least the prerequisites, if not a claim, to join this group. For instance, of the 136,000 full-time librarians in the United States, might not some or many be intellectuals? And what about booksellers and editors, lawyers and doctors, journalists and foundation managers? Are they forever excluded from the ranks of intellectuals simply for the lack of a university letter-head? (p. 220)

Having been a professional librarian in New York City for four years and employed in a book-publishing house for two years, I can support Jacoby's claims for librarian intellectuals through my own professional contacts. I encountered as well erudite people among editors, doctors, lawyers, engineers and others. Also, these types of professionals possess skills, worldly connections, private-and public-institution experience and other expertise that the average academic might well envy, and from which s/he could learn much. Moreover, in view of how long male academics (both intellectual and non-intellectual) have readily tolerated or even implemented job discrimination against female academics, they should ponder more than they apparently do the deeper implications of being a part of non-equalitarian social structure which has also seriously compromised itself morally for decades by contracting research from the Defense industry (though some academic scientists are refusing to engage in research of this nature).

An even larger stricture of academe and academics of both sexes is centered in Ivan Illich's charge that schools (including universities), while flaunting the myth of an equalitarian society, actually certify a "class-conscious reality" (p. 80—a position also forwarded persuasively in Paul Fussell's *Class*). Illich's critique is a powerful one indeed, though not to be pursued here. Academics, however personally libertarian, iconoclastic or rebellious, participate in a certification of student marketability or "commodification" that, according to Illich, gives professionalism vast sway over modern societies and puts people at the mercy of experts, professionalists, specialists. This technocracy sizably reduces the room for individual and communal learning, discovery and creativity, and rigidifies society into a caste structure. College professors, intellectual or otherwise, participate in this constricting, anti-libertarian certifying activity (such rebellion as giving all As being childish and unethical for obvious reasons). Thus the academic institutionalization of intellectuals, according to Illich's thesis, almost automatically bends them into certifiers of a far more subtle and pervasive authoritarianism than even a crafty lunatic like Josef Stalin could devise. However, getting outside of academe by joining non-academic intellectuals, artists, and others for various significant social, political, artistic, spiritual activities could counter a college professor's involvement in academic technocracy, and perhaps even give him or her ideas, motivation or courage to battle the degree mill and bullying professionalism.

The association of academic and non-academic intellectuals could even be organized and centered to deal with national and international crises that require a unified, bold and trenchantly critical voice (something resembling this was set up in the early 1980s when some academics began to fear Ronald Reagan was going to have American troops invade Nicaragua; on the other hand, the silence or silencing of the American intelligentsia during the 1991 Gulf War suggests both the weakness of our intelligentsia and the sinister scope of power of the Government, the Pentagon and the mass media when working in unison). It would take some will and drive and of course some organizing skills, and perhaps a loose-knit governing board or association to develop, order, and sustain activities, purposes, scope and potential. Another invaluable medium for organizing and informing an intelligentsia, as it has been for developing and stimulating an intellectual audience, is the listener-supported radio station, like KPFA in Berkeley, KPFK in Los Angeles, and WBAI in New York. This type of radio-programming has for decades featured artists, intellectuals and academics in a rich variety of culturally serious formats, and could easily veer even more than it has towards centralizing and expediting intelligentsia goals of a public or socially critical nature. Another valuable media dimension of course is PBS television, which, with its basic visual orientation, can through image dramatize certain topics—waste hazards, for example—more effectively than radio can (though its dependence on big corporation sponsorship can be inhibiting).

One reason such a broad-based group (or, perhaps, groups) is needed is to apply insuperable pressure to critical public institutions or corporate organizations capable of disastrous evil such as the American Presidency, Congress, the big corporations, mass media, special-interest lobbies (NRA, AMA, NAM, for example), the Pentagon, the FBI, the CIA, the NSA, and industrial polluters. There are, certainly, special, disciplined organizations (such as Ralph Nader's consumer-defense groups) already dealing specifically and technically with these problems; these organizations, no doubt, do more *practical* good than all the finest insights of an intelligentsia combined. According to Andrew Ross, "it has been argued, most cogently by Foucault, that 'technical' or 'specific' intellectuals, whose purview of political action is linked to specific struggles that demand their specific knowledge and expertise, must increasingly form the basis of decentralized opposition. From the time of the first postwar pressure groups against the development of the hydrogen bomb, it has been scientific intellectuals rather than humanists who have been at the forefront of this professional activism" (p. 210). One reason such intellectuals are needed is that many problems and evils today are in themselves technical matters, and require more than a general intelligence and cultivation to understand, let alone deal with (for example, the exact nature of the danger of nuclear plants).

Yet other events or developments—crises, symptomatic and misunderstood issues, events, trends—might better be met by astute *general* analysis and moral, humanistic evaluation by artists, philosophers, social scientists, writers and scientists throughout the country. For example, such topics as the impact of Puritanism on American society or culture, American mobility, the American attitude towards art and artists, the nature of racism in modern America, the role of food or sex or sports or time or charity or leisure in American society are matters deliberations upon which are likely to benefit as much from the general intellectual as from specialists or technical intellectuals, because the former probably speaks from a broader base of knowledge and values than the specialist and thus offers a crucially needed spaciousness of context that the historian of early 18th Century Connecticut Puritanism might fail to provide. Indeed, one valuable function of the general or public intellectual is to prevent ideas or knowledge from becoming so specialized or technical as to be beyond general educated understanding or criticism. For example, we have been told repeatedly that computers are revolutionizing knowledge and its accessibility, transmission and quantity, without being told what the costs of this modern technology are economically, philosophically, ethically, psychologically—and ecologically (a critical consideration, because discarded computers when crushed give off toxic lubricants dangerous to natural resources like underground water). The ethical or psychological impact of computers—that's a broad, crucial subject for broadly learned, richly speculative minds, and the more individual the response, the greater the number and sharing of such responses, the more likely a fertile creativity and consensus of ideas, insights, realizations and proposals could result.

Also, in times of national (and international) crisis, such as whether to go to war, our major poets, novelists, philosophers should be given a platform on such issues in view of their general wisdom about human nature and human societies. Lewis Mumford once pointed out that public places (including buildings) would have been far more beautiful—and thus society itself—had artists played a role in city planning instead of undergoing the alienation from our society integral to esthetic modernism. Artist intellectuals possess a heightened sense of the Beautiful (and the Ugly) woefully untapped by some modern societies, certainly the United States. The result has been a strident sinister ugliness both in public places and in the general sense of the esthetic pervading modern societies.

Individualist dissent, to be sure, can be a hazard of the intellectual mind and habit; such individualized (and, sometimes, egoistic) dedication to pursuing and grasping the truth no matter how labyrinthine or unpopular can lead to serious paralysis of social action as polarized or even allied intellectuals battle a point to the death. Further, intellectuals and artists are as prone to the Seven Deadly Sins as anyone else. All this is the price one pays for intellectual involvement, and it could be high. But it must be risked.

Of course some people have no use for intellectuals at all. Joseph Epstein in an essay review of James Gould Cozzens designed to restore Cozzens to a high place after his critical demolition by the left-wing likes of Dwight Macdonald, discusses Cozzens's attack on intellectuals in *Guard of Honor*. One character refers to the "differences that always arise between those who have to deal with fact, and those who are free to deal with theories." And "Another character feels himself obliged to admire a simple, unlimited integrity that accepted as the law of nature such elevated concepts as the Military Academy's Duty-Honor-Country, convinced that these were the only solid goods; that everyone knew what the words meant" (p. 343). Contempt for or suspicion of theory is of course very American, theory to some native minds redolent of intellectuals, professors, communism, Karl Marx, certainly of foreign ideas. But Cozzens's wording, ignored by Epstein, bears a closer look. The people who "have to deal with fact" are usually those that cannot or will not theorize to begin with, doing little or no reading (or, at least, no conceptual reading) and thus having no grasp of any serious tradition or system of ideas, and thus none of their own ideas, having no idea of what had been thought before by which to place or measure their own thinking or ideas. Also, some of those people forced to confront facts misuse or abuse them. Cozzens implies that factualists are somehow innately decent people, facts supposedly being a close neighbor to practicality and thus truth, whereas theorists are slick types ready to pull some ideology over one's eyes (or head). Cozzens and his fact-fellows (including Epstein) conveniently forget that the human mind is as capable of generality and generalization as it is of facts, that the two can work together to expand human awareness, possibility, and effective planning and action, and that human beings can think and act as evilly with facts as they can virtuously or ideally with theories. As far as "simple, unlimited integrity" goes, some integrity is not simple; there are times when one can agonize morally about one's duty to one's country and one's duty to another moral "law" (calling duty, honor, country laws of nature is simplistic and question-begging, anyway), surely something some American soldiers felt—retrospectively, at least—about invading Panama in 1989 to capture one man, perhaps killing 3000-4000 civilians in the process. How simple is duty for a person working in a chemical manufacturing plant that is polluting his town? Duty to the company? To the town? To one's family? Or oneself? These are often not easy matters to decide, certainly not likely to be solved merely by "simple, unlimited integrity." Complexity of thought, awareness of options, clarity of thought process—these are activities or states of intellection, and one need not have read Plato in Greek or Pascal or Kierkegaard or even Bertrand Russell's simpler books to see the value of major thinkers attempting to confront reality complexly, thoroughly or justly.

In the meantime the major societal problems and evils go on seething, and it will take not only Nader's groups or Common Cause or the Union of Concerned Scientists or Educators for Social Responsibility but also an aroused and reasonably cohesive intelligentsia to confront the crises and trends that could ruin our country. Our Government built a stealth bomber a few years back at a cost of around half a billion dollars, and it had planned to build 132 more at a total cost of 68 *billion* dollars. Both that monstrous invention and any rationale for it are the sort of thing to be vigorously criticized not only by organizations like UCS or by formidable activists like Dr. Helen Caldicott, but also, if more generally or broadly, by an organized intelligentsia with the power or connections to transmit its critical position on such matters to the strategic power sectors of American society, or, at least, to social officials or media that can have a real impact on those sectors.

One familiar reason why both the American intellectual and his country have suffered is the traditional alienation between the two. The result has been a nation without the benefit of perception and vision from some of its most humanistically acute, creative or learned minds, and an intelligentsia without a broader or socialized function, and thus without significant contact with and impact on society and reality. The prevailing attitude, that the critical issues often underlying the important decisions in big business, in politics, in the military, in social services are best left to the "practical" people—the politicians, merchants, lawyers, CEOs—and that the intellectuals should stick to their classrooms and little magazines, is pernicious. Letting former CEO Roger Smith "take care" of Detroit's Poletown led to the leveling of an old residential district and the eviction of its inhabitants (many elderly) for a new, city-tax-supported GM center. Paul Goodman's book title, *The Society I Live In Is Mine*, certainly applies here: the business of America should *not* be business; it should be enhancing the quality of life for as many people as possible, regardless of race, creed, or sex, and that submerged American ideal will be more deeply realized if the ethical vision and humane awareness of a society is sizably informed by its most compassionate and humane intellectuals.

Furthermore, intellectuals are an important source of ideas in at least two senses. First, they generally can provide more new ideas about life, society, art, politics, philosophy, religion than the average person because they spend more time reading and thinking than most people do. Ideas might not always be practical or realistic or "business-oriented," but at their best they offer (as Denis Donoghue observes in the Matthew Arnold epigraph to this chapter) the possibility of "social redemption," vitalized media for renewing human and societal creativity and meaning. Secondly, they can clear the path for the New by astute analysis and criticism of the Old. Whatever is oppressive, paralyzing, inhumane, wasteful or simply meaningless in the status quo needs the confrontation with and strictures of a society's best and boldest minds (not always intellectuals) to liberate and develop both society and the individual.

As isolated or institutionalized persons, intellectuals can be ridiculed or ignored. But united, they could embody a significant force for far more moral, esthetic, and humane refinement of societal purpose and individual potential than now exists. It all lies initially in believing that an operative, effective, unifiable intelligentsia is a viable possibility, and that the times are sufficiently imperiling to demand an intelligentsia. What, after all, is the worth of a "fine intellect" and a heightened sensibility if they are not used to articulate and promulgate the highest moral, esthetic and humanistic ideals conceivable for a society and to rigorously assess, expose and resolve a society's besetting evils and manias? One thing is certain: without such a class or community, the general moral character and life quality of American society will likely continue to deteriorate, possibly to a point of no return.

Works Cited

Curtius, Ernst Robert. *The Civilization of France*. New York: Random House, 1982.
Epstein, Joseph. *Plausible Prejudices*. New York: Norton, c1985.
Fussell, Paul. *Class*. New York: Ballantine Books, 1987.
Goodman, Paul. *The Society I Live In Is Mine*.
Hauser, Arnold. *The Social History of Art* 4. New York: Knopf, 1958.
Hofstadter, Richard. *Anti-Intellectualism in American Life*.
Howe, Irving. *A Margin of Hope: An Intellectual Biography*. New York: Harcourt, Brace, Jovanovich, 1982.
Illich, Ivan. *Towards a History of Needs*. New York: Bantam, 1980.
Jacoby, Russell. *The Last Intellectuals: American Culture and the Age of Academe*. New York: Basic Books, 1987.
Mumford, Lewis. *The Story of Utopias*. New York: Viking Press, 1962.
Porter, Melinda Camber. *Through Partisan Eyes: Reflections on Contemporary French Arts and Culture*. New York: Oxford University Press, 1986.
Rexroth, Kenneth. *Bird in the Bush: Obvious Essays*. New York: New Directions, c1959.
Riesman, David. *Selected Essays from Individualism Considered*. New York: Doubleday, 1954.
Ross, Andrew. *No Respect: Intellectuals and Popular Culture*. New York: Routledge, 1989.
Zeldin, Theodore. *France 1845-1945: Taste and Corruption*. New York: Oxford University Press, 1980.
—. *The French*. New York, Random House. c1983.

Index

Abel, Lionel 169
Abrams, M. H.
   Natural Supernaturalism 51
academic intellectuals 164, 174, 175, 177
Alger's (Horatio) myth 156
Ali, Muhammad 2
   The Greatest: My Own Story 80, 90, 95, 96
altruism 16
American culture 174
American society 154
American universities 166, 167
anality 51, 52
animism 26
apocalyptic 3, 36
Armstrong, Louis 138
art 149
artist 149
artist intellectuals 179
Bantu Philosophy 82
Barrett, William 171
Bartlett, Lee 118
Baudelaire, Charles Pierre 155
Beats, the 170, 171
beau lieu 144, 148
beautiful place 144
Berdyaev, Nicolas 122
Berry, Thomas 30
Berry, Wendell 33
Berryman, John 168
Bischoff, Elmer 171
Black Muslimism 84, 97, 98
Blake, William 39, 148
Bloom, Harold 173

Bogart, Humphrey 156
Book of Revelation 37, 41, 42, 49, 51
"Break on Through to the Other Side!" 36
Briggs, Ernest 171
Brower, David 33
Brown, Bundini 80
Bufithis, Philip H. 76
Burgess, Anthony 26
Bush, George 174
Caldicott, Dr. Helen 180
Carlyle, Thomas 160
Carson, Rachel 33
Carter, Jimmy 169
CEOs 154
Cezanne, Paul 155
Chamard, Henri 9
Charles I, King 54
Chomsky, Noam 173
Christianity 54
Clark, Henry 89
Clinton, Bill 174
Cohn, Norman
   The Pursuit of the Millenium 51
"commercial totalitarianism" 159
computers 178
Conrad, Joseph 75
Corso, Gregory 170
Cozzens, James Gould 179, 180
Crane, Hart 174
Crawford, Joan 156
Crich, Gerald 30, 31
Curtius, Ernst Robert
   The Civilization of France 173
Daleski, H. M. 66

de La Fayette, Mme. 9, 14
de Mourgues, Odette 9
de Sablon, Mme. 9, 14
de Sévigné, Mme. 14
death 40
Delany, Paul 27
Diebenkorn, Richard 170, 171
Donne, John
  "The Canonization" 37
Donoghue, Denis 45, 51, 181
  Thieves of Prometheus 51
Douglas, Justice William O. 24, 25
Dreyfus, Alfred 172
Duncan, Robert 1, 2, 5, 170, 171
  "Often I Am Permitted to Return to a Meadow" 5
  The Opening of the Field 145
Dundee, Angelo 93
Duponts, the 157
Dutcher, Andrée 170
Early, Gerald 95
  "Hot Spics Versus Cool Spades: Three Notes Towards a Cultural Definition of Prize-fighting" 83
eco-monism 2, 24
egotism 38
Eliot, T. S. 55, 127
emotions, the 12, 19
Epstein, Joseph 179, 180
eschatology 42
Eshleman, Clayton 117
esthetic impersonalism 127
Etruscans 28
Everson, William (Brother Antoninus) 170, 171
Ferlinghetti, Lawrence 170
Ford, Ford Madox 155
Foreman, George 77, 88
Foster, Jodie 156
Frank, Joseph 169
Franklin, Benjamin 32
Frazier, Joe 84, 85
French intelligentsia 172
Freud, Sigmund 8, 10, 17
Friedman, Alan 53
Frye, Northrop 1
Fussell, Paul 157
  Class 176
Gardner, Ava 157

general intellectuals 178
Gibson, Morgan 131
Gilbert, Sandra 49
Ginsberg, Allen 170
Goodman, Paul
  The Society I Live In Is Mine 181
Grant, Cary 156
Grant, Ulysses S. 13
gratitude 16
Graves, Morris 170
Greenberg, Clement 169
Greer, Germaine 64, 68
Groddeck, Georg 15
Gulf War (1991) 177
Hamalian, Linda 129
Hardy, Barbara 49
Hardy, Thomas 18, 153
  "In Tenebris II" 18
Hauser, Arnold 162
Hemingway, Ernest 74, 75, 78, 87, 95
Hinckley, John 156
Hofstadter, Richard 161
  Anti-Intellectualism in American Life 161
Hook, Sidney 169
Howe, Irving 169, 173
"Howl" 170
Hudson, Rock 156
human survival 35
hylozoism 26, 28, 29, 47
Illich, Ivan 176
intellectuals 5
intelligentsia in France 161
investment bankers 154
Jackson, Michael 153
Jacoby, Russell 166
Joachim of Floris 52
Johnson, Magic 77
Johnson, Shirley 120
Jordan, Michael 75
Jung, Carl 144
  Collective Unconscious 145
Kabat, Reverend Carl 172
Kael, Pauline 155, 169
Kees, Weldon 170
Kennedy, John F. 163
Kenyon Review 117
Kermode, Frank 37, 51, 66
  D. H. Lawrence 52

Index

Kerouac, Jack 170
King, Don 86
Kissinger, Henry 164
Kropotkin, Peter 172
La Rouchefoucauld, Francois (Duc de) 2, 8
   The Maxims 8
Lawrence, D. H. 1, 2, 3, 24, 25, 26, 27, 79, 83, 121, 122
   blood consciousness 26, 74
   "dark gods" 32, 33
   Rananim 24, 39
   Works:
      "All Souls" 44
      Apocalypse 32, 37, 50, 83
      "Apropos of *Lady Chatterley's Lover*" 67
      Birds, Beasts and Flowers 122
      "December Night" 44
      "Dies Illa" 37
      "Dies Irae" 37
      Etruscan Places 29, 32, 33, 50, 54, 83
      "Everlasting Flowers: For a Dead Mother" 44
      "Fish" 27
      "The Flying Fish" 50
      "Forsaken and Forlorn" 44
      "Gloire de Dijon" 44
      "The Horse Dealer's Daughter" 55
      "Humiliation" 44
      "Hymn to Priapus" 45
      "Indians and an Englishman" 35
      "Introduction to His Paintings" 54
      Lady Chatterley's Lover 3, 31, 32, 37, 40, 51, 53, 54, 55, 57, 63, 64, 65, 66, 67, 68
      "Last Poems" 50
      Look! We Have Come Through! 2, 36, 44, 45, 47, 142
      The Man Who Died 40, 50, 54, 63
      "Manifesto" 45, 49, 52
      Movements in European History 52, 53
      "Mutilation" 44
      "New Heaven and Earth" 1, 2, 3, 36, 45
      "New Mexico" 28, 83
      "New Year's Eve" 44
      Pansies 37
      The Princess 31, 55
      The Rainbow 31, 37, 40, 53, 54
      Sea and Sardinia 34
      "Sex Isn't Sin" 53
      "She Looks Back" 44
      "Snake" 122
      "Song of a Man Who Has Come Through" 45
      "Song of a Man Who is Loved" 44
      "Song of a Man Who is Not Loved" 44
      Sons and Lovers 3, 53, 54, 55, 56, 57, 67
      "Spirit of Place" 24
      "Spring Morning" 44
      St. Mawr 25, 26, 31, 37, 55
      Studies in Classic American Literature 25, 32, 54
      Twilight in Italy 30
      The Virgin and the Gipsy 3, 55, 57, 63
      Women in Love 3, 30, 31, 34, 37, 40, 44, 46, 51, 53, 54, 57, 67
         "Rabbit" 58, 59, 60, 62
         "The Industrial Magnate" 58
Lawrence, Frieda 26
Leite, George *Circle* 171
Lewis, Carl 76
Lipton, Lawrence 137
listener-supported radio stations 177
Liston, Sonny 85, 90
Macdonald, Dwight 169, 179
   Guard of Honor 179
   Politics 168
Mailer, Norman 2, 3, 54, 159
   Works:
      Advertisements for Myself 73
      An American Dream 77
      Armies of the Night 76
      Existential Errands 72, 75
      The Fight 3
      "King of the Hill" 73, 85
      The Prisoner of Sex 83
      "The White Negro" 73
Manilow, Barry 155
Mann, Thomas 173

Mann, Thomas (cont'd.)
  Dr. Faustus 173
mass-media celebrity 5
Maturin
  Melmoth the Wanderer 107
McCarthy, Mary 169
McDonald, Dwight 163
Mediterranean culture 132
Melville, Herman
  Moby Dick 31
minotaur 18
monism 2, 26, 28, 29, 145
Monk, Thelonious 155
Montand, Yves 173
Moore, Marianne 81
Moore, W. G. 10
Morrison, Jim 1
Morrow, Bradford 120
movie stars 154
movies
  National Velvet 155
Mozart, Wolfgang Amadeus 155
Muhammad Ali-George Foreman Fight 3
Mumford, Lewis 179
Nader, Ralph 157
Namath, Joe 92
narcissism 13
Native Americans, Southwest 28
Nevelson, Louise 155
New Criticism 116
New Critics 117
New Jerusalem, the 40
New York Abstract Expressionists 167
New York intelligentsia 169
Nicholson, Jack 153
Nisbet, Robert A. 172
Nixon administration 164
non-academic intellectuals 174, 175, 177
Norton, Ken 88
Novak, Kim 157
ontology 53
Orwell, George
  1984 107
Pacific Coast of America 170
Park, David 171

Partisan Review 117, 168, 169, 170, 171
"passions," the 10, 12
People 155
Perot, Ross 174
personalist poetics 127
Phillips, William 171
philosophical anarchism 117
Podhoretz, Norman 75, 76
poetry as communication 116
Poggioli, Renato 169
political hysteria in America 165
political ideologies 165
Pollnitz, Christopher 26, 27
positive thinking 19
Pound, Ezra 41, 172
Poussin, Nicolas
  Painting: "A Dance to The Music of Time" 4, 99
Powell, Anthony 2, 4
  A Dance to the Music of Time 2, 4, 100
  conservatism in 112
  genre in 100
  power in 107
  radical ideology in 112
  satire in 101, 112
  sex in 107
  snobbery in 105, 106
Pritchard, R. E. 51
  D. H. Lawrence: Body of Darkness 51
professional athletes 154
professionalism 176
profits 158
Proust, Marcel 155
public intellectuals 174, 175
Pussums 58
Pynchon, Thomas 163, 174
Quarry, Jerry 98
Rahv, Philip 171
Ransom, John Crowe 116
Reagan, Ronald 157, 169, 177
  Reagan decade 158
rebirth 40
reminiscence 120
Renoir, Jean 155
Rexroth, Kenneth 1, 2, 4, 5, 36, 122,

170, 171, 172
prosody 137
Works:
  Andrée-Rexroth elegies 118, 126, 139
  "Another Spring" 118, 124
  "August 22, 1939" 118
  "The Bad Old Days" 119
  Collected Short Poems 127
  The Dragon and the Unicorn 118, 138
  "An Easy Song" 123
  "Falling Leaves and Early Snow" 118
  "For a Masseuse and Prostitute" 118
  "Growing" 124
  "The Heart of Herakles" 141
  The Heart's Garden, the Garden's Heart 118, 141
  In Defense of the Earth 127, 131, 138
  In What Hour? 119
  "Inversely, As the Square of Their Distances Apart" 5, 137
  "A Letter to William Carlos Williams" 123
  "The Lights in the Sky Are Stars" 138, 141
  "Loneliness" 128, 129, 130
  The Love Poems of Marichiko 118, 133, 134, 136
  "Lyell's Hypothesis Again" 118, 121, 139
  "Marthe" poems 118
  Natural Numbers 123, 138
  "New Poems" 138
  "Northhampton, 1992-San Francisco, 1939" 119
  The Phoenix and the Tortoise 118, 120, 137
  "Quietly" 131, 132
  "She Is Away" 128
  "The Signature of All Things" 118, 138
  "Still on Water" 121
  "A Sword in a Cloud of Light" 138

  "Time Is the Mercy of Eternity" 1, 118, 139, 141
  "Towards An Organic Philosophy" 118
  "The Visionary Painting of Morris Graves" 140
  "When We With Sappho" 118, 120, 122
  "Yugao" 118, 139
Richards, Hubert J. 43
Riesman, David 163
rock stars 154
Rockefellers, the 157
Ross, Andrew 162, 164,
Rothko, Mark 155, 169
Russell, Bertrand 75
Sacco-Vanzetti trial and execution 172
sadism 59, 60
Sagan, Carl 167
San Francisco Renaissance 170
Sartre, Jean-Paul 172, 173
Scandinavian sagas 136
Schapiro, Meyer 169
Schickel, Richard 153, 154, 156
  Intimate Stranger 153
Schneider, Daniel J. 62
Schorer, Mark 44
Schwartz, Delmore 168
scientific intellectuals 178
Self 155
self-love 12, 14, 17, 19
Seven Deadly Sins 20
Sierra Club vs. Morton—1972 U. S. Supreme Court case 25
Signoret, Simone 173
Smith, Emmet 75
Smith, Roger 181
Snyder, Gary 170
social structure 176
sodomy 66
Spicer, Jack 170
Spilka, Mark 66
St. John 42
Stalin, Josef 177
stealth bomber 180
Still, Clifford 171
Stravinsky, Igor 155
Streep, Meryl 155

subject-object 26, 27, 145
subject-subject 26, 27, 33
Sun King, the 11
syphilis 54
Tancock, L. W. (La Rouchefoucauld's
   editor) 17
Tate, Allen 116
Taylor, Elizabeth 155
technocracy 176
tenemos 144
The Plumed Serpent 32
Thomas, Dylan
   "The Force That Through the Green
   Fuse Drives the Flower" 47
Thoreau, Henry David 172
Tobey, Mark 170
Trillings, the 169
TV commentators 154
Tyson, Mike 158
Unique Homes 158
Utopian thinking 164
vanity 12, 13, 14, 16, 17, 19, 20
Veblen, Thorstein
   "Conspicuous Consumption" 158
Vietnam War 172
virtue 16
von Rilke, Rainer Maria 163
Walt Disney business enterprises 25
Weekley, Ernest 44, 45
Wells, H. G. *War of the Worlds* 30
Whalen, Philip 170
Widmer, Kingsley 66
Williams, Esther 157
Williams, William Carlos 127
Wilson, Edmund 169
Wordsworth, William 27, 148
   The Prelude 121
World War One 40
Worthy, James 75
Wright, James 142
Yeats, William Butler 55, 155
Zeldin, Theodore 174
Zola, Emile 172
Zusne, Leonard 144